S0-ECL-869

Mental Illness and Due Process

Report and Recommendations
on Admission to
Mental Hospitals under New York Law

Special Committee to Study Commitment Procedures

THE COMMITTEE

Allen T. Klots, *Chairman*
A. Edward Gottesman, *Secretary*
J. Kenneth Campbell
William A. Delano
Richard V. Foster, M.D.
The Honorable Abraham N. Geller
Paul H. Hoch, M.D.
The Honorable Jacob Markowitz
Francis J. O'Neill, M.D.
The Honorable Samuel R. Pierce
The Honorable Samuel I. Rosenman
Simon Rosenzweig
Gray Thoron

Orison S. Marden, *President of The Association (ex officio)*
Roger B. Oresman, *Liaison Member with the Executive Committee of The Association*

THE STAFF

Bertram F. Willcox, *Director*
Ruth Roemer, *Associate Director*
Peter J. McQuillan, *Assistant Director*
Edward J. Bloustein, *Associate*

MENTAL ILLNESS *and* DUE PROCESS

Report and Recommendations on Admission to Mental Hospitals under New York Law

BY THE SPECIAL COMMITTEE TO STUDY COMMITMENT PROCEDURES OF THE ASSOCIATION OF THE BAR OF THE CITY OF NEW YORK

in cooperation with

THE CORNELL LAW SCHOOL

Cornell University Press

Ithaca, New York

© 1962 by the Association of the Bar
of the City of New York Fund, Inc.

CORNELL UNIVERSITY PRESS

First published 1962

Library of Congress Catalog Card Number: 62-18213

PRINTED IN THE UNITED STATES OF AMERICA
BY VAIL-BALLOU PRESS, INC.

FOREWORD

THE next time you go to a small party of about ten or twelve guests, look around the room carefully. If it is a statistically average group, one of the people there has been, is, or will be mentally ill during his lifetime and a patient in a mental hospital. It is likely, however, that his mental illness will be temporary and amenable to treatment, and many of the friends and associates of the patient may never know that he has suffered and recovered from this widespread disease.

Ten per cent of all Americans have a personal brush with mental disturbance so serious as to require hospitalization. Far greater numbers suffer from lesser degrees of mental illness. To these, and to all thinking citizens, the system of admission to hospitals for the mentally ill is an immediate and pressing problem.

This volume reports the study, conclusions, and recommendations of a special committee of judges, doctors, and lawyers which has reviewed the law and procedure for admission to and release from mental hospitals in New York State. The formation of the committee was prompted partly by the importance of sound practices for hospitalization in view of the great number of persons afflicted by this disease. At the same time, it has not been lost sight of that a single case of improper treatment or injustice for a single mental patient is an evil which should be avoided insofar as laws and men can avoid it.

This committee, established by The Association of the Bar of the City of New York, has spent almost two years studying the laws and procedures for admission of the mentally ill to hospitals in New York State and many of the ancillary problems surrounding this central issue. This report is and, of necessity, must be a consensus of many points of view on the complex issues which we have faced. It is a product of the collective judgment of all members of the committee. We have reached unanimous agreement on a full set of recommendations, although some individual members of the group may not subscribe to all the comments in the study. We offer the report and recommendations in the hope that our work will relieve some of the difficulties and problems in administration of the law and will point the way to new steps toward the future.

The committee has received untiring and indispensable help from many individuals and organizations throughout the state. We acknowledge with gratitude the significant debts which we owe:

To almost a hundred New York State judges who gave time and thought in answering lengthy questionnaires and in writing their comments on the problems involved and to the justices of the Supreme Court from the metropolitan area of New York City who met with the committee;

To the directors of state mental hospitals, licensed private institutions, and receiving hospitals and to the members of their staffs, who held extended personal interviews with the staff of the committee on the operation of admission procedures in their hospitals and in their communities;

To almost 150 physicians throughout the state, 100 health officers and their designees, and 30 chiefs of police who answered questionnaires, a number of whom took the trouble to give thoughtful comments; and to the many psychiatrists and other physicians who met with our staff and generously gave of their experience;

To the many persons who consulted with us in person, by letter, or by questionnaire, including the district attorneys of the state of New York and other lawyers in government service, the referees appointed by the Appellate Division of the Supreme Court relating to matters of incompetency, many lawyers in private practice, social workers, ministers, and interested and informed citizens;

To the New York State Department of Mental Hygiene for its whole-hearted cooperation in providing information requested by the committee; particularly to Mr. Robert E. Patton, its Director of Statistical Services, for prompt and skillful preparation of special statistical data; to Mr. E. David Wiley, its counsel, for many items of specific information essential to the study; to Mr. Hyman M. Forstenzer, its Director of Community Mental Health Services for able help on large and small questions; and to Dr. John R. Cumming and Dr. Elaine Cumming of the Mental Health Research Unit of the Department for their stimulating advice at the outset of the study;

To Dr. Milton I. Roemer, Dr. Alexander H. Leighton, Dr. Dorothea C. Leighton, and Professor Rose K. Goldsen of Cornell University for their invaluable help in the planning stage of this study;

To Fountain House Foundation and Mr. John H. Beard, its Executive Director, for undertaking an independent study of the experience with various methods of admission and the attitudes toward them of former mental patients, and particularly to Mr. Raymond B. Pitt, Acting Research Director of Fountain House, and his associates in this study;

To the committee's direct predecessors: The Committee on Legal Aid of The Association of the Bar of the City of New York, which worked under the chairmanship of Mr. Kenneth Campbell, and later under that of Mr. Peter Ward, in exploring the fundamental need for a study and report on this subject and in laying the groundwork for support of this committee's work; and to the McRoberts Research Group at the Cornell Law School, which had begun a study of the problem in an upstate rural area before the commencement of the present project;

To the Commonwealth Fund, the New Land Foundation, and the McRoberts Research Endowment Fund of the Cornell Law School for financial support of this work.

The committee wishes to express its appreciation to its own staff members for their untiring and devoted application to the job in hand and for their scholarly approach to the extensive research tasks involved:

To Professor Bertram F. Willcox, McRoberts Research Professor in Administration of the Law, Cornell Law School, our Staff Director, who as a scholar as well as a man of deep human sensibilities guided this work from its inception to its completion;

To Mrs. Ruth Roemer, the Associate Director, for her devoted work on the entire project and for her study during the summer of 1960 of methods of admission in several European countries; to Mr. Peter J. McQuillan, the Assistant Director; to Dr. Edward J. Bloustein, who served as consultant on various phases of the work; to Mr. David L. Willcox, a member of the staff; to Miss Mary E. Curtis, an experienced psychiatric nurse, for her study during the summer of 1960 of individual patients admitted by different methods to three upstate hospitals.

Finally, the chairman would like personally to thank each one of the devoted members of the committee, who surely stole many hours in the past two years from lighter and more pleasant matters to bring a searching and objective scrutiny to all of the many aspects of the study. My special thanks go to Mr. William A. Delano, who served as acting secretary of the committee during a major part of its work while the secretary was absent, and to Mr. A. Edward Gottesman, our secretary, for his invaluable contribution in shaping up the final stages of the work.

The study was completed in January 1962, but a few significant judicial and legislative developments of recent months have been incorporated in appropriate places. We hope that the effects of this study will continue to be felt for many years, years which we trust will mark a brighter era in the care of the mentally ill.

ALLEN T. KLOTS
Chairman

New York, New York
May 31, 1962

CONTENTS

Appendixes and Index

PART ONE

Conclusions and Recommendations

I

Basic Principles

Revolution against Violence

THE bars are disappearing—from most of the windows. The wards are quiet—save for an occasional moaning or outburst of shouts. The harsh words—asylum, lunatic, straitjacket—are dying out, as new ways of thinking replace the old. In mental hospitals in New York State, as elsewhere throughout the world, the last ten years have been years of revolution, the revolution against violence.

The startling change has come largely through the introduction of new medical measures. The use of tranquilizers has spread quickly and widely in the few years since their introduction in 1955. Tranquilizers, while apparently not a specific or cure for mental disturbance, ease some of the worst and most savage symptoms of the mentally ill and open the way for more personal treatment. A quiet patient can get help: the doctors can talk to him; nurses and attendants can give him small responsibilities and a feeling of contact with the world. Everyday tasks, such as eating, working in the garden, reading, and going to the movies, are now an integral part of the patient's treatment.

These and other changes have helped turn the insane asylum into a hospital. Open-door wards, some of which leave those under care free to come and go as they please during the day, have changed the prisoner into a patient. At the same time more people are being treated in the community, in out-patient clinics and day-and-night hospitals which let part-time patients work at their regular jobs. After-care and rehabilitation centers outside the hospitals have been introduced and expanded. For the first time mental patients everywhere—not just in a few places—can be treated like human beings with a disease.

Since the law must remain responsive to changing social needs and conditions, the advent of these changes in the conception and treatment of mental illness necessitates a review of the legal procedures for admission to and discharge from mental hospitals.

Most of New York State's mental patients now go through "certification" to a state or private mental hospital—the softer term replaced "commitment" in 1933. The New York Mental Hygiene Law, which is the statute governing admission and discharge, gives the patient a right, before certification, to a hearing by a judge to determine whether he needs care and treatment in an institution. Notice of the right to a hearing may be waived on a showing that the notice would be useless or harmful to the patient. In practice only a small proportion of patients—less than 10 per cent throughout the state—ever have a hearing. Outside New York City the hearing is hardly ever held; the patient generally gets no notice of his right to one.

For the increasing number of elderly persons who are sent to a mental hospital, lack of a hearing may be particularly shocking. Many of them are mentally ill, but many are suffering primarily from the advanced toll of age. Because most are mild or timid, they do not request a hearing and they often end up in a mental hospital, alone, bewildered, and sometimes forgotten by their families.

Even where hearings are held, it is hard to probe much beneath the surface. The stories are bare; the judge has little chance to learn the patient's background, the home or lodgings from which he has come, the surrounding facts and influences. On the basis of skeleton evidence, the judge must decide whether a man or woman will be "sent away," that is, confined in a state mental institution for an initial period of sixty days, which may become six months or six years.

In the vast majority of cases, where no hearing is held, the judge signs the certification order on nothing more than a petition for hospitalization and the report of two physicians. He never sees the patient. He never hears his side.

Not all patients enter state mental hospitals by certification. Early in this century, with the first tentative steps toward modern treatment of mental illness, the state saw the value of a method of voluntary admission to mental institutions. The present Mental Hygiene Law contains procedures for hospitalizing patients who recognize their illness and want to seek care and treatment. But because a large proportion of mental patients have until recently been forced by the pressures of their disturbance and real or imagined fears of mental hospitals to resist admission, the main emphasis of the law, which had its last thorough revision in the 1930's, is still on certification, or nonvoluntary admission to a state hospital.

The focus is beginning to change. A patient who is not faced with the fear and stigma of commitment to an asylum often sees more clearly than the committed patient the indecisions and dilemmas of mental illness, even his own mental illness, and realizes that he can be helped by professional care. These patients, an increasingly large part of the mentally ill who get into the hospital system, are willing and able to enter voluntarily. This very act may help in their treatment.

The majority of patients, however, still come to a hospital through one of the six statutory procedures for more or less compulsory admission. The different nonvoluntary procedures reflect the widely diverse conditions of the large number of patients who enter state and private institutions each day and, to some degree, the varied kinds of facilities available in different parts of the state.

Compulsory Admissions

In New York City and other cities where special receiving hospitals for psychiatric patients exist, a patient may be sent to one of these hospitals for sixty days under Sections 81(2) and 81(5) of the Mental Hygiene Law if, in the judgment of the hospital's director, he is "in immediate need of care and treatment or observation."

Every day of the year, Monday through Sunday, the telephone at a receiving hospital like Bellevue in New York City or at a police precinct house anywhere in the state will ring with an urgent request for an ambulance and attendant for someone whose mental and emotional apparatus has broken under continued or sudden strain. Some of the cases are dramatic: attempted suicides or raving violence. Most are more drab: the elderly lady next door, found living alone and neglected, who mumbles endlessly about times long since past; the bus driver or secretary, suddenly unable one morning to get up and go to work, who sits in bed staring for hours at a blank wall.

Where receiving hospitals do not exist, or in some areas even where they do, patients are generally sent directly to state mental hospitals or licensed private institutions by the standard court certification, under Section 74 of the Mental Hygiene Law. This procedure requires a petition and a certificate of two physicians that the patient needs care and treatment and a court order "committing" the patient. (Although the word "commitment" is now archaic in this context, in some circumstances it is both easy and descriptive.) An examining physician need not be a psychiatrist; he may be any "reputable physician, duly licensed to practice medicine" in New York, who has been in practice for three years. The initial order authorizes the institution to keep the patient sixty days for observation and treatment, and if the hospital director files a certificate before that time stating that the patient needs further care, he may be kept without any specific time limit until he no longer requires hospitalization.

Most patients come to state mental hospitals under Section 74. The petition for certification may come from a member of the patient's family, from someone else with whom he is living, from certain charitable organizations, or from public welfare officers. Patients go to state hospitals from receiving hospitals in this same way; and the number of certifications each week at a receiving hospital like Bellevue is so large that the Supreme Court, New York County, in the person of one of its judges, sits twice a week in a special courtroom at the hospital.

Here the process of admission to a mental hospital takes on somber reality: in the corridor outside, the patients who have requested a hearing, dressed in pajamas and hospital bathrobes, wait in a straggly gray line to present their protests against being "sent away." A psychiatrist reads to the judge the physician's report setting out the initial observations and recommendations on the need for care. Most patients, when called into the courtroom, talk up in their "defense"; their stories are sometimes rambling and incoherent, sometimes only a pitiful plea to go home. There is no regular representation of the patient's rights; many observers point out that the hearing may not meet minimum constitutional requirements. The judges can and do try to explore the patient's side of the case, but often they must make a decision on the grave issue of personal liberty with little more than scanty evidence.

Emergency Admissions

A third method of admission allows a state, county, or city health officer to send a patient directly to a state mental hospital on his certificate alone, but only in an emergency, or when the patient is dangerous to himself or others. This health-officer certification is used for many cases which would otherwise be handled by a receiving hospital if one existed in the local area. A health officer's certification, like admission to a receiving hospital, is limited to a sixty-day period and cannot be extended without court certification.

Another emergency provision, contained in Section 75 of the Law, allows admission and detention of a patient for ten days on a petition and certificates like those presented under Section 74, but without the court order. This form is most often used when a judge is not immediately available and a health-officer admission cannot be made. In these cases the ten-day detention period is for the purpose of getting a court order to keep the patient longer, and not for observation and treatment.

Newer Procedures

In 1960 Section 73-a of the Mental Hygiene Law was enacted at the request of the New York State Department of Mental Hygiene, which runs the eighteen state mental hospitals in New York and is charged generally with the problems of mental illness among New York's sixteen million population. On petition by any of the persons who may make application under Section 74 and with the certificate of two doctors (one of whom, unlike the doctors making a Section 74 certificate, must be a psychiatrist), a patient can be admitted directly to a state hospital for up to sixty days. Two things distinguish this from a regular court commitment. First, the patient cannot be kept beyond the sixty-day period on just the hospital director's certificate, but must be regularly certified; second, if the patient or someone acting for him objects at any time *after admission,* the hospital must either release the patient or begin a regular court commitment proceeding within five days after the notice of objection, or within ten days after admission. Detention over protest without court review can therefore last a week or two at most. Notice of the patient's right to object is given to him and his nearest relative three days after admission.

Section 73-a makes no provision for judicial review of the patient's admission during the initial sixty-day period of hospitalization. Without such protection of the patient's rights, this can be a dangerous procedure. Safeguards such as those proposed in this report must be put into the law, either through adoption of this committee's recommendations or through amendment of Section 73-a in the near future.

A procedure like that of Section 73-a can serve two main needs: to provide an easy emergency admission in many cases and to avoid the delay of passing a patient through a receiving hospital or a court proceeding before admission to a state hospital. Although new and so far only rarely used, it takes advantage of one of the recent medical findings in the continuing study of mental illness: that the first few days after a psychotic outburst are crucial ones. Some doctors believe that a psychosis which drives a person to irrational behavior or to seek help may be treated more effectively in its early stages than later when it has hardened into a tight ball of emotional disturbance. Under the present practice, a person admitted to a receiving hospital often gets little intensive therapy in the first days of hospitalization because of the administrative demands made on the staff in processing incoming patients; the mentally ill person kept at home while his family and doctor have him certified often gets less help. Section 73-a provides a way for shortening the period before the patient can get real therapy. But any procedure for prompt admission of patients to mental hospitals on medical authority alone should be backed up by immediate judicial review.

The sixth method of nonvoluntary admission under present law is specially designed for a different and growing class of patients—those who do not object to admission but are unable or unwilling to go on their own volition. Under Section 73 of the Mental Hygiene Law, patients who do not object may be admitted directly to a state hospital on the certificate of *one* physician (who need not be a psychiatrist). This procedure provides for an initial sixty-day stay. But it differs from regular court commitment in that the patient cannot be kept after the sixty-day period *if he then objects.* Hospitals appear to be careful not to take a patient under a Section 73 admission if he shows any tendency to object prior to admission. During the initial sixty-day period, however, the hospital is authorized to keep the patient in spite of his protests, and there is no regular provision for judicial review.

Because the one-physician certificate is probably the easiest method of getting a patient into a state mental institution for the initial sixty-day period, and because the patient may stay indefinitely if he never protests, its use has increased in recent years with older, nonviolent patients suffering from some mental illness resulting from senility. These patients pose particular problems in mental health administration as a whole, and the use of one-physician certificates for older patients has been strongly criticized in many quarters.

Although the main reason for the diverse methods of nonvoluntary admission is to provide for the varying needs of the large number of mentally ill from every walk of life and in very different states of mental difficulty, recent trends in the use of the procedures reflect changing attitudes toward the care of mental disturbance. The increased use of one-physician certificates, for instance, is partly because of the ability of tranquilizers to quiet a patient and remove his imagined fears of the pits and traps of the mental hospital. The new Section 73-a procedure was proposed by the Department of Mental Hygiene in order to eliminate the eight-to-ten-day waiting period that commonly accompanies processing through a court commitment. Unfortunately, Section 73-a is not accompanied by adequate safeguards of the patient's rights. In eliminating part of the delay before starting therapy, however, Section 73-a admissions may allow the patient who is provided with treatment in the vital early days of his illness to be helped and discharged in a period of time that would have been considered extraordinary fifteen years ago.

Indeed, the figures for recent years indicate a much shorter average period of stay in state mental hospitals than was formerly customary; from 1955 to 1961 the average stay for all newly admitted patients in New York institutions dropped from eight months to six months. Not only are mental illnesses once thought incurable being alleviated, but patients with many forms of disorder are often home again within a month or two after the outbreak of mental illness first required their hospitalization.

Practical Problems

Shortening the treatment period has become particularly important because of the increasing number of mental patients admitted. In fact, while admissions to mental hospitals in New York have continued a general rise since the Second World War, the hospital population has shown steady declines in every year since 1955. If the treatment period had not been shortened, the problem of overcrowding would by now be overwhelming.

Every day of the year about seventy persons in New York State begin the road to admission to a state mental hospital, making more than twenty-five thousand every twelve months. Even with recent declines, the total population of New York State mental hospitals is about eighty-five thousand. If all the patients were hospitalized in one place, they would make the state's ninth largest city, larger than Schenectady and just smaller than Utica. Pilgrim State, which is the largest of the state hospitals, is as big as a fair-sized town, with fourteen thousand patients.

Court certification for every patient, after a hearing on the merits, is practically impossible. Even the simpler methods of compulsory admission pose major administrative difficulties. But more important, unwilling admission can be an initial setback to treatment. Voluntary admission combines therapeutic advantages with a practical means of large-scale hospitalization.

Voluntary Admissions

For the patient who recognizes his mental illness and is able and willing to do something about it, voluntary admission, particularly to an open-door ward if he is eligible, sweeps away many of the old bugaboos of commitment and asylums. By his own act he asks for admission to the hospital and is accepted; in this respect it is not unlike entering a general hospital for the treatment of any disease.

The voluntary form of admission under present law, embodied in Section 71 of the Mental Hygiene Law, does involve some obligations to stay. The patient cannot leave for fifteen days after admission and not until ten days after he gives notice of his intention to leave. These periods, which were sixty and fifteen days respectively before a 1958 amendment, were shortened to increase the attractiveness of voluntary admissions; the retention of a period after notice of intention to leave is to give the hospital time to apply for certification if the patient should and can be detained under Section 74.

Though voluntary admissions are on the rise, they still represent only about a fifth of new admissions each year. Some hospitals have a much larger voluntary rate than others, but even St. Lawrence Hospital, which has the highest voluntary rate and is a completely open-ward hospital, had only about 56 per cent voluntary admissions in 1960. It is hard to say what influences the rate of voluntary admission. It seems that the hospital director's attitude, as much as patients' understanding, is a major factor.

Some doctors minimize the importance of the method of admission, even of voluntary admission, as an aid in therapy, but most agree that voluntary patients are generally better patients, with good chances of recovery. For many reasons, not the least of which is the elimination of the detention spirit, the voluntary admission, along with the open ward and increased emphasis on keeping the mental patient in contact with the world, is part of the essence of modern mental health treatment.

Because the present form of voluntary admission requires the patient to agree to stay in the hospital for a certain period, the Department of Mental Hygiene was reluctant, until recently, to accept voluntary patients unless they clearly understood the bargain they were making. Since 1956, in order to ease the way for voluntary admission, the Department has taken a more liberal view of the right of a patient who is mentally disturbed to ask for help in exchange for a promise to give up his freedom to leave for a certain period. This question, on which there are conflicting opinions, is only one of many about the status of the mental patient which have come in for serious review in the new era of mental health care and treatment. The basic problem involves the needs of the mentally ill for therapy, the protection of their personal freedom, and the interests of the community.

The Physicians and the Lawyers

Few mental patients read the Bill of Rights. The immediate problems which they are unable to bear seem remote from the honored stricture: "No person . . . shall be . . . deprived of life, liberty or property, without due process of law." Yet the whole problem of admission of the mentally ill to hospitals is tied to the question of depriving a citizen of his personal liberty.

Few contest the need to deprive some mentally ill persons of their freedom: many patients are dangerous either to themselves or others. Even when a patient is not dangerous, most patients with serious mental illness are detained in hospitals insofar as necessary to make treatment possible.

On the other hand, if treatment can be given without restraint, both the rights of the patient and the chances of his successful return to normal mental health are more readily assured.

These two positions are cornerstones; on them we can lay down certain fundamental principles about the admission and discharge of mental patients. The principles deserve special attention:

> Every person with serious mental illness needs some care and in many cases must go to a hospital, even if he does not want to.
>
> Mental hospitals are not prisons, but they do, by force on body or mind, deprive patients of some freedom.
>
> Rapid, noncompulsory admission to mental hospitals is good for most patients and helps in allowing effective treatment and early release.
>
> When a person must be sent to a mental hospital against his will, he should not be treated like a criminal and be tried and convicted of being sick. Procedures for his admission are only stepping-stones to treatment.
>
> Any person hospitalized against his will is entitled to watchful protection of his rights, because he is a citizen first and a mental patient second.

A few years ago many lawyers and doctors did not believe one or more of these fundamentals; some still do not. But because enough lawyers and enough doctors believed some of them, several independent groups of judges, lawyers, researchers, doctors, and administrators began to urge a general review of the law and practice of hospitalization for mental illness in New York State.

Tentative beginnings were made by the Committee on Legal Aid of The Association of the Bar of the City of New York; the Department of Mental Hygiene was receptive to discussions of the issues. Some universities, notably Cornell, were independently studying similar problems. Presiding Justice Bernard Botein, of the Appellate Division, First Department, which generally oversees the administration of the largest single court certification process in the state, the commitment term at Bellevue, was a sympathetic observer.

One step in bringing together judges, lawyers, doctors, and administrators came in 1959, when the Commissioner of Mental Hygiene, Dr. Paul Hoch, submitted for comment to the Presiding Justices of the Appellate Division in the state's four judicial departments a legislative proposal to amend the Mental Hygiene Law. Justice Botein and Justice Gerald Nolan, of the First and Second Departments, jointly asked for advice on the proposal from The Association of the Bar and the New York State Bar Association. A meeting was arranged at which the counsel of the Mental Hygiene Department was present, along with the two judges and representatives of the bar associations. The immediate practical result was a revision of the Department's draft statute. The more important effect was the beginning of intensive joint efforts to form a state-wide group representing law and medicine, with the aim of thorough review of the whole problem.

Formation of the committee which presents this report was announced on March 28, 1960, by the President of The Association of the Bar of the City of New York. The members include a Supreme Court justice and a judge of the Court of General Sessions, the Commissioner of Mental Hygiene, a law school dean, the head of a state mental hospital and another representative of the Department of Mental Hygiene, and several practicing lawyers. The staff director is a university law school professor.

Each member of the committee began with the problem of learning to talk the others' language. There were long sessions and hard ones. The members began to realize that many very fundamental questions had to be expressly raised before progress could be made. But every member turned to the task with a will.

Several specific problems that the committee found important are broader than the question of revising the law and procedures.

There is a necessary balance in the hospitalization procedures between medical considerations and legal ones. Looking back at the principles stated above, we note that some of them are mainly concerned with promoting therapy, others with protecting civil liberties. This does not suggest that there is a dilemma, or that the demands of one are incompatible with the needs of the other. It does rightly suggest, however, that no process of admission to mental hospitals will ever be entirely satisfactory unless it meets certain minimal requirements both of legal rights and therapeutic policies.

This study is mainly aimed at marking out those requirements. On the one hand, this report will suggest that the increased use of voluntary admission has become closely tied up with modern therapy and should be encouraged. The committee proposes the immediate addition of fully informal admission as an advance from present voluntary procedures. On the other hand, the report recognizes that both voluntary patients and all patients who are or must be admitted against their will should get organized and continuing legal safeguards of their rights. For this purpose the report recommends the establishment of a special agency devoted solely to this function.

Another question which runs through all the deliberations and recommendations of the committee is the difficult one of defining the persons who should be hospitalized for mental illness. In most cases this problem solves itself, either because the patient wants to go to the hospital or because he clearly needs treatment, even against his will. But there is a critical area where the decision may be a close one, particularly if the patient is to be detained without his consent.

Who Is Mentally Ill?

Some say all of us. A few say none. We have no pat answer. The present New York law provides a variety of criteria for admission to a mental hospital, beginning with the definition of a "mentally ill person" as "any person afflicted with mental disease to such an extent that for his own welfare or the welfare of others, or of the community, he requires care and treatment." A person may be admitted to a hospital if he is mentally ill "to a degree which warrants institutional care," or "where the condition of such person is such that it would be for his benefit to receive immediate care or treatment." On the other hand, Section 74, which only requires certification that the allegedly mentally ill person "is in need of care and treatment," goes on to say that if it "appears that such mentally ill person is harmless and his relatives or a committee of his person are willing and able properly to care for him, at some place other than an institution," the judge may order that he be allowed to stay outside a hospital. There are a variety of other ways of saying almost the same thing. But none of them provides a clear demarcation between those who are ill and those who are well.

Even a casual reader of the statute can see that the present criteria are far from consistent. The committee recognizes that an important additional help both in protecting the rights and assuring the treatment of the mentally ill would be use of consistent criteria for determining who should be hospitalized. Good definition would relieve some of the physician's problems, as well as the lawyer's.

Considerable effort by various groups has been given to defining mental illness for the purpose of hospitalization. Further development in psychiatry may point the way to a more precise definition. The committee which presents this report has been concerned with this question, but it has not been able to give it the time or detailed expert study that the issue requires. We can only hope and urge that other groups will carry forward this work in the context of the improved treatment and new admission procedures now in process of development.

The Study and the Recommendations

The work done by the committee, including the extensive study done by its able staff under the leadership of Professor Bertram F. Willcox, McRoberts Research Professor in Administration of the Law at Cornell University, has led to conclusions and recommendations which are set out in the next chapter. These are the distilled essence of much research, pondering, discussion, and a little banging on the table. The committee has agreed that the conclusions and recommendations provide a positive program for direct action in repairing some of the defects in present law.

If the public and the legislature also agree, we can now begin.

II

Recommendations

THE CENTRAL ISSUES: ADMISSION AND DISCHARGE

Mental Health Review Service

UNDER the headline "FORGOTTEN MEN" the occasional newspaper article may tell the story of people admitted to a mental hospital ten years ago, living the regular, monotonous life of the patient without hope of release. The story may be true, for some mental illnesses cannot be cured with known treatments, and some patients are destined to spend the rest of their lives under custody and care. But they should not be forgotten.

We have pointed out in Chapter I that the vast majority of patients certified to state hospitals under Section 74 receive no hearing, and many do not even receive a notice indicating that they are entitled to a hearing. In the small percentage of cases (principally in New York City) where hearings are held, the hearings tend to be brief, informal, and lacking in any organized presentation of the patient's side of the case.

The committee has found that there is a need during the entire stay in a mental hospital for objective and periodic examination of a patient's status and right to release. Especially for the nonvoluntary patient, full representation promptly upon initial admission and regular review of the grounds of his detention are essential to continuing protection of his rights as a citizen. A voluntary patient should also be kept aware of the terms of his hospitalization, if only to make sure that he does not get a mistaken idea that he is being held against his will.

Present judicial certification procedures, even when accompanied by a hearing, seldom sketch a full picture of the patient's background. The hearing may not even meet basic requirements of due process of law. Although the details of due process in a hearing involving mental illness are and probably should be different from the details of due process in trial of a criminal offense, certain fundamentals are not provided by the present kind of hearing. Ordinarily, no one represents the patient or outlines the possible alternatives to care in a state hospital. No one points out the factors and developments in his work or family life which may have created temporary emotional strain or which may now ease his return to normal life in the community. No one is charged with this responsibility.

To fill in these blank areas and to implement the changed methods of admission proposed by the committee in this report, we make the following recommendation:

> *Recommendation No. 1* (*Mental Health Review Service*). A new state-wide agency, called provisionally the Mental Health Review Service, shall be established as an agency independent of the hospitals and of the Department of Mental Hygiene and shall be responsible to the courts handling mental hospital admissions.
>
> The Mental Health Review Service will have the duty of studying and reviewing the admission and retention of every nonvoluntary patient. It shall have two aims: (1) to explain to the patient and his family the procedures under which a patient enters and is retained in a mental hospital, and to inform them of the patient's right to a hearing before a judge, his right to be represented by a lawyer, and his right to seek an independent medical opinion, if desired; and (2) to provide the court with informa-

tion on the patient's case to establish the need for his care and treatment in the hospital or his right to discharge. The Service will also recommend to the court, in all cases where the Service sees the need, the desirability of the patient's having legal representation or of his being examined by another psychiatrist.

Staffed by persons trained for this work, the Mental Health Review Service will have a primary duty to guarantee that patients know their rights and that the court has before it the facts necessary for deciding the question of the propriety of a patient's retention.

The Mental Health Review Service shall be available in state hospitals, in licensed private institutions, and in psychiatric receiving hospitals—in short, in all mental hospitals which any patients enter against their will.

Although the primary functions of the Service will relate to nonvoluntary patients, it will also have the duty of explaining to voluntary patients their status and rights and will be available to aid voluntary patients who ask for its help.

The establishment of a Mental Health Review Service will probably not increase substantially the number of hearings held or the work load of the courts. Even today in New York County, where almost all patients are given notice of their right to a hearing, about 85 per cent of the patients do not demand a hearing. The establishment of the Mental Health Review Service will ensure that when hearings are demanded and held there will be an opportunity for a full presentation of facts upon which the court may base an informed judgment.

The Mental Health Review Service will help to assure that no patient becomes a "forgotten man." But it will have a more important function: it will pave the way for the introduction of regular methods of nonvoluntary admission to mental hospitals without the necessity for a court order prior to hospitalization and the beginning of therapy.

Medical Admission

New York has already begun to move away from court certification. As indicated in Chapter I, Section 73 of the Mental Hygiene Law, which allows admission of nonobjecting patients, and new Section 73-a, which allows admission even of patients who protest, require no court order for an initial detention period in state hospitals of two weeks to sixty days. Admission to psychiatric receiving hospitals under Section 81(2) has also long been made without judicial order.

The committee has concluded that admission to receiving hospitals and to state institutions should be on the same footing. Some critics say there is time-wasting formality in the initial admission to state hospitals; others view with alarm the lack of safeguards in admission to receiving wards. We have sought a uniform method of admission for both kinds of facilities.

The path away from court certification leads toward fully medical admission to any mental hospital. By "medical admission" we mean a system in which the need for initial hospitalization is a decision for doctors, not for a court.

The present law reflects the recent search for a method of fully medical admission which will allow early help for the mentally ill and prompt beginning of treatment. The committee approves this trend toward medical admission. We have adopted the basic principle that prompt therapy is good therapy.

Detention of a mental patient raises legal questions, but the problems of detention are different from those of admission and can, to some degree, be met separately.

The trend toward medical admission has spread widely. In England a comprehensive study of the law relating to hospitalization of the mentally ill began in 1954, and the new British Mental Health Act of 1959, one result of the study, sanctions not only fully medical admission, but a system of review of detention by nonjudicial agencies. We see no need to go that far.

We recommend that New York adopt a procedure for prompt, informal medical admission to mental hospitals. At the same time we recommend effective, continuing legal safeguards of the rights of all patients who are kept or stay in mental hospitals more than a few days.

To provide a workable form of medical admission for all patients who object to hospitalization, the committee recommends a revision of the basic form of nonvoluntary admission:

> *Recommendation No. 2 (Basic Method of Admission).* Initial admission to a state mental hospital, licensed private institution, or psychiatric receiving hospital shall be authorized on an application for admission by the patient's family or other named persons and the certificates of two physicians, and on confirmation of the need for hospitalization by the medical staff of the institution. This initial admission shall be for a period of sixty days. The admission shall be subject to the right of the patient to a judicial hearing promptly after admission, as provided in Recommendations No. 4, No. 5, and No. 6.

This provision should be supplemented by a special admission procedure for patients who do not object to admission. Since medical admission already exists for this limited sector, only a small change is required in the substance of the present law:

> *Recommendation No. 3 (Nonobjecting Patients).* Initial admission to a state mental hospital, licensed private institution, or psychiatric receiving hospital of a patient who does not object to admission shall be authorized on an

application for admission by the patient's family or other named persons and the certificate of one physician, and on the confirmation of the need for hospitalization by the staff of the institution. This initial admission shall be for a period of sixty days. Within fifteen days after such admission and as a condition of continued retention of the patient, the certificate of a second examining physician, who may be a psychiatrist on the staff of a state hospital or psychiatric receiving hospital (but not of a private institution) shall be made. The admission shall be subject to the right of the patient to a judicial hearing promptly after admission, as provided in Recommendations No. 4, No. 5, and No. 6.

These proposals eliminate court certification prior to initial admission. They are primarily aimed at allowing prompt initiation of useful treatment. They will also help to eliminate the fear and stigma that have been and still are associated with commitment and certification.

Notice and Right to Hearing

Fully medical admission helps to solve some of the problems of therapy. But it must be qualified with appropriate safeguards of the patient's rights. Therefore the committee recommends:

Recommendation No. 4 (Notice). Within five working days after a patient's admission, the hospital shall be required to serve written notice on the patient and his relatives of their right to request a judicial hearing on the need for care and treatment of the patient in a mental hospital and of the right to obtain representation by a lawyer at the hearing. The patient shall be authorized to designate up to three persons, in addition to those now specified in Section 74(3) of the Mental Hygiene Law, on whom the notice should also be served. The Mental Health Review Service will make certain that notice has been served under this recommendation and that the patient has been informed of his rights.

Recommendation No. 5 (Court Review with Judicial Hearing). If the patient or other interested person requests a hearing, or if the Mental Health Review Service recommends a hearing, a judicial hearing shall be held promptly. No time limit shall be placed on the right to demand a hearing; the right shall remain open at all times during the first sixty days of hospitalization. The person requesting the hearing shall be allowed to choose whether it will be held in the county of the patient's residence, the county from which he was admitted, or the county where the hospital is located. Any interested party, including the hospital, may apply to change the place of hearing to any other county in order to serve the convenience of the parties or the condition of the patient. Before the hearing the Mental Health Review Service shall investigate the patient's case and report its findings to the judge.

Recommendation No. 6 (Hospitalization after Hearing). After hearing, the judge shall either order discharge of the patient or make an order authorizing the hospital to retain the patient for care and treatment for a period not to exceed six months. In appropriate cases, the order may authorize transfer of the patient from the hospital of admission (which may be a psychiatric receiving hospital) to any state hospital or to a licensed private institution.

So far we have concentrated on the patient who requests release or a hearing, either himself or through his family. As we noted in Chapter I, an increasing number of the mentally ill have a clearer view of their problems and do not object to continued hospitalization, even in some cases where they are unable or unwilling to become voluntary patients. If a patient will remain in a hospital voluntarily, we encourage his transfer to voluntary status, even after a nonvoluntary admission. However, if a patient will not or cannot stay voluntarily, but does not request a hearing or object positively to remaining, he must still have proper safeguards for his personal liberty.

Tranquilizers create special concern about nonobjecting patients. No one quite knows how a tranquilizer works in calming the violence and fears, the indecision and depression, of the mentally ill. Some laymen and lawyers look at tranquilizers as "drugs." They do not claim that they have a narcotic or habit-forming effect. But tranquilizers may reach the very source of the will to resist. Since a patient who has been admitted to a mental hospital without his consent may not be in a position to object to his continued detention because of the nature of his illness or the initial steps in its treatment, his rights must be protected as fully as those of the patient who voices his protest.

The Mental Health Review Service can provide these safeguards in part through its authority to recommend a hearing during the initial sixty-day hospitalization, even though the patient or someone acting on his behalf does not ask for a hearing. Nevertheless, the committee recommends that initial medical admission be supplemented by judicial review if it is necessary or advisable to detain beyond sixty days any patient for whom a hearing is not requested or held.

> *Recommendation No. 7* (*Court Review without Hearing*). If, after service of the notice proposed in Recommendation No. 4, no hearing is requested by the patient or his relatives within the first sixty days of hospitalization and no hearing is recommended by the Mental Health Review Service, and if the patient does not agree to remain in the hospital as a voluntary patient; then, upon an application for authority to retain the patient and upon a

certificate of the hospital director that further care and treatment of the patient is necessary, presented to a judge before the expiration of the first sixty days of hospitalization, the judge may make an order authorizing the hospital to retain the patient for care and treatment for a period not to exceed six months.

Notice of this application for authority to retain shall be served on the patient and his relatives by the hospital and explained to them by the Mental Health Review Service, and relevant information about the case shall be furnished by the Mental Health Review Service to the judge, all in the same way as the notice and review proposed in Recommendations No. 4 and No. 5.

The committee's proposals are aimed at quashing the specter of the "forgotten man" by abolishing any method of hospitalization without time limit. In the place of certification for an indefinite period, a patient may be retained for a period reasonably related to the length of treatment under modern methods of therapy.

Some patients cannot be significantly helped in six months; others can be discharged in two. For the patient whose stay in the hospital must be extended beyond the original six-month period after the first court review, we recommend periodic reexamination of the need for hospitalization:

Recommendation No. 8 (*Renewal of Authority to Retain*). The judicial authorization for the retention of a patient for care and treatment in a hospital shall be renewed periodically. Before the expiration of any period of retention, the hospital may apply for renewed authority to retain the patient, and notice of such application shall be served on the patient in the same way as the notice proposed in Recommendation No. 4. The Mental Health Review Service shall also make a further investigation of the patient's case. Within fifteen days of the notice of application, the patient and his relatives shall be given an opportunity for a full hearing.

After the initial six-month judicial authorization, an order may be made authorizing retention of the patient for an additional year; after the additional year, an order may be made from time to time authorizing retention of the patient for a period not to exceed two years.

The time periods are intended as maximums, and the judge should have full authority to shorten the time periods. The time periods should be applied so that minor errors or delays will not subject the hospital to liability for false imprisonment.

If the hospital makes an application for renewal of authority to retain before expiration of the prior period, the existing authority shall continue until judicial action on the application.

Voluntary Admission

Medical admission of mental patients is a long step away from commitment. The next step comes when the patient himself asks for help.

How can you *detain* a patient in an open ward? The question poses its own dilemma. As treatment of mental patients moves more toward keeping the patients in touch with the world outside the hospital, voluntary hospitalization follows naturally on its heels.

The present method of voluntary admission is a good one, and its increasing use should be encouraged. If it will help to put that in black and white, we suggest that it be added to the law.

Voluntary patients now make what is essentially a bargain with the hospital; they agree to stay for fifteen days after admission and for ten days after they give notice that they want to leave. This bargain is not really a contract, and the committee approves the new determination of the Department of Mental Hygiene, which began with the amendment in 1956 of the general order on voluntary admissions (General Order 2 of the Regulations of the Department), to accept voluntary admissions without proof that the patient has legal capacity to contract.

Voluntary admission should be simple. The Department has already said: "A person may be accepted for voluntary admission if he appreciates that he is in need of hospital care and treatment and presents himself and signs a proper form willingly with appreciation of what he is doing."

We approve this principle and therefore make the following specific proposal:

> *Recommendation No. 9 (Encouragement of Voluntary Admissions).* Section 71 of the Mental Hygiene Law, providing for voluntary admissions, shall be continued and amended to state expressly that voluntary admission of suitable mentally ill persons is encouraged and that persons may be received in a state hospital or licensed private institution upon making application for treatment.

One of the findings of the committee's staff is that some voluntary patients are not aware of their right to ask for discharge. This is understandable, considering the atmosphere of compulsion that has surrounded hospitalization of the mentally ill for many decades. Moreover, certain types of treatment, such as electric shock therapy, may also cause a patient to forget how or why he entered the hospital. Therefore, we suggest that each patient be kept fully informed of his status:

> *Recommendation No. 10 (Information to Voluntary Patients).* It shall be the duty of a state hospital or licensed private institution to inform the voluntary patient in writ-

> ing at the time of his admission, and thereafter before the expiration of sixty days, thereafter before the expiration of one year, and thereafter before the expiration of each two-year period, of his status as a voluntary patient. The Mental Health Review Service shall explain to the patient at the time of his admission, and at each of the other times, the conditions of his hospitalization and his rights as a voluntary patient.

The full development of modern treatment of mental illness may lead to an even more liberal view of voluntary admission. True voluntary admission would leave the patient free to discharge himself from the hospital at any time. This would finally make hospitalization for mental illness just like hospitalization for any other disease.

We recommend that the law anticipate the possible wider use of informal, essentially nonstatutory admission:

> *Recommendation No. 11 (Informal Admissions).* Informal admission to state hospitals and psychiatric receiving hospitals shall be permitted if the hospital is willing to accept the patient. No formalities shall be required for admission, and the patient shall be free to leave at will.
>
> The names of all informal patients shall be reported to the Department of Mental Hygiene and to the Mental Health Review Service within ten days after admission.
>
> It shall be the duty of the hospital to inform the patient in writing, at least as often as required in the case of voluntary patients in Recommendation No. 10, of his status as an informal patient and of his freedom to leave the hospital.

For the present we expect that the current voluntary admission procedure will continue to exist side by side with the proposed informal admission. In the near future, however, we look forward to gradual replacement of the older method by the informal procedure suggested, in line with the development of treatment and the progress of the community's thinking about mental disturbance.

One development in sensible progress toward true voluntary admission to a mental hospital should be elimination of the civil disabilities that may exist even for voluntary patients. The right to a driver's license may present some questions, just as physical illness sometimes warrants restriction of the privilege to drive. But, so far as possible, no other normal privilege should be denied the voluntary mental patient.

> *Recommendation No. 12* (*Civil Rights of Voluntary Patients*). Voluntary and informal patients shall not be deprived of the right to vote while in the hospital or after their discharge (this restates present law); nor shall they suffer any other deprivation of civil rights because of their hospitalization, such as prejudice to their civil service ranking.
>
> The right of voluntary and informal patients to a driver's license shall remain as at present, with the Commissioner of Motor Vehicles making the decision whether or not a license should be issued or continued for a person who has been or is hospitalized for mental illness. The hospital may make a recommendation to the Commissioner of Motor Vehicles in cases in which the hospital believes it is not safe for the patient to drive.

Admission to Receiving Hospitals

More than half the patients who are brought or come willingly to the psychiatric receiving hospitals that exist in some cities in New York State go home without being admitted to a state mental institution. This fact is a key to the valuable role which receiving hospitals can play in the treatment of mental illness.

The receiving hospital or ward has a chance to treat the patient in the first crucial days after his illness becomes apparent. Present methods of admission to receiving facilities, discussed fully in Chapter IV, are quite informal: on a report that a patient is mentally ill, and on confirmation by the hospital that he is in immediate need of care and treatment, he may be admitted. In practice, as well, admission to a receiving hospital is accompanied by a minimum of formality and red tape.

In spite of this, the potential resources of the receiving hospital have not yet been tapped. It remains chiefly a place to keep patients who are awaiting admission to another institution. The seventeen hundred beds available at the four receiving hospitals in New York City, at the one serving Westchester and the one in Nassau, and the three receiving facilities in Buffalo, Rochester, and Albany are mainly occupied by patients awaiting transfer to a state hospital. If these beds were all available for intensive local treatment, the already good record of the receiving hospitals in returning patients to the community without sending them on for treatment elsewhere would undoubtedly improve.

The committee's proposals for medical admission to state hospitals should relieve in great measure the overcrowding of receiving hospitals by patients awaiting court commitment. This in turn will allow the receiving hospitals to use their extensive facilities mainly for the purpose of immediate therapy of patients who may not need transfer to a state institution.

Receiving hospitals require two special powers different from those of state institutions. One is the power to bring persons to the hospital from any one of the several places where the person's illness may first be detected or reported. In most cases, the first report of mental illness comes from a doctor or from a general hospital; in many cases, the police pick up a person who is mentally ill or he comes before a magistrate on a minor criminal charge such as disturbing the peace. We recommend that provision be made for the admission of persons to a receiving hospital from any one of these sources.

Recommendation No. 13 (*Removal to Receiving Hospitals*). The following agencies shall have authority to direct the removal of a person to a psychiatric receiving hospital for the purpose of admission:

(a) Receiving hospitals throughout the state shall be authorized to direct the removal to such a hospital of persons appearing to be mentally ill, on the written statement of the need for hospitalization by a physician;

(b) The police throughout the state shall be authorized to take custody of a person and to provide for his removal to a psychiatric receiving hospital or to another safe and comfortable place if the person appears to be mentally ill and is conducting himself in a manner which in a sane person would be disorderly;

(c) A magistrate may issue a civil order directing the removal to a psychiatric receiving hospital of any person who appears to be mentally ill and who is arraigned before the magistrate on a minor criminal charge if the magistrate finds the person to be in immediate need of examination and treatment in such a hospital.

In the event of admission to a receiving hospital at the instance of the police or a magistrate, fingerprint records of the patient shall be expunged from the police files and no criminal order shall be issued under Section 870 of the Code of Criminal Procedure.

Section 81(2) of the Mental Hygiene Law shall be amended to eliminate the authority of a nurse to direct removal to a psychiatric receiving hospital; Section 82 of the Mental Hygiene Law shall be amended to eliminate

> the removal of a patient to a psychiatric receiving hospital on a "precept"; [1] and Section 81(5) of the Mental Hygiene Law shall be amended to eliminate the warrant procedure for removal to a psychiatric receiving hospital.

The second special power of receiving hospitals should allow them to act as way stations for a patient going to a state hospital. For this purpose, they need not keep a patient more than twenty-four hours. We have already recommended that patients be admitted to receiving hospitals on the certificate of two doctors in the same way as to state mental hospitals and licensed private institutions. This method of admission is mainly designed for a patient who may get sufficient treatment during his stay in the receiving hospital to allow his discharge directly back into the community. Receiving hospitals, however, should also have available a method of admission which allows temporary care of the patient for a short period, with the expectation that he will either be sent to a state hospital for further care and treatment or formally admitted to the receiving hospital for the full sixty-day period. For this purpose the committee proposes:

> *Recommendation No. 14 (Admission to Receiving Hospitals).* Initial admission to a psychiatric receiving hospital shall be authorized after examination by a single physician on the staff of the hospital and on his written opinion that the person requires immediate care and treatment, and on acceptance of the patient by the hospital. This admission shall be for a period of twenty-four hours. If, within the twenty-four-hour period, a second medical opinion in writing from another physician, who may be a physician on the staff of the receiving hospital, confirms the need for admission, the person may be admitted for sixty days as

[1] The "precept" procedure involves a court order directing the apprehension and confinement of certain mentally ill persons.

provided in Recommendation No. 3. The admission shall be subject to the right of the patient to a judicial hearing promptly after admission, as provided in Recommendations No. 4, No. 5, and No. 6.

An essential element in relieving receiving hospitals of one administrative burden is to allow transfer of patients who have been fully admitted to such hospitals to a state mental hospital without any formal proceeding. Since our recommendations provide the same safeguards for full admission to a receiving hospital which are provided in the case of admission to a state institution, we propose that transfer from the receiving hospital to the state hospital be allowed without judicial order:

> *Recommendation No. 15 (Transfer from Receiving Hospitals to State Hospitals).* If, at any time after admission to a psychiatric receiving hospital under the proposals contained in Recommendations No. 2, No. 3, or No. 14, no hearing has been requested or recommended by the patient or someone on his behalf, a patient may be transferred without judicial order from a psychiatric receiving hospital to a state mental hospital, and the sixty-day period of the initial admission shall run from the time of admission to the transferring hospital. Notice of the proposed transfer shall be given to the Mental Health Review Service and to the persons notified of initial admission as proposed in Recommendation No. 4.

Emergency Admissions

Admission to psychiatric receiving hospitals is at present the best form of emergency admission for a mentally ill person who is in immediate need of care and treatment. Unfortunately, receiving hospitals are available in only a few areas. Outside those areas the present emergency procedures for admission of patients on the certificate of a health officer fulfill the basic needs of the emergency patient.

The secondary method of emergency admission, the incomplete court order authorized by Section 75 of the Mental Hygiene Law, is only a stopgap measure, which allows detention of the patient in a state mental hospital while the judge's signature on a certification order is obtained.

With the trend toward medical admission rather than court certification, the health-officer admission appears the most sound and workable method of allowing patients to enter state mental hospitals in emergency cases. The committee therefore recommends the continuance of the health-officer admission with slight modifications and the abolition of the emergency admission on incomplete court order.

> *Recommendation No. 16 (Emergency Admissions)*. In cases of emergency, initial admission to a state mental hospital, licensed private institution, or psychiatric receiving hospital shall be authorized on the certificate of a health officer, a director of a community mental health service, or a designee of either of them, after examination of the patient and on confirmation of the need for hospitalization by the staff of the institution. This initial admission shall be for a period of sixty days. Within fifteen days after such admission and as a condition of continued retention of the patient, an application for admission shall be made, to be accompanied by the certificate of a second examining physician, who may be a psychiatrist on the staff of a state hospital or psychiatric receiving hospital (but not of a private institution). The admission shall be subject to the right of the patient to a judicial hearing promptly after admission, as provided in Recommendations No. 4, No. 5, and No. 6.

> Efforts should be made to provide adequate places for temporary lodging of persons prior to admission on the certificate of a health officer or director of a community mental health service. Budgets of health officers and community mental health services should make allowance for the costs of administering health-officer admissions.

The committee contemplates that the hearing and review procedures proposed in Recommendations No. 4 through No. 7 shall apply to health-officer admissions as well. With these protections, the health-officer admission can be used as a substitute for the regular forms of admission proposed in Recommendations No. 2 and No. 3, though, of course, only in emergency cases where the patient is in immediate need of care and treatment.

Release

The goal of all admission and review procedures is discharge of the patient and his return to the community as a well and useful citizen.

Under existing law a patient already admitted to a mental hospital may seek his release

(1) by a writ of habeas corpus;

(2) under the procedure in Section 76 of the Mental Hygiene Law which provides for a jury trial of the need for hospitalization; and

(3) under the procedures in Section 87 of the Mental Hygiene Law for judicial review of the decision of a hospital director against release or for discharge by the Commissioner of Mental Hygiene.

Admission to a mental hospital has long implied the legal steps of court commitment and detention; discharge, on the other hand, has historically been left to the doctors. The emphasis therefore has been on progress toward medical admission. The recommendations of the committee for fully medical admission procedures and for periodic review of the status of every mental patient require no change in the basic provisions as to release.

As a practical matter, the hospitals are quick to release patients as soon as they are able to return to the community. The pressure of admissions at the front door precludes retention of patients after the need for their treatment in the hospital has passed. Indeed, there has been some criticism that patients are often discharged to the community only to return to the hospital within a few months. As doctors learn more about the sources of mental illness and the causes of recurrence, they are attempting to solve this problem, so that a patient once discharged will be able to continue his rehabilitation in the community. After-care clinics aid in this process.

In general, therefore, medical considerations will continue to determine when a patient may be released and whether his release and return to the community will be permanent and successful.

> *Recommendation No. 17 (Medical Release)*. The present provisions for release and discharge of patients on the certificate of the director of a state hospital or the person in charge of a licensed private institution shall be continued.

> *Recommendation No. 18 (Judicial Release)*. Present provisions for release of mental patients by the courts shall be implemented with the assistance of the Mental Health Review Service. These provisions include (1) the right to a writ of habeas corpus, (2) the right to review of the admission by a judge acting on the verdict of a jury as provided in Section 76 of the Mental Hygiene Law, and (3) judicial review of the decision of a hospital director against

release, and provisions allowing release by the Commissioner of Mental Hygiene, pursuant to Section 87 of the Mental Hygiene Law. An application under any of these provisions may be made in the county of the patient's residence, the county from which he was admitted, or the county where the hospital is located. Any interested party, including the hospital, may apply to change the place of hearing the application to any other county in order to serve the convenience of the parties or the condition of the patient. There shall be no filing fee in any judicial proceeding involving the personal liberty of any person found or alleged to be mentally ill.

RELATED PROBLEMS

Three satellite problems revolve around the central questions of hospitalization of the mentally ill. The first, and perhaps most pressing, is the available group of procedures for looking after the property and business interests of mental patients or, in some cases, of persons who are mentally disturbed but do not require hospitalization. This question is discussed in Chapter VI, and we outline below only some of the general conclusions and recommendations which the committee has reached.

The second problem is care of the aged and senile. Many older persons who passively submit to hospitalization at the instance of their families or others could and probably should be cared for outside a mental hospital. There has been considerable criticism of the admission of such persons to hospitals under Section 73 of the Mental Hygiene Law, which allows their indefinite retention in the hospital as long as the patient does not protest.

The third problem is the admission to mental hospitals of persons accused of crime.

Property and Business Interests

The problem of administering the property and other financial interests of the mentally ill touches on a series of sensitive areas in which distinctions largely without differences have multiplied through the years.

On the one hand, patients hospitalized in state institutions were historically thought of as indigents at a time when accepting public care was in itself considered embarrassing. Today state mental hospitals house the overwhelming proportion of the hospitalized mentally ill, and persons who can afford to pay for their care are as often patients in state hospitals as in private institutions. All but a very small percentage of patients, who can and will undertake the high charges of private hospitals, seek admission to a state institution for care and treatment of mental illness. This means that patients in state hospitals may have social security benefits and financial and business interests on a sizable scale, which may provide funds for their hospital charges and for their own use in appropriate cases.

Existing law contains three major provisions for the administration of the funds and property of those deemed incompetent or mentally ill.

(1) Article 81 of the Civil Practice Act provides for the appointment of a committee in an elaborate procedure involving a jury trial, the appointment of a special guardian to represent the alleged incompetent, and an ultimate finding that the person is "incompetent to manage himself or his affairs."

(2) Section 1374 of the Civil Practice Act provides for the summary appointment of a committee upon a showing that the alleged incompetent has been "committed to a state hospital . . . and is an inmate thereof." This summary proceeding is not

available in the case of those who have not been certified to a state hospital and is not available in the case of those who have voluntarily entered state hospitals.

(3) Section 34(14) of the Mental Hygiene Law permits directors of state institutions to receive personal property (other than jewelry) of patients having no committee up to a value of $2,500 and to disburse funds of patients for certain specified purposes.

These provisions of present law do not go far enough in establishing simple, informal, inexpensive procedures for the conservation and protection of the property of persons unable properly to care for their interests, whether or not such persons are in mental hospitals and without regard to the method of admission.

Provision should be made for managing the property of some persons whose mental illness is not serious enough to require hospitalization but who are unable to deal with the financial problems they must regularly face. In some cases, persons who cannot handle their affairs but who could be treated and cared for without entering a mental hospital are sent to an institution in order to simplify the procedure for appointment of a committee. For these persons, simple and informal procedures for the appointment of a conservator of their property might mean a chance for useful treatment in the community rather than admission to a mental institution.

The committee therefore makes the following proposals, which are set forth in more detail in Chapter VI:

> *Recommendation No. 19* (*Protection of Property of Patients*). The director of a state mental hospital shall have the authority, under regulations to be promulgated by the Commissioner of Mental Hygiene, to provide protection for the property of patients in his hospital up to a fixed amount without respect to the method of admission or

to the power of a court to appoint a committee or other guardian.

Recommendation No. 20 (Appointment of Conservator for Patients in Hospitals). Section 1374 of the Civil Practice Act, relating to committees of an incompetent, should be repealed, and a new statute should be enacted to provide for an inexpensive, flexible, and nontraumatic method for the appointment of a "conservator" for any person in a state mental hospital, licensed private institution, or psychiatric receiving hospital, regardless of the method of admission of the patient, if the patient cannot properly care for his property and business interests by reason of old age, mental weakness, or mental illness.

The statute shall require a written judicial finding of the need for the appointment or discharge of a conservator or for any grant of powers to or change in powers of a conservator, but it shall not require that a finding of "incompetency" be made.

The statute shall authorize the court to grant to the conservator in each case powers appropriate to the condition and needs of the patient, whether such powers are greater or less than those now granted to a committee under Article 81 of the Civil Practice Act.

The act shall also provide for a temporary conservator pending a permanent appointment and shall allow a jury trial in a discharge proceeding only.

Recommendation No. 21 (Possible Extension of Use of Conservator). If experience with the conservator provisions proposed in Recommendation No. 20 suggests extension of this use, a conservator should be authorized in the case of persons who are unable to care for their property and business interests whether or not they are hospitalized.

Elderly and Senile Patients

Recent increase in general life expectancy means that many older people must face continuing and increasing problems in their late years. The committee has not been able to study the special problems of older patients in the detail which should be given to the subject.

We recognize that some older persons have mental illnesses which occur because of their age, particularly those brought on by progressive arteriosclerosis and other physical maladies. Although many of these patients cannot be cured, it may be necessary to care for them in mental hospitals.

A large number of older people, on the other hand, have no mental disturbance which comes under the heading of mental illness. They may be forgetful, or difficult to take care of, but their problems are not ones which require professional psychiatric care. These patients should not be in mental institutions. Even if there were no stigma whatever to hospitalization of older persons, they should be cared for in facilities specially designed to meet their needs. The committee has been unable to investigate or outline in detail the provisions that should be made for these elderly people, but because their problems are sometimes intertwined with those of mental patients and mental hospitals, we make the following recommendation:

> *Recommendation No. 22 (Elderly and Senile Patients).* After study of the needs of elderly and senile patients, the legislature should appropriate funds to aid in the construction and maintenance, at both state and local levels, of additional facilities of high quality for the care of those aged who are without major mental impairment.

The availability of such facilities will be the only permanent answer to the problems of caring for the aged. Until implementation of this proposal, however, we trust that the recommendations on nonvoluntary admissions to mental hospitals which we have made in this report will provide increased protection of the rights and interests of elderly patients.

Voting Rights

We have recommended above that the civil rights of voluntary patients, including the right to vote and any civil service status, should not be prejudiced by admission to a mental hospital. We also recommend that the voting rights of nonvoluntary patients be protected:

> *Recommendation No. 23* (*Voting Rights*). Section 152(6) of the Election Law shall be amended to eliminate the statutory disqualification from voting of persons "committed to an institution for the care and treatment of the mentally ill." However, appropriate provisions shall continue to allow disqualification from voting of persons adjudged incompetent or persons committed to an institution for the care and treatment of the mentally defective.

Formal Provisions

In connection with the admission procedures proposed by the committee in this report, a few details require filling in. The first of these is the form, name, and content of the application for admission of nonvoluntary patients to a mental hospital, which has been discussed in connection with all nonvoluntary admissions. The committee has adopted the present form of petition with minor changes:

> *Recommendation No. 24* (*Application for Admission*). The application for initial admission of a person to a state hospital, licensed private institution, or psychiatric receiv-

ing hospital shall be executed not more than ten days prior to admission by any one of the persons now authorized to make a petition under Section 74 of the Mental Hygiene Law, or, where none of these is available and able and willing to execute such an application, by the director of a state hospital or psychiatric receiving hospital (but not the director of a licensed private institution). The signature on the application should be made under penalties of perjury, but need not be witnessed or acknowledged by a notary public.

In the case of the doctors' certificates which we have proposed as the basic document of initial admission, we propose the following formal requirements:

Recommendation No. 25 (Examining Physicians). The certificates of examining physicians required for admission to a state mental hospital, licensed private institution, or psychiatric receiving hospital shall be made after examination of the patient not more than ten days prior to admission, and (1) in the case of state mental hospitals, one of the required certificates may be executed by a physician on the staff of the hospital to which admission is made; (2) in the case of psychiatric receiving hospitals, both of the required certificates may be executed by physicians on the staff of the hospital to which admission is made; (3) in the case of licensed private institutions, neither of the required certificates may be executed by a physician on the staff of the institution to which admission is made.

Recommendation No. 26 (Confirmation by Hospital). The examination of the patient and confirmation by a state hospital or licensed private institution of the patient's need for admission shall be made by some psychiatrist on the staff of the hospital other than the examining physician in the particular case.

While we have already provided for notice to a patient of his status and rights after admission, the committee has also approved a formal requirement, which is at present the practice of the Department of Mental Hygiene, of informing the patient of the nature of the hospital and his reason for being there immediately upon arrival. We also propose that the patient be given an opportunity at that time to make a telephone call anywhere within the state.

> *Recommendation No. 27 (Information to All Patients on Arrival).* Immediately upon the arrival of any patient at a state mental hospital, licensed private institution, or psychiatric receiving hospital, a medical officer of the institution shall inform the patient in writing of the character of the institution and the reason for his being there and shall give the patient the opportunity to make a telephone call anywhere within the state.

Admissions in Criminal Cases

A special class of admissions, both to state mental hospitals and psychiatric receiving hospitals, is admission of persons accused of crime. Since these admissions are quite different from ordinary admissions, this report devotes a separate chapter, Chapter VII, to this problem, and the committee's Recommendations No. 28 through No. 34 will be found outlined there in detail. Because most of the recommendations deal with specialized, somewhat technical problems, we do not summarize them here.

Proposed Legislation

Our study has been ambitious. We feel certain that it is not complete. The conclusions we have reached and the proposals we have made do form the framework for a major revision of the law relating to admission and discharge of mental patients in this state.

The program requires action. The proposals outlined here, even when filled in with the details presented in Part Two of this report, will not change the law by themselves. New legislation will be necessary to implement these recommendations. When the long and tortuous job of adopting new legislation has been done, we hope that it will lean heavily on the recommendations of this report.

Then a new era of mental health law in New York State will have begun.

PART TWO

The Study

Introduction

IN New York State patients may enter mental hospitals in seven different ways. They may enter voluntarily, or they may enter by any one of six different nonvoluntary methods. One of the nonvoluntary methods is used for psychiatric receiving hospitals, to which patients may be brought in various ways. The other five nonvoluntary methods admit patients to state hospitals and licensed private institutions, whether the admission is from the community directly or from the community indirectly by way of a receiving hospital.

In theory, all these methods of admission are made available because of the various circumstances, conditions, and needs of the patients. In practice, the policies of the hospital and the habits of local doctors and judges seem to determine the choice of method far more than do the needs of the particular patient.

Flexibility is claimed as a virtue of present New York law, but diversity might be a more appropriate word. Although the same law—with some minor variations—applies throughout the state, different patterns of admission have grown up in different localities. The most striking difference is that between the large cities which have psychiatric receiving hospitals and the rest of the state, where patients are admitted directly to state hospitals. But this is not all. In addition, every receiving hospital and every state hospital handles admissions according to its own particular policies and its own particular practice. Because of all this diversity, the percentage of voluntary admissions varies widely among the various hospitals, as do the percentages of the patients admitted by the several nonvoluntary methods.

Moreover, even the specific steps followed in any method of admission may vary from place to place according to local custom. Since the statute allows great latitude in dispensing with its requirements of notice to the patient and opportunity for a judicial hearing, customary procedures followed in any given method have come to differ sharply in different parts of the state.

Flexibility to meet the individual needs of patients may be desirable if it is appropriate to their varying conditions. But the variations in their condition do not depend, obviously, upon the accident of the patient's proximity to one hospital or another; and yet that accident does to a large extent determine what will happen. The vaunted flexibility is in fact, as already noted, rather an accidental diversity—a diversity which must fail to provide many patients with the method of admission and the procedures which accord best not only with their individual needs but also with modern developments in psychiatric care and the basic principles of due process.

To try to assess how well or how poorly the present New York law meets these objectives, we present the following description and analysis of how the law actually works in practice in various parts of the state. We examined the state's admission practices in the light of the revolution in the care of the mentally ill which is now in progress—in hospitals that are being transformed from locked custodial institutions into treatment centers with open doors and in communities that are developing diagnostic services, treatment, and after-care services in the community as supplements or alternatives to care in mental hospitals. Our task would perhaps have been simpler if we could have waited until these changes should have reached into every ward of every hospital and into every community of the state. But the interests of the 70,000 persons who are admitted each year to all kinds of mental facilities in New York State—to state hospitals, licensed private institutions, and psychiatric receiving hospitals—could not wait. Methods of admission fitted to the modern temper are themselves an aspect of improved care of the mentally ill.

The main body of this study is concerned with admission in civil cases for three groups of patients—voluntary patients, nonvoluntary patients admitted for limited periods of time, and nonvoluntary patients retained for longer periods of time. A special problem related to admission is also considered—the management of the property and business interests of the hospitalized mentally ill and aged who are incapable of handling their affairs. In addition, certain aspects of admission to mental hospitals in criminal cases are examined. This analysis is intended as a basis for determining whether the admission law of New York has kept pace with recent dramatic advances in psychiatric care and whether, at the same time, it provides adequate safeguards for the patient's liberty.

III

Voluntary Admissions

Rapid, noncompulsory admission to mental hospitals is good for most patients and helps in allowing effective treatment and early release.

TO encourage voluntary admissions, to improve the statutory framework in which they take place, and to reinforce the patient's knowledge of his right to release, the committee has made the following recommendations on voluntary admissions:

> *Recommendation No. 9 (Encouragement of Voluntary Admissions)*. Section 71 of the Mental Hygiene Law, providing for voluntary admissions, shall be continued and amended to state expressly that voluntary admission of suitable mentally ill persons is encouraged and that persons may be received in a state hospital or licensed private institution upon making application for treatment.
>
> *Recommendation No. 10 (Information to Voluntary Patients)*. It shall be the duty of a state hospital or licensed private institution to inform the voluntary patient in writing at the time of his admission, and thereafter before the expiration of sixty days, thereafter before the expiration of one year, and thereafter before the expiration of each two-year period, of his status as a voluntary patient. The Mental Health Review Service shall explain to the patient at the time of his admission, and at each of these other times, the

conditions of his hospitalization and his rights as a voluntary patient.

Recommendation No. 12 (*Civil Rights of Voluntary Patients*). Voluntary and informal patients shall not be deprived of the right to vote while in the hospital or after their discharge (this restates present law); nor shall they suffer any other deprivation of civil rights because of their hospitalization, such as prejudice to their civil service ranking.

The right of voluntary and informal patients to a driver's license shall remain as at present, with the Commissioner of Motor Vehicles making the decision whether or not a license should be issued or continued for a person who has been or is hospitalized for mental illness. The hospital may make a recommendation to the Commissioner of Motor Vehicles in cases in which the hospital believes it is not safe for the patient to drive.

The most sweeping change we envision in procedures for voluntary admission is the introduction of a fully informal method of entering and leaving mental hospitals.

Recommendation No. 11 (*Informal Admissions*). Informal admission to state hospitals and psychiatric receiving hospitals shall be permitted if the hospital is willing to accept the patient. No formalities shall be required for admission, and the patient shall be free to leave at will.

The names of all informal patients shall be reported to the Department of Mental Hygiene and to the Mental Health Review Service within ten days after admission.

It shall be the duty of the hospital to inform the patient in writing, at least as often as required in the case of voluntary patients in Recommendation No. 10, of his status as an informal patient and of his freedom to leave the hospital.

As mental hospitals have unlocked their doors and shifted their emphasis from custody to treatment, persons suffering from mental illness have become more willing to enter a mental hospital voluntarily. The use of tranquilizing drugs and open wards and the spreading realization that many patients can now be returned quickly to their communities have contributed to the new public attitude. Patients who know of these developments are less terrified by the thought of hospitalization, less determined to avoid it as worse than death itself. More are willing to seek the benefits of treatment in a hospital voluntarily, and their doctors, too, encourage it.

Voluntary admission to a mental hospital, many psychiatrists tell us, brings some special benefits to the patient. Treatment at an earlier stage; maintenance of better morale, which induces a more cooperative attitude on the patient's part; and preservation of the patient's dignity and sense of self-direction are all assumed to help with his recovery.[1] Psychiatrists and other

[1] New York State Department of Mental Hygiene, Report of Interdepartmental Committee on Laws Governing Hospitalization of the Mentally Ill 41 (unpublished, dated June 10, 1954, and made available to our committee by the New York State Department of Mental Hygiene); see also A Draft Act Governing Hospitalization of the Mentally Ill, Public Health Service Pub. No. 51 (rev. ed. 1952), Commentary, Part II, 19:

"A fully operating program of voluntary admissions will reduce materially the harmful experiences often associated with compulsory hospitalization and at the same time encourage the mentally ill and their families to obtain care at an early stage, when the promise of recovery is greatest. Another important consideration is the need, from the standpoint of effective treatment, for the patient's cooperation with his physician. This is most likely to be obtained if the patient is in a hospital environment because he recognizes his need for it and affirmatively seeks it. Making hospitalization so far as possible as readily available to the mentally ill as to the physically ill should reduce the financial and human cost of mental illness which is greatest when the patient's condition has been aggravated by delay in treatment or by the experience of forcible hospitalization, and when, recovery having become impossible, lifelong custody is the only prospect."

physicians in New York State who answered a questionnaire from our committee generally agreed that the form of admission entailing the least compulsion is the best. Many of their statements deplored the formalities of compulsory admission, which exaggerate and perpetuate the fear of hospitalization in patients and their families.

Despite this strong preference for voluntary admission, these same physicians believe that the method of admission does not have a major and direct long-term effect upon the patient's medical progress. In this vein they commented: motivation toward recovery is not determined by the method of admission; the method of admission is unimportant during the period of severe symptoms; the method of admission has no lasting medical effect; the method of admission must be adapted to the individual case and is much less important than the kind of treatment used. One physician noted that a voluntary admission is likely to be used when the patient is aware of his need for help; such a patient has a better prognosis, not because of the kind of admission used, but because of the kind of patient he is.[2]

Our staff found no evidence that the voluntary patient, once hospitalized, receives any special privileges or treatment because of the method of his admission, although some patients think it advantageous to be a voluntary. In a survey of a limited number of former mental patients by Fountain House Foundation,[3] twenty-six of the thirty former patients questioned

[2] Controverting the assumption that a voluntary patient does have a better prognosis, however, was the comment of one physician that many voluntary patients with awareness of their need for treatment have chronic illnesses that respond poorly to treatment, whereas many patients who must be admitted compulsorily respond quickly to drugs or shock therapy or both, and make excellent, prompt recoveries. Some of the patients readmitted as voluntaries (see text *infra* at note 9) may of course be voluntaries who have insight but who also have some chronic mental illness which does not respond to treatment.

[3] Mr. John H. Beard, Executive Director of Fountain House Founda-

said that it does make a difference whether a person signs himself in on a voluntary basis or is legally committed. These respondents mentioned the following advantages of a voluntary admission: the patient can sign himself out; the patient receives better treatment and greater respect from the doctors or the hospital staff; the patient's mental health is considered to be better if he is known to be a voluntary patient.[4]

An effort was made to ascertain whether a voluntary admission might in fact sometimes result in a program of treatment different from that which would be undertaken if the patient

---

tion, a voluntary agency in New York City devoted to psychiatric rehabilitation of the mentally ill, generously offered, as a service to our committee, to expand the research program of Fountain House in order to include a survey of the understanding and experience which some patients had of voluntary admissions and of legal commitment.

The study was based on interviews with 30 Fountain House members selected at random from members (1) who were over twenty-one years of age at the time of their latest hospitalization, (2) who were living in the New York City area before their latest hospitalization, (3) whose latest hospitalization occurred after January 1958, (4) whose latest hospitalization was in a state mental hospital or city psychopathic hospital, not in a veterans' hospital, and (5) who used Fountain House during the day and thus were available for an interview. Of the 30 Fountain House members interviewed, 14 had first been hospitalized at Bellevue Hospital, 11 at Kings County Hospital, and 3 at voluntary hospitals. Only 2 had gone directly to state hospitals.

The typical subject in the sample was a white, single male, between the ages of thirty and forty, a high-school graduate who had had at least two hospitalizations and who had been hospitalized for a total period of time of at least one year. The number of hospitalizations in the sample runs at a slightly higher rate than that for the schizophrenic population of the New York State hospital system.

[4] It is interesting to note that although most of the respondents thought voluntary admission advantageous to their hospital stay, it was thought to be of less significance for their readjustment in the community. Joining a club, getting help from the family, holding a job, dating, were seen by only five respondents as being facilitated by a voluntary admission. Ten felt, however, that it would be easier to secure a new job after having been a voluntary patient, since they felt that employers associated a legal commitment with "loss of control."

were admitted in another way. Might electric shock therapy, for example, be rejected or delayed because a voluntary patient might refuse or fail to sign the consent for it? Or might the hospital staff, perhaps, tend to work on voluntary patients more promptly than on others because the voluntaries can be detained for a short time only? These questions, and others similar to them, were investigated in a study of individual patients admitted by different methods in three upstate hospitals.[5] Although this study, again, was based on a small sample, so that its results are far from conclusive, no evidence was found that the method of treatment varies significantly with the method of admission. The method of treatment appears to vary, as would be expected, with the condition of the patient, the facilities of the hospital, and the hospital's medical and administrative policies—but not with the legal method of the patient's admission.

We have thus been unable to adduce statistical or scientific proof of the superiority of voluntary admission over compulsory from the point of view of the patient's long-term medical welfare. No significant evidence was found, however, militating against the avowed preference of many physicians for the voluntary admission. If, therefore, the seemingly reasonable view of most doctors is to be accepted, albeit without rigid proof, that voluntary admission facilitates prompt and early care and tends to promote an attitude favorable to effective treatment, it is important to consider the extent of use of the voluntary admission.

[5] The study was conducted in the summer of 1960 for our committee by Miss Mary E. Curtis, an experienced psychiatric nurse, to determine whether there are differences in the treatments, conditions, or privileges of patients which depend upon the method of admission.

RECENT INCREASES IN VOLUNTARY ADMISSIONS

During the last twelve years voluntary admissions to state mental hospitals in New York have increased significantly, until in 1960 more than one-fifth of all admissions were voluntary. From 1949 through 1960 voluntary admissions rose from 6 to 21 per cent of all admissions to state mental hospitals, nearly a fourfold increase. Chart 1 shows the trend for those years in voluntary admissions to state hospitals.

Although voluntary admissions are on the rise in all state hospitals, the percentages of voluntary admissions vary greatly from one hospital to another. Table 2 in the Appendix shows this variation for the year ending March 31, 1960, with a range of from 56 per cent in one hospital to 7 per cent in another. Similar variations in the use of the voluntary admission are shown by county in Table 3 (Appendix).

Differing conditions throughout the state help to explain these variations, since changes in treatment, in hospital administration, and in public attitudes have naturally occurred at different rates in different communities and different hospitals. One factor is the availability of psychiatric clinics where patients are seen on an out-patient basis and can be urged to enter the hospital voluntarily. Another may be the attitude of doctors, social workers, and others toward voluntary admissions. In some areas doctors seem quite unaware of this method of admission and initiate emergency or court-ordered admissions, or send the patient to a receiving hospital for observation, as a matter of course. Where doctors are aware of the possibility, their attitudes toward voluntary admission and the importance they attach to it vary greatly.

A factor that depresses the voluntary rate is the practice in some receiving hospitals of sending all patients to state hos-

CHART 1. Trends in voluntary admissions to selected New York State mental hospitals: Percentages of total admissions that were voluntary, 1949–1960

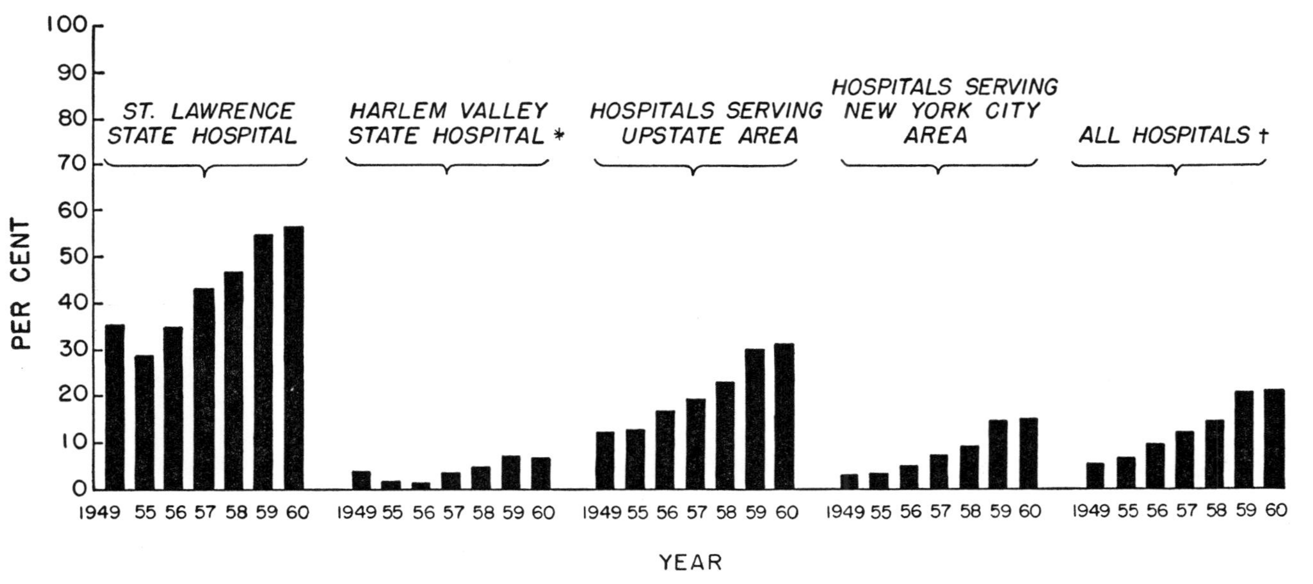

Source: New York State Department of Mental Hygiene, Division of Statistical Services. (See Table 1, Appendix, for supporting data.)

* See text of Chapter III for explanation of low voluntary rate.

† The Psychiatric Institute is omitted because, with its special role, almost all its patients enter voluntarily.

pitals either on a single physician's certificate (for nonobjecting patients under Section 73) or on a court order. For example, Harlem Valley State Hospital (mentioned in Chart 1) receives nearly all the adult patients of Jacobi Hospital, which routinely uses one-physician certificates for transferring its patients. Many of the patients admitted by this method would be suitable for voluntary admission and would be accepted as such; indeed, the staff at this receiving hospital even refer to the one-physician certificate as a "voluntary" admission.

The relationship between the state mental hospital and its community, including the public's image of it as a hospital rather than an asylum, might be expected to influence voluntary admissions. Since open wards are one indication of a hospital therapeutically oriented, one might expect to find a clear correlation between the use of open wards and voluntary admissions. St. Lawrence State Hospital with the highest percentage of voluntary admissions does also have the highest percentage of patients on open wards—100 per cent. But otherwise the expectation is not supported, for no correlation appears to exist, surprisingly, in New York State between the percentage of patients admitted voluntarily and the percentage of patients on open wards. (See Table 2, Appendix.)

Finally, the interest—or lack of interest—of state hospital directors in having patients enter voluntarily may be an important factor. In interviews with our staff some directors recognized that their own attitudes must influence the methods of admission used. These attitudes were found to be reflected in the actions of hospital personnel at all levels.[6] The percentage

[6] From the interviews and observations of Miss Curtis in three upstate hospitals, *supra* note 5, it appeared that hospital personnel handling admissions tend to agree with the philosophy of the director of the hospital on admission methods. Thus, in a hospital where the director was favorably inclined toward voluntary admissions, the chief clerk admitted that the greater volume of voluntary admissions increased the time spent on records because of the shorter stays and frequent re-

of voluntary admissions is higher in those hospitals where hospital policy aggressively favors voluntary admissions—where the admitting doctors take the time and trouble to show patients the hospital, its wards where they will stay and its facilities, and to urge patients to enter "on their own." By contrast, in a hospital not energetically favoring voluntary admissions, several patients commented that they had not known of the possibility of entering voluntarily and that they would have preferred a voluntary admission had they known of it.[7]

The patient's familiarity with mental hospitals seems to affect the voluntary admission rate. Our staff asked several state hospital directors about the tendency of patients originally admitted as voluntaries to return as voluntaries and about the methods of readmission used for patients originally admitted by a nonvoluntary method. The directors were in general agreement that if a patient felt that he had been helped by an earlier hospitalization he would be likely to return as a voluntary. Policy in several hospitals encourages such a return by explaining to the patient at his discharge that, if he ever again needs help, a particular doctor at the hospital whom the patient knows will always be available. Of thirty Fountain House members questioned on their preference for a voluntary admission or a legal commitment if they should ever need hospitalization again, twenty-five answered that they would prefer to sign themselves in as voluntary patients, and twenty-two specified

---

admissions of the voluntary patients, but she felt that this was not a waste of time. In another hospital where the director was not enthusiastic about voluntary admissions, the chief clerk commented that voluntary patients are a nuisance and a waste of the time of doctors and social workers in readmissions. Similar differences in attitude were found among nurses and doctors in different hospitals, but within each hospital the attitudes toward voluntary admission were fairly consistent at all levels of personnel. For an exception, see *infra* note 18 and accompanying text.

[7] Statements made to Miss Curtis in the course of her study, *supra* note 5.

for this a hospital in which they had been previously hospitalized.[8]

The influence of previous hospital experience on the patient's attitude toward admission can be strikingly demonstrated. In 1960 only 17 per cent of first admissions were voluntary. Among the readmissions that year, however, 32 per cent, or nearly twice as large a proportion, were voluntary.[9] There is manifestly a much greater willingness on the part of mental patients in need of care to enter a hospital voluntarily after they have had some experience with it than there was before such experience.

In addition to the impetus which voluntary admissions can receive from the practicing doctor, the social worker, the hospital, and the community, law and its administration can also encourage such admissions. Two specific measures have been taken in the last five years toward this end. One was the amendment in 1956 of a general order of the Regulations of the Department of Mental Hygiene so as to broaden the definition of persons suitable for voluntary admission. The rewriting of this order assured hospital directors that the policy of the Department favored such admissions, even if some risks might be incurred in connection with patients who wanted to leave too soon. The second step was the amendment in 1958 of Section 71 of the Mental Hygiene Law so as to reduce from sixty to fifteen days the initial period for which a voluntary patient can be detained in the hospital and from fifteen to ten days the period of time thereafter during which a voluntary patient can be detained after he has given written notice of intention to leave.[10]

[8] Survey conducted for the committee by Fountain House Foundation, *supra* note 3.

[9] New York State Department of Mental Hygiene, Division of Statistical Services, communication of March 30, 1961.

[10] N.Y. Sess. Laws 1958, ch. 108, § 1, eff. March 5, 1958. The detention period specified applies only to state hospitals and licensed private institutions. Some psychiatric receiving hospitals require voluntary pa-

Both these measures were aimed at giving the benefits of voluntary status to more patients. To some extent this has been accomplished. The fact remains, however, that only 21 per cent of all admissions to state hospitals in 1960 were voluntary, and the rate varied widely among different hospitals. The general rate is low, furthermore, in comparison with that in England and Wales, where 75 per cent of all admissions to mental hospitals—and in some hospitals more than 90 per cent—were voluntary in 1957.[11]

PROBLEMS IN VOLUNTARY ADMISSIONS

To understand this varying and limited growth of the voluntary admission, one must examine it in operation and see the problems which both patients and hospital administrators face in its use—problems involving the suitability of patients for voluntary admission, the period of time during which they may be detained, their right to discharge, and the effect of hospitalization upon their civil and property rights.

Suitability for Voluntary Admission

The Mental Hygiene Law gives authority to state hospitals and licensed private institutions to receive as a voluntary patient "any person suitable for care and treatment, who volun-

---

tients to give ten days' notice of intention to leave, but this is a regulation of the hospital rather than a statute; and the regulation specifies no minimum detention period.

[11] Royal Commission on the Law Relating to Mental Illness and Mental Deficiency, Report, para. 221 (1957): "It has been found possible to admit as voluntary patients many more than those suffering from the milder forms or the early stages of illness; many patients whose illness is such that they could be certified quite properly as 'of unsound mind' have sufficient insight into their condition to wish to receive treatment and are accepted as voluntary patients."

tarily makes written application therefor." [12] The hospital has discretion on whether or not to accept a patient as a voluntary admission, subject to review by the Department of Mental Hygiene.[13] Before 1956 the regulation of the Department on voluntary patients explicitly required that the patient be competent to make an application for admission at the time of admission and that after his admission he continue to be competent to choose to stay. This meant that if the patient's mental condition changed so that he could no longer understand the voluntary condition of the contract, another form of admission had to be secured or the patient had to be discharged.[14]

With such provisions, many hospital directors felt constrained to refuse voluntary admission to patients who were so un-

[12] Mental Hygiene Law, § 71. If the person is under eighteen years of age, the written application must be made by his parent, legal guardian, or next of kin. The Section 71 voluntary admission is not used in psychiatric receiving hospitals, to which patients may be admitted without any application or formality as in admission to a general hospital for a physical illness.

[13] Section 71 requires the hospital director to notify the Department of Mental Hygiene of all voluntary admissions within ten days after admission, and the Department is required to examine such cases to "determine if they belong to the voluntary class." Immediate compliance with the Department's recommendation on discharge or certification is required. Failure to comply is ground for revocation of a license issued to a private institution.

[14] General Order 3 of the Regulations of the Department of Mental Hygiene, effective December 23, 1954, stated:

"When the mental condition of such individuals changes following admission so that they are unable to understand the voluntary condition of the contract they should no longer be held on a voluntary application but, depending upon his condition, another form of admission should be secured or the patient should be discharged. This stand is taken in the belief that one of the essential conditions of the contract, i.e. the patient's competency, has been removed.

"Good judgment should be used in applying this procedure. A patient who may be reasonably expected to recover shortly from an episode may continue on a voluntary status. The medical inspector under ordinary circumstances will recommend that action in such a case be held in abeyance until the next medical inspection."

stable that their understanding of their status might change. They were not much reassured by a qualification in the regulation which directed them to use "good judgment" and gave some leeway in its application. Some hospitals, furthermore, refused routinely to admit as a voluntary patient anyone thought to be suicidal. Concerned as they were about the validity of contract [15] with an acutely disturbed or vacillating patient, these hospitals accepted as a voluntary patient only one who could express clearly and unequivocally his desire to enter the hospital.

On April 5, 1956, the general order on voluntary admissions was amended to eliminate these restrictions and to encourage voluntary admissions in fact as well as in words. (It has become General Order 2.) It now reads:

> Voluntary admission of suitable mentally ill persons should be encouraged as providing optimum conditions for the treatment of the patient and the establishment of good relations with the family

[15] Voluntary admission has been considered by the Attorney General to be a constitutionally valid contract between the hospital and the patient. "I am further of the opinion that the provisions of Section 83-A of the Insanity Law [the predecessor of Section 71 of the Mental Hygiene Law] requiring a voluntary patient to give ten days notice in writing of intention to leave are valid and enforceable. If all the conditions mentioned in the statute are complied with by the voluntary patient, the execution of the application blank by the patient creates a contractual relation and the patient surrenders his freedom for a period of ten days so that the patient may come under observation and receive care and treatment in the institution. No rights of the patient are invaded by compliance with the statute. If during the ten days period the condition of the patient warrants, the patient may be formally committed to the institution under the order of the court, or may be discharged." N.Y. Ops. Atty. Gen. 332, 334 (1923).

Nearly a quarter of a century later, however, and two thousand miles away, the Supreme Court of New Mexico, in *Ex parte* Romero, 51 N.M. 201, 181 P. 2d 811 (1947), held unconstitutional a voluntary admission statute that provided for detention for ten days after written notice of desire to leave. The New Mexico court rejected the reasoning of the New York Attorney General because a contract with a person so disordered as to require hospitalization is not enforceable.

and the community. Such persons may be received in a state hospital or licensed private institutions upon making voluntary application for treatment therein. A person may be accepted for voluntary admission if he appreciates that he is in need of hospital care and treatment and presents himself and signs a proper form willingly with appreciation of what he is doing.

Under the revised regulation, hospitals are becoming more willing than formerly to accept the voluntary admission of all kinds of patients, even the suicidal, the delusional, or the violently aggressive, provided only that they apply for admission. Less and less, therefore, is behavior or diagnosis a criterion for voluntary admission.[16]

The director of one hospital with a high proportion of voluntary admissions reported that anyone may be hospitalized voluntarily in his hospital if he can answer "yes" intelligently to three questions:

1. Do you know that this is a state hospital?
2. Do you know that there is something wrong with you mentally?
3. Do you want to come in?

Even though the patient changes his mind after admission, he will be retained nevertheless. He need not be able at every moment of his stay to reaffirm his desire to be a voluntary patient, since he may be disoriented, forgetful, or apprehensive

[16] Beyond the scope of this study are the characteristics of patients who tend to be admitted as voluntary patients. An interesting and valuable study of social class and hospitalization has shown that the chance of entering a mental hospital voluntarily, on the one hand, or by court order, on the other, is strongly related to social class. In the highest social class, the authors found that almost equal proportions enter by the two procedures. In the lowest social class, the probability of entering by court certification is four and one-half times that of entering by voluntary admission. Hardt and Feinhandler, Social Class and Schizophrenic Prognosis 7 and Table 4 (page 9) (unpublished study, 1958, by the New York State Mental Health Research Unit and Harvard University).

while under treatment. Other hospitals, however, still follow a stricter policy and keep as voluntary patients only those who have an understanding of their status at all times.

Various kinds of patients may be admitted under Section 71: patients who have insight into their illness and affirmatively want hospital care; patients who sign a form for a voluntary admission but have little understanding of its significance; and "forced voluntaries"—contradictory though this phrase seems—who sign a form for a voluntary admission under pressure from a family or from a court.

Hospital directors differ on the wisdom of accepting patients in this last group, voluntaries "forced" to enter by threat or coercion. One director said that a patient admitted under threat of court action will usually want to leave after the initial detention period, when the charges against him will have been dropped. Other directors favored such admissions on the ground that these patients often respond well to treatment. In a licensed private institution of high caliber visited by the staff, the director said that he is not concerned with the pressures that may have induced a patient to sign a voluntary admission so long as they were not of such a nature as to interfere with the possibility of successful treatment. One psychiatrist with extensive experience in after-care clinics commented that an element of coercion in bringing about a voluntary admission is not necessarily bad; a patient who is offered the choice of being admitted voluntarily or certified may make excellent progress as a voluntary patient in spite of the initial pressure put upon him.

Cases of overzealous admission of "voluntary" patients doubtless do exist, where the language of Section 71 is stretched to cover a person who really objects. Many cases at the other extreme also exist: patients who might have come into the hospital voluntarily are brought in by the compulsory process. Cases were reported to our staff of patients thus willing to enter voluntarily who were nevertheless sent in on a health officer's certificate or a court's order.[17]

Significant departures from the spirit of General Order 2 were found with respect to accepting as voluntary patients all who signify their willingness. A few hospitals even refuse readmission to a voluntary patient who has once been admitted as a voluntary and has then left against the hospital's advice.[18] This may be an explicit policy of the hospital, or it may be a defensive measure adopted by the admitting staff against repeated work-ups of voluntary patients who refuse to stay long enough for treatment.[19] Some voluntary admissions may also be discouraged by the hospital's insistence that the patient sign a consent to shock therapy at the time of admission.[20]

[17] Insufficient use of voluntary admission procedures was also shown in a study of 109 cases in Connecticut in which more than half the decisions to hospitalize were initiated by the patients or by their families, but in which only four voluntary admissions occurred. Lewis and Zeichner, Impact of Admission to a Mental Hospital on the Patient's Family, 44 Mental Hygiene 503, 504 (Oct. 1960).

[18] See discussion of readmissions *supra* at note 9 and accompanying text.

[19] One hospital director requires a report from his admitting staff on all patients refused voluntary admission; thus strong justification must be presented to the supervisory staff for refusal to admit voluntary patients. In this very hospital, however, the staff took it upon themselves to record in a little black book the names of all voluntary patients who left against advice as persons who should not be readmitted as voluntaries.

[20] A voluntary patient must himself sign a special consent for shock therapy, although a relative may sign on behalf of a nonvoluntary patient. If a voluntary patient refuses to sign such a consent at the time of admission, he is usually admitted as a voluntary anyway. But at least one case came to the staff's attention in which acceptance of a hesitant voluntary patient was delayed several hours while he was urged to sign the consent for shock therapy; on the insistence of the patient's doctor that this requirement was improper, the patient was finally admitted without signing.

A voluntary patient who refuses to sign a consent for shock therapy may receive other treatment and may later be persuaded to accept

Evidence that many patients are admitted by compulsory methods who might have entered voluntarily may be found in the variation in the rate of voluntaries among different hospitals. The generally low rate of voluntary admissions from New York City is shown by Chart 1. In an effort to combat routine certification, receiving hospitals have undertaken to screen patients for voluntary admission to state hospitals. State hospitals serving the New York City area have also, from time to time, sent staff doctors to the receiving hospitals to talk with groups of patients and urge them to enter a state hospital voluntarily. This practice of screening patients for voluntary admission while they are in the receiving hospitals has not, however, yielded the hoped-for increases in voluntary patients.[21] The risk is that such patients, on actual arrival at the state hospital, may have to be returned for certification after all, and this risk deters acceptance of all but clear cases. Thus the director of one large state hospital near New York City pointed out that it is hard to decide on voluntary admissions without ex-

---

shock therapy. Occasionally a patient who is obdurate may be certified for the express purpose of giving him shock treatment on consent signed by a relative. The best solution may be that of one licensed private institution which has abandoned the practice of requesting consent for shock therapy, from either patient or relative, at the time of admission. This hospital believes that since shock therapy is used today in only 1 per cent of all cases, it is unwise to require consent for the other 99 per cent; consent for the one can be asked for when needed.

[21] In February 1958 one state hospital undertook to have a doctor from its staff at Bellevue daily to talk with patients about voluntary admission. In 1958, 305 patients were admitted to state hospitals from Bellevue as voluntary patients. In 1959, as a result of this same project, 606 patients at Bellevue were cleared for voluntary admission to state hospitals, but in 1960 only 430 patients were thus cleared.

At least one doctor involved in this program is of the opinion that it is still valuable, even though a small percentage of patients may need to be returned to the receiving hospital for certification. The danger that patients may consider their return a breach of faith is met by explaining to them at the outset that this may happen if they do not cooperate or if they fail to improve.

amining the patient at the state hospital. For this reason almost all his voluntary patients come from the county where his hospital is located. It is not practicable, in short, for the state hospital to decide to admit a voluntary patient at long range.

The hospital's right to decide whether a patient is suitable for voluntary admission may create practical problems for the patient, his family, and his physician. So long as the hospital is near the patient's home or near the receiving hospital from which he comes, little inconvenience arises from a rejection. But when the state hospital is far away, the inconvenience and expense are likely to be serious, since the cost of transportation in voluntary admissions is borne by the patient or his family.

In general, broadening the definition of persons suitable for voluntary admission has given authority to admit all who sign the voluntary admission form. But vestiges of former restrictions remain and inhibit some voluntary admissions. The New York State Interdepartmental Committee on Laws Governing Hospitalization of the Mentally Ill made a specific suggestion:

> If community psychiatric clinics were more numerous and were held more frequently, they could be used by the hospital staffs to pass on the propriety of voluntary admission for many patients being considered for such admission by physicians in the communities.[22]

Certainly, as state hospitals reach out into the community in this way, psychiatrists from state hospitals will be able to provide advance clearance for voluntary admissions and even to encourage them. It should be recognized, however, that some restriction is inherent in a form of admission which requires the patient to sign an affirmative consent and gives the hospital discretion to determine his suitability for such admission subject to review in each case by the Department of Mental Hygiene.

[22] Report, *op. cit. supra* note 1, at 24.

Detention of Voluntary Patients

The scheme of a voluntary admission under Section 71 is that the patient agrees to enter the hospital and then "may be detained for a period not exceeding fifteen days . . . and thereafter until ten days after receipt of notice in writing from such person of his intention or desire to leave."[23] Although this detention period is considerably shorter than that in force prior to 1958, as mentioned above,[24] it is nevertheless a limitation on the patient's right to discharge.

Some psychiatrists in hospitals and in private practice criticized the shortened period as not allowing enough time for diagnosis and progress with treatment, since patients almost always require more than twenty-five days for treatment. More than this, the shortage of psychiatrists in state hospitals slows the pace of diagnosis and work-up of patients' cases, so that hospital staffs may be hard pressed even to diagnose the cases

[23] The statute presents a possible question of interpretation. The voluntary application form provided by the Department of Mental Hygiene reads:

"I desire to be received as a voluntary patient for care and treatment in the . . . [name of institution] . . . and promise, if my request is granted, to obey all the rules and regulations. It is understood that I may be detained at this institution for a period not exceeding 15 days, at your discretion, if my condition warrants it. I further agree, *at any time after this period,* to give 10 days' notice, in writing before leaving without your permission." (Emphasis supplied.)

This form interprets the statute as requiring that the notice be given at or after the end of the first fifteen days—not earlier. Does the statute mean that the "notice" must be "thereafter" as the form assumes? Or does it mean "detained . . . thereafter," which would let the notice be given during the fifteen-day period? No case law has been found. The interpretation adopted by the Department's form makes the minimum period, in effect, twenty-five days. The other reading would make it fifteen days, if the notice should be given within the first five days. The Department's reading of the form appears to be generally accepted.

[24] *Supra* note 10 and accompanying text.

before the shortened deadline—let alone to treat them. Another problem caused by the shortened period concerns alcoholic patients admitted as voluntaries. They usually want to leave before their treatment is completed and of course cannot be held more than twenty-five days against their will. The admission and readmission of these patients puts a heavy burden on the hospital without doing the patients any lasting good.

Despite these problems, most of the hospital directors approve the shortened detention period and find no fault with the ten days during which a voluntary patient may be detained after receipt of notice of intention to leave. (Such notice may be given by the patient himself or by a relative or spouse.) Only two hospital directors suggested lengthening the entire period of retention of voluntaries, and then only by five days. Most hospital directors feel that the encouragement of voluntary admissions given by the shortened minimum stay outweighs any hardship imposed on the hospital staff.

Perhaps the general satisfaction with the shortened period stems in part from the likelihood that most voluntary patients who need further care can be persuaded to stay. Several directors said that because of this they rarely need to certify a voluntary patient. In one New York City hospital, out of 377 voluntary admissions in 1959, only 9 patients, or 2 per cent, were certified. This was considered an unusually large number. In one upstate hospital, the only voluntary patient whom the director could recall having certified was a woman considered dangerous to her children.

Under General Order 2 a patient who presents his notice to leave should be judicially certified if at that time "he does not appreciate his mental condition, and he is considered dangerous to himself or others." [25] This standard is more rigor-

[25] General Order 41 of the Regulations of the Department of Mental Hygiene authorizes the director of the hospital to petition for judicial certification when the authority to detain a dangerous patient held under

ous than that required for an original nonvoluntary admission; but we found that this rigorous standard is usually applied in practice, so that a voluntary patient is rarely certified merely because he would be "better off hospitalized." The growth of the open hospital has shown that many patients who are not well can still function in society without danger to themselves or others, and therefore hospital directors are reluctant to detain by compulsion voluntary patients who are not dangerous.

A minor voluntary patient, one under eighteen whose parent, legal guardian, or next of kin signs the application,[26] must be released on reaching the age of eighteen, or he must execute the form for voluntary admission himself. The only other possibility is for him to be judicially certified. If the minor voluntary is a psychopathic personality but without psychosis, he cannot be thus certified. In that case the only way by which he can receive further treatment in the hospital is for him to sign the voluntary admission, which he usually will not do.[27]

As we have seen, few voluntary patients become compulsory

---

a voluntary or health officer's admission is about to expire and no other proper person is willing to take action.

[26] Children's units now exist in nine state hospitals—Rochester, Binghamton, Marcy, Middletown, Rockland, Creedmoor, Central Islip, Kings Park, and Hudson River State Hospitals (Mental Hygiene News, Feb. 1961). In some of these units the demand for admission has been so great that admission as a minor voluntary is not used, but children are judicially certified when they first enter, with all the trauma and stigma that such certification entails.

[27] Note that the British Mental Health Act, 7 & 8 Eliz. 2, ch. 72 (1959), provides for compulsory admission of a psychopath under the age of twenty-one and detention until age twenty-five unless it is found that if he were released he would be dangerous to himself or others. Sections 26(5), 44(2). There was opposition to these provisions because of fear that they might create a new criminal code for psychopaths who have not had any brush with the law. But it was enacted, nevertheless, on the basis of prevalent medical opinion that if there is any hope of helping these patients it must be while they are young. Royal Commission's Report, *op. cit. supra* note 11, para. 354.

patients. Few compulsory patients, moreover, become voluntary patients, although once treatment is started they may often be willing to remain voluntarily. The Mental Hygiene Law does not expressly recognize the possibility of such a change in the patient's status except in the case of one who entered on a health-officer admission.[28] Hospitals can, however, without statutory authorization, discharge any compulsory patient and readmit him as a voluntary patient. In practice, however, this is rarely done.

British mental hospitals, by contrast, have found their own noncompulsory admission so helpful to a patient's cure that they discharge patients from compulsory powers wherever practicable. The patients then remain in the hospital informally, like any patient in a hospital for a physical illness, free to leave at will. During the first few months after the passage of the British Mental Health Act of 1959, 25,000 patients were thus changed from the compulsory status to an informal one.[29]

Discharge

The right to a prompt discharge on recovery or where the patient is not dangerous is of crucial importance as an inducement to voluntary admissions. But the right is meaningless unless the patient knows of it. General Order 4 of the Regulations of the Department of Mental Hygiene requires the director or a medical officer to inform all patients, at the time of admission, about the character of the institution and

[28] Section 72 (1) (c) says that a patient admitted on a health-officer admission may be certified under certain circumstances "unless the patient shall sign a request to remain as a voluntary patient under the provisions of section seventy-one." In one upstate hospital half of the patients originally admitted on a health-officer admission did in fact become voluntary patients.

[29] Communications from the Ministry of Health, London, March 1960 and May 12, 1960.

the reason for their detention. In addition, a representative of the Department interviews each voluntary patient every six months to make certain that he understands his status. Our study of individual patients admitted by different methods in three upstate hospitals [30] indicated that voluntary patients are much more aware and much more intelligently informed of their rights and the legal consequences of their hospitalization than are compulsory patients.

Discharge of voluntary patients is absolute. They cannot be discharged conditionally—as certified patients can—into convalescent care during which they must attend an after-care clinic. Of course they may agree to attend such a clinic voluntarily, and one inducement to do so is that drugs are furnished without charge in such clinics. Administrators of after-care clinics assured our staff that all patients are encouraged to attend such clinics, regardless of how they were admitted to the hospital.

Nevertheless, some patients seem to believe that after-care is more readily available to certified patients than to voluntary ones. Of the 30 former mental patients questioned by Fountain House Foundation,[31] 9 said that they thought it would be easier to secure help from after-care clinics if they had been legally committed. Of these, 7 thought after-care could be denied to voluntary patients but could not be denied to certified patients. This was the only item in a long series of questions relating to community adjustment in which certification was seen as having more favorable consequences than a voluntary admission.

From the point of view of the patient's rights, the most important feature of a voluntary admission is the right to leave the hospital at will after short periods of detention which merely allow the hospital time to start treatment and opportunity to persuade the patient to remain. The right to leave the

[30] *Supra* note 5.

[31] Fountain House Foundation survey, *supra* note 3.

hospital after that is clearly spelled out in the voluntary admission form which the patient signs, and our staff found that in practice voluntaries are well informed of their right to leave. The certification of those few voluntary patients who must be detained for further care seems to present no serious problems.

In practice, voluntary patients may, in spite of the statutory detention periods, leave at any time and even without giving notice. They may go home for the week-end and not return; or they may simply walk away from an open hospital at any time. One hospital director commented that he construes such an action by a patient as legally equivalent to due notice, and that he therefore discharges the patient from the hospital records. With increasing numbers of all patients, compulsory as well as voluntary, on open wards and free to leave the hospital whenever they wish, the problem of retention is a general one, not confined to voluntaries. It is largely met today by the effective use of drugs and by milieu therapy. These measures win the patient's cooperation in most cases, and the patient who runs away and does not return is rare.

Rights of Voluntary Patients

By entering a mental hospital and subjecting himself to its regulations, a voluntary patient necessarily suffers some curtailment of his civil and property rights. The regulations may be fair and reasonable, but they deprive all patients, voluntary along with all others, of some rights which they would continue to exercise if they were not hospitalized, or if they were hospitalized in a general hospital for a physical illness. New York's regulation concerning patients' correspondence, for instance, though called "an ideal model for a state which wishes to incorporate the communication privilege in its statutes," [32] does nevertheless allow censorship of mail under cer-

[32] Ross, Commitment of the Mentally Ill: Problems of Law and Policy,

tain circumstances.[33] General Order 10 regulating service of documents on patients and execution of legal instruments by patients deprives patients of freedom in the management of their affairs and requires hospital supervision of certain business transactions. One difference between the legal positions of a voluntary and a certified patient is that a committee, or legal guardian, for a voluntary patient can be appointed only after adjudication of incompetency after a jury trial, a proceeding which may be traumatic, expensive, and cumbersome, whereas a certified patient may have a committee appointed after ad-

57 Mich. L. Rev. 945, 998 (1959). See statement of Dr. Jack Ewalt for the American Psychiatric Association that patients should have free access to communication facilities (telephone and uncensored mail) and free visitation with their families, clergymen, attorneys, and people of this sort. Subcommittee on Constitutional Rights of the Committee on Judiciary, U.S. Senate, 87th Cong., 1st Sess., Hearings, Part 1, p. 75 (1961).

[33] General Order 26, Correspondence of Patients, permits the hospital director to withhold incoming mail if delivery to the patient would be unsafe or unwise and prejudicial to the patient or the institution and to prevent the transmission of outgoing mail that is obscene, profane, illegible, incoherent, or otherwise objectionable. All letters addressed to the Governor, certain public officials, judges, lawyers, and certain officers of the Department of Mental Hygiene must be forwarded at once and without examination, and all mail in reply must be delivered to the patient. The spirit with which General Order 26 is to be interpreted is explained in subdivision (d):

"The 'proper discretion' which institution authorities may, in the opinion of the post-office department, rightly exercise as to preventing the transmission of mail matter addressed by a patient to parties outside, should be exercised in good faith and with fair judgment, erring if at all, on the side of a liberal view of each individual case. The commissioner thinks that comparatively few letters of patients ought to be suppressed, and those only where the objection to transmission is clear and conclusive."

See two cases in New York that led to this regulation guaranteeing a patient's right to free communication with his attorney and favoring the inviolability of mail. Hoff v. State, 279 N.Y. 490, 18 N.E. 2d 671 (1939); People *ex rel.* Jacobs v. Worthing, 167 Misc. 702, 4 N.Y.S. 2d 630 (Sup. Ct. Nassau Co. 1938).

judication by a much less elaborate procedure under Section 1374 of the Civil Practice Act.[34]

After release from the hospital, other rights, such as the right to a driver's license [35] and the right to practice a profession,[36] are related to the condition of the patient rather than to the method of admission. And hospitalization for mental illness,

[34] See Chapter VI *infra*.

[35] N.Y. Vehicle and Traffic Law, § 510(3)(b) provides that a license to drive "may be" suspended or revoked "because of some physical or mental disability of the holder, the court commitment of the holder to an institution under the jurisdiction of the department of mental hygiene or the disability of the holder by reason of intoxication or the use of drugs." In practice, when a person enters a mental hospital, the hospital usually takes charge of his operator's license, along with his other valuables, for safekeeping. No official action is taken then to suspend or revoke his license. The Department of Motor Vehicles has never suspended or revoked a license merely because of the certification of the holder to a mental hospital. Under an informal agreement between the Commissioner of Motor Vehicles and the Department of Mental Hygiene, the director of a state hospital notifies the Commissioner in writing at the time of the patient's release if the hospital believes the patient not fit to drive. The license is then suspended, and the person is entitled to a hearing on the suspension. He may obtain court review of the decision to revoke his license. In the past fifteen years no lawsuit has been brought by a person denied a license on the ground of mental illness. Information from the Commissioner of Motor Vehicles, Mr. William S. Hults.

Our staff was told of the anomalous situation in which a person has obtained or renewed his license and is then hospitalized for a period, say, of six months. He may drive thereafter for two and a half years before the renewal of his license requires a statement on his application about any hospitalization for mental illness within the past three years, thus bringing about a reconsideration of his driving qualifications. This, our committee felt, might well be a matter for consideration by the Commissioner of Motor Vehicles.

[36] See New York Education Law, § 6514(2)(c) for revocation of the professional license of a physician, osteopath, or physiotherapist who is an alcoholic or a drug addict, or who "has become insane," and New York Education Law, § 6911(1)(f) for revocation of the license of a nurse who is an alcoholic or a drug addict, or who "has become mentally incompetent." All our inquiries indicated that cases of actual revocation of a professional license are rare.

again regardless of the method of admission, is a matter of record important for jury service, for civil service positions, and for some other kinds of employment.[37] Discrimination in these matters is unfortunate and unfair. The remedy lies in better education rather than in better law.

The legal status of the voluntary patient in New York differs in one important way from that of the certified patient. The voluntary patient does not lose his right to vote. The statutory disqualification because of hospitalization for mental illness operates upon a certified patient or upon a patient, whether certified or not, who has been adjudicated incompetent.[38] A voluntary patient who has never been adjudicated incompetent is therefore permitted to vote, whereas a certified patient is not. The right to vote is so important that, even though the law imposes no disability in this regard on voluntary patients, their right to vote while in the hospital or after discharge should be made crystal clear.

Moreover, it should be added, many nonvoluntary patients are competent to vote. Some mental disturbances may be quite compatible with wisdom about matters of state. And as one member of the committee half-seriously said, when you see how sane people vote, any general disqualification seems unfair. For these reasons and because the present disenfranchisement of

[37] The Fountain House Foundation survey, *supra* note 3, indicated that many patients were confused about the effect of hospitalization. For example, almost two-thirds of those questioned thought that they could lose their jobs for not having revealed that they had been hospitalized for a mental illness; one-half believed that this could occur after discharge from after-care.

[38] N.Y. Sess. Laws 1962, ch. 11, § 2, eff. Feb. 13, 1962, amended Election Law § 152 (6) to provide that a mentally ill or defective person committed to an institution by a court order shall not be disqualified from voting when he has been "certified by the head of such institution to have been released or discharged therefrom in accordance with regulations of the commissioner of mental hygiene and to have a mental condition which fully warrants his proper exercise of his right to vote."

"committed" patients is stigmatizing, is generally unenforced, and is perhaps unenforceable, this disqualification from voting should be repealed.

INFORMAL ADMISSIONS

As early as 1952 England began to experiment with informal or nonstatutory admission as an alternative to voluntary admission. By it a patient is admitted to a mental hospital without any application and without any order for detention, just as he would be admitted to a general hospital for treatment of a physical illness. This is, in fact, the method in general use in the United States in psychiatric wards of general hospitals; and these admissions, it should be noted, constitute about 60 per cent of the 315,000 annual admissions to hospitals treating the mentally ill.[39] The Royal Commission on the Law Relating to Mental Illness and Mental Deficiency considered it

> wrong that treatment without detention should still depend on the patient's ability to make a valid positive application for treatment . . . it is no longer right for the law to assume that mentally disordered patients must be subject to detention while under care in hospital unless they can give positive evidence of their wish to receive care. In our view the assumption should now be, as it is with all other patients, that they are willing or content to enter hospital unless they or their relatives positively object.[40]

The Royal Commission therefore recommended

> abandoning the assumption that compulsory powers must be used unless the patient can express a positive desire for treatment, and

[39] Joint Commission on Mental Illness and Health, Action for Mental Health 177 (1961). See also the statement by Miss Gladys Harrison, former Assistant General Counsel, Department of Health, Education, and Welfare, based on information from the National Association for Mental Health, that in 1958 psychiatric admissions to psychiatric units in general hospitals exceeded the number of admissions to public mental hospitals. Hearings before the Subcommittee on Constitutional Rights of the Senate Committee on the Judiciary, *op. cit. supra* note 32, at 100.

[40] Royal Commission's Report, *op. cit. supra* note 11, para. 288.

replacing this by the offer of care, without deprivation of liberty, to all who need it and are not unwilling to receive it.[41]

The British Mental Health Act, passed on July 29, 1959, turned this recommendation into law. The voluntary admission by which a patient signs an application for admission has been replaced by nonstatutory admission.[42]

Patients admitted informally are discharged by the hospital doctor when he believes them fit to leave. If they wish to leave before that, the doctor tries to persuade them to complete their treatment. But the hospital has no power to detain them against their will unless one of the compulsory admission procedures is followed. In the rare event that an informal patient who needs further hospitalization cannot be persuaded to stay, the act gives power to change his status quickly to that of a detained patient.

The success of nonstatutory admission in England is related, no doubt, to the total program of care in England. By this program mental hospitals have been opened and are being transformed everywhere into therapeutic institutions; many patients are being treated in the community rather than in hospitals; and public attitudes toward mental illness are being educated to greater tolerance.

The use of the nonstatutory, or informal, admission avoids the troublesome legal feature of the voluntary admission discussed above—the need, express or implied, to determine the capacity of the patient who makes an application for a voluntary admission.[43] England, by substituting the informal for the

[41] *Id.* para. 291.

[42] British Mental Health Act, 7 & 8 Eliz. 2, ch. 72, § 5 (1959). For a discussion of the act, see Willcox and Roemer, Hospitalization under the British Mental Health Act, 1959, 9 Am. J. Comp. L. 606 (autumn 1960).

[43] Ross, Hospitalization of the Voluntary Mental Patient, 53 Mich. L. Rev. 353, 361 (1955). See above text and related footnotes 11 through 14.

voluntary, seeks to avoid this difficulty and achieve the same desired end—early, noncompulsory hospitalization without stigma or formalities for any patient who does not affirmatively object.

The informal admission avoids a second problem with the voluntary admission. For a patient to enter a mental hospital willingly, he must know, so far as possible, that he may also leave it at will.[44] As has been well said, "For the voluntary patient the door must swing open outward as readily as it opens in."[45] Under the nonstatutory admission this right to leave is unrestricted. Under it, too, there is no possible implication of curtailment of the civil rights of patients. They become subject to the rules of the hospital, but suffer no more curtailment of their civil rights than they would suffer by reason of hospitalization for a physical illness.

An informal method of admission in New York State would have several advantages: (1) it would encourage the admission of some patients who may today be deterred from a voluntary admission (Section 71) by the twenty-five-day detention period; (2) it would eliminate the natural psychological urge which now makes many voluntary patients avail themselves of their right to leave at the end of twenty-five days whether leaving then is advisable or not; and (3) it would provide a method of admission that would be free from compulsion, more nearly free from delays, and as free as possible from stigma.

[44] *Id.* at 374–85.

[45] Testimony of Miss Gladys Harrison before the Subcommittee on Constitutional Rights of the Senate Committee on the Judiciary, *op. cit. supra* note 32, at 91.

IV

Initial Admissions of Nonvoluntary Patients

Every person with serious mental illness needs some care and in many cases must go to a hospital, even if he does not want to.

When a person must be sent to a mental hospital against his will, he should not be treated like a criminal and be tried and convicted of being sick. Procedures for his admission are only stepping-stones to treatment.

INITIAL admission of a nonvoluntary patient to a mental hospital should be a medical admission, decided by doctors, not by the court, but immediately after admission the court should provide prompt and thorough review of the patient's need to stay in the hospital. The committee recommends one basic method of initial nonvoluntary admission to all psychiatric facilities—to state hospitals, licensed private institutions, and receiving hospitals. For those patients for whom a more summary method of admission is essential or advisable, this summary method should be backed up with the same requirements as in the case of that basic method of admission. The committee's recommendations spell out the fundamental steps in initial admission:

Recommendation No. 2 (Basic Method of Admission). Initial admission to a state mental hospital, licensed private institution, or psychiatric receiving hospital shall be authorized on an application for admission by the patient's family or other named persons and the certificates of two physicians, and on confirmation of the need for hospitalization by the medical staff of the institution. This initial admission shall be for a period of sixty days. The admission shall be subject to the right of the patient to a judicial hearing promptly after admission, as provided in Recommendations No. 4, No. 5, and No. 6.

Recommendation No. 3 (Nonobjecting Patients). Initial admission to a state mental hospital, licensed private institution, or psychiatric receiving hospital of a patient who does not object to admission shall be authorized on an application for admission by the patient's family or other named persons and the certificate of one physician, and on the confirmation of the need for hospitalization by the staff of the institution. This initial admission shall be for a period of sixty days. Within fifteen days after such admission and as a condition of continued retention of the patient, the certificate of a second examining physician, who may be a psychiatrist on the staff of a state hospital or psychiatric receiving hospital (but not of a private institution) shall be made. The admission shall be subject to the right of the patient to a judicial hearing promptly after admission, as provided in Recommendations No. 4, No. 5, and No. 6.

Recommendation No. 16 (Emergency Admissions). In cases of emergency, initial admission to a state mental hospital, licensed private institution, or psychiatric receiving hospital shall be authorized on the certificate of a health officer, a director of a community mental health service, or a designee of either of them, after examination of the patient and on the confirmation of the need for hospitalization by the staff of the institution. This initial admission shall be for a period of sixty days. Within fifteen days after such admission and as a condition of continued retention of the patient, an application for admission shall be made, to be accompanied by the certificate of a second examining physician, who may be a psychiatrist on the staff of a state hospital or psychiatric receiving hospital (but not of a private institution). The admission shall be subject to the right of the patient to a judicial hearing promptly after admission, as provided in Recommendations No. 4, No. 5, and No. 6.

Efforts should be made to provide adequate places for temporary lodging of persons prior to admission on the certificate of a health officer or director of a community mental health service. Budgets of health officers and community mental health services should make allowance for the costs of administering health-officer admissions.

To bring a patient to a psychiatric receiving hospital and to effect his admission to this kind of hospital, the committee recommends:

Recommendation No. 13 (Removal to Receiving Hospitals). The following agencies shall have authority to direct the removal of a person to a psychiatric receiving hospital for the purpose of admission:

(a) Receiving hospitals throughout the state shall be authorized to direct the removal to such a hospital of persons appearing to be mentally ill, on the written statement of the need for hospitalization by a physician;

(b) The police throughout the state shall be authorized to take custody of a person and to provide for his removal to a psychiatric receiving hospital or to another safe and comfortable place if the person appears to be mentally ill and is conducting himself in a manner which in a sane person would be disorderly;

(c) A magistrate may issue a civil order directing the removal to a psychiatric receiving hospital of any person who appears to be mentally ill and who is arraigned before the magistrate on a minor criminal charge if the magistrate finds the person to be in immediate need of examination and treatment in such a hospital.

In the event of admission to a receiving hospital at the instance of the police or a magistrate, fingerprint records of the patient shall be expunged from the police files and no criminal order shall be issued under Section 870 of the Code of Criminal Procedure.

Section 81(2) of the Mental Hygiene Law shall be amended to eliminate the authority of a nurse to direct removal to a psychiatric receiving hospital; Section 82 of the Mental Hygiene Law shall be amended to eliminate the removal of a patient to a psychiatric receiving hospital on a "precept"; and Section 81(5) of the Mental Hygiene Law shall be amended to eliminate the warrant procedure for removal to a psychiatric receiving hospital.

Recommendation No. 14 (Admission to Receiving Hospitals). Initial admission to a psychiatric receiving hospital shall be authorized after examination by a single physician on the staff of the hospital and on his written opinion that the person requires immediate care and treatment, and on acceptance of the patient by the hospital. This admission shall be for a period of twenty-four hours. If, within the twenty-four-hour period, a second medical opinion in writing from another physician, who may be a physician on the staff of the receiving hospital, confirms the need for admission, the person may be admitted for sixty days as provided in Recommendation No. 3. The admission shall be subject to the right of the patient to a judicial hearing promptly after admission, as provided in Recommendations No. 4, No. 5, and No. 6.

The committee has also made certain additional detailed recommendations on initial admission:

Recommendation No. 24 (Application for Admission). The application for initial admission of a person to a state hospital, licensed private institution, or psychiatric receiving hospital shall be executed not more than ten days prior to admission by any one of the persons now authorized to make a petition under Section 74 of the Mental Hygiene Law, or, where none of these is available and able and willing to execute such an application, by the director of a state hospital or psychiatric receiving hospital (but not the director of a licensed private institution). The signature on the application should be made under penalties of perjury, but need not be witnessed or acknowledged by a notary public.

Recommendation No. 25 (Examining Physicians). The certificates of examining physicians required for admission to a state mental hospital, licensed private institution, or psychiatric receiving hospital shall be made after examination of the patient not more than ten days prior to admission, and (1) in the case of state mental hospitals, one of the required certificates may be executed by a physician on the staff of the hospital to which admission is made; (2) in the case of psychiatric receiving hospitals, both of the required certificates may be executed by physicians on the staff of the hospital to which admission is made; (3) in the case of licensed private institutions, neither of the required certificates may be executed by a physician on the staff of the institution to which admission is made.

Recommendation No. 26 (Confirmation by Hospital). The examination of the patient and confirmation by a state hospital or licensed private institution of the patient's need for admission shall be made by some psychiatrist on the staff of the hospital other than the examining physician in the particular case.

Recommendation No. 27 (Information to All Patients on Arrival). Immediately upon the arrival of any patient at a state mental hospital, licensed private institution, or psychiatric receiving hospital, a medical officer of the institution shall inform the patient in writing of the character of the institution and the reason for his being there and shall give the patient the opportunity to make a telephone call anywhere within the state.

Finally, the committee has proposed new and additional facilities for the care of the aged:

Recommendation No. 22 (Elderly and Senile Patients). After study of the needs of elderly and senile patients, the legislature should appropriate funds to aid in the construction and maintenance, at both state and local levels, of additional facilities of high quality for the care of those aged who are without major mental impairment.

In New York State all patients who go to a mental hospital, except those who go voluntarily, are admitted for a period of time which is limited by law. Patients thus admitted may be discharged and returned to the community after a brief period of treatment. They cannot be held beyond the limited period except by certification of a court, which authorizes detention for an indeterminate period of time.

The initial admission of a patient who is unwilling or unable to enter a hospital voluntarily may occur in one of several ways, depending on the patient's condition, on the psychiatric facilities available in the community, or on other factors. We have described these forms of admission briefly in Part One of this report and now turn to a more detailed consideration of them.

Under the Mental Hygiene Law, a broad distinction is made between admission to psychiatric receiving hospitals, operated by a unit of local government, either a city or a county, and admission to state mental hospitals and to private institutions licensed and inspected by the State Department of Mental Hygiene. We shall therefore describe in turn the ways that nonvoluntary patients are admitted (1) to psychiatric receiving hospitals and (2) directly to state hospitals and licensed private institutions.

ADMISSION TO PSYCHIATRIC RECEIVING HOSPITALS

A number of psychiatric hospitals or psychiatric wards of general hospitals in cities throughout the state have been designated by the State Department of Mental Hygiene as receiving hospitals authorized to admit patients for observation under Section 81(2) of the Mental Hygiene Law. The powers conferred by that section and the duties imposed by it are limited in their application to areas having the facilities specified by that law. Thus the section is introduced by language which limits its effect to New York City, Erie County, and other places where the state or any subdivision operates "a psychopathic hospital, or a psychopathic ward in a general hospital, for the *temporary* observation, examination, care and *certification* of mentally ill . . . persons." The words which we have italicized exclude state mental hospitals themselves and also exclude licensed private institutions, and none of these do in fact exercise the powers or perform the duties here in question.[1]

[1] Warner v. State of New York, 297 N.Y. 395, 403–04, 79 N.E. 2d 459, 464 (1948).

Four receiving hospitals in New York City are authorized to admit patients under Section 81(2) (Bellevue, in Manhattan; Kings County, in Brooklyn; Jacobi, in the Bronx; and Elmhurst, in Queens); two in the environs of New York City (Grasslands Hospital serving Westchester County and Meadowbrook Hospital serving Nassau County); and three in other cities (the psychiatric department of the E. J. Meyer Memorial Hospital in Buffalo, the Monroe County Infirmary in Rochester, and Mosher Memorial, which is the psychiatric wing of Albany Hospital).

The primary function of these hospitals is observation, diagnosis, and determination as to future care. Some treatment may be given, but receiving hospitals differ in the variety, extent, and intensiveness of the treatment offered. Overcrowded hospitals beset with shortages of staff and rapid turnover of patients are forced, understandably, to concentrate their efforts on screening and processing cases for admission to state hospitals. Other hospitals, in which the resources are more adequate to the patient load, can operate mainly as community treatment centers, referring to the state hospitals only those patients who need long-term treatment.

As an indication of the overcrowding and of the extent to which some of these receiving hospitals are used for both emergency and nonemergency cases, note that Bellevue Hospital with an authorized capacity of 630 patients had in 1960 an average of 719, and on one night in December of that year had 800. Intense overcrowding appears also in Kings County Hospital in Brooklyn.[2]

[2] As a result of a series of newspaper articles in the *New York World-Telegram* in March 1961 by a reporter, Michael Mok (who had had himself admitted to Kings County Hospital as a mental patient), the Commissioner of Hospitals, Dr. Ray E. Trussell, appointed a committee, headed by Dr. Lawrence C. Kolb, Director of the Psychiatric Institute, to investigate conditions in the New York City psychopathic hospitals and to make recommendations for their improvement.

The psychiatric division of Bellevue admitted 17,477 patients during 1960; some 3,600 more were interviewed in the admission ward but were denied admission. The average length of a patient's stay at Bellevue is two weeks. Of the 17,477 patients admitted in 1960, 1,977 patients were on convalescent status from state hospitals, or were "on escape" from such hospitals, i.e., recorded as having left without permission. These were all returned to the state hospitals by informal administrative transfers. Fifty-two per cent of all admissions, 9,166 patients, were discharged directly to the community after observation and treatment. The remaining 8,014 or 46 per cent of all admissions (including the 1,977 on convalescent care or on escape) were transferred to state or other mental hospitals. (About 2 per cent of the patients admitted to Bellevue died during their hospitalization there.)

In 1960, of the 10,871 patients admitted to the psychiatric division of Kings County Hospital, 244 were on convalescent status from state hospitals; 3,746 patients, or 34 per cent of all admissions, were discharged directly to the community after observation and treatment; 4,978, or 46 per cent of all admissions, were transferred to state or other mental hospitals. The remaining 20 per cent included parolees, escapees, interhospital transfers, and deaths. The average length of stay for patients admitted to Kings County Hospital in 1960 was 13.4 days.

The other two receiving hospitals in New York City—Jacobi, in Bronx County, and Elmhurst, in Queens County—differ from Bellevue and Kings County Hospitals in that each refuses to admit more patients than its authorized capacity. When this ceiling is reached, persons requiring immediate hospitalization are referred either to Bellevue or to Kings County Hospital. This practice is designed to maintain a high quality of care at these two hospitals, but it aggravates the overcrowding at Bellevue and Kings County. The emphasis of these hospitals on treatment rather than on screening of patients results in a high percentage of patients discharged to the community. At Jacobi in 1960, 63 per cent of all admissions were discharged directly to the community, and at Elmhurst in that year 68 per cent of all admissions were so discharged.

Even outside New York City, the receiving hospitals handle a large flow of psychiatric patients. Grasslands admits approximately 1,500 a year; Meadowbrook, about 1,300; Meyer Memorial, about 2,800; Monroe County Infirmary, 1,200–1,300; and Mosher Memorial, about 1,800.

Statutory Provisions for Admissions to Receiving Hospitals

Under Section 81(2) of the Mental Hygiene Law, the officers of a psychopathic hospital or a psychopathic ward in a general hospital, public or private, are responsible for having a decision made upon the mental condition of any doubtful person who comes under their observation, or who is reported to them by certain persons specified in the statute as appearing to be mentally ill. These officers must also institute proceedings for the certification of such a person to a mental hospital when that is necessary.

A patient admitted to a receiving hospital under Section 81(2) may be kept there for up to sixty days, and for even longer than that—subject to his right to leave on fifteen days' notice—if the receiving hospital is a psychopathic department of a county hospital or of a general hospital used for teaching as part of a medical school. No legal process is required so to detain a patient.

This nonvoluntary method of admission to a receiving hospital requires no petition or special application and no medical certificate. The controlling decision, to hospitalize the patient because he is in immediate need of care and treatment or observation or not to hospitalize him because he is not, is made by the hospital psychiatrist.

As an alternative to this procedure, a patient may be admitted to a receiving hospital on a noncriminal judicial admission. Section 81(2) also provides that a local magistrate may certify a person brought before him who seems to be mentally ill to such a receiving hospital for not more than sixty days if the hospital agrees. Such a certification is civil in nature; no criminal information needs to be presented. Justices of the Domestic Relations Court of New York City presiding in the Children's Court Division may send any child within their jurisdiction to the New York City Department of Hospitals for psychiatric observation for a period not to exceed thirty days, and such justices presiding in the Family Court Division may similarly send for observation adults before the court who appear to be insane.[3] Similarly, New York City magistrates presiding in Girls' Term Court may send any girl brought before that court to the Department of Hospitals for psychiatric observation for not over thirty days, after a hearing and certification by the court that there is reasonable ground to believe that a psychiatric examination is necessary.[4]

Patients may also come into receiving hospitals in New York City or in Erie County under Section 81(5), which provides: "Any person, apparently mentally ill, and conducting himself in a manner which in a sane person would be disorderly, may be arrested by any peace officer and confined in some safe and comfortable place until the question of his sanity be determined." In New York City and in Erie County, under this section, an information may be laid before a magistrate alleging that a person appears to be mentally ill.[5] The magistrate must

[3] Domestic Relations Court Act of the City of New York, §§ 85, 92(19) (McKinney's Consol. Laws of N.Y. Ann. Bk. 66, Pt. 4).

[4] Girls' Term Court Act, § 21 (McKinney's Consol. Laws of N.Y. Ann. Bk. 66, Pt. 4).

[5] Code Cr. Proc., § 147 defines who are magistrates.

then issue a warrant directed to a peace officer commanding the officer to arrest the patient and bring him before the magistrate's court which issued the warrant.[6] If, upon arraignment, the person appears to the magistrate to be mentally ill, the magistrate must certify him to the care and custody of a receiving hospital for not more than sixty days, until the question of such person's mental illness is determined. This section is rarely used in New York City, but in Erie County it is a usual procedure for admissions to the Meyer Memorial Hospital in Buffalo.[7]

A peace officer in New York City or in Erie County often has discretion on whether or not to seek a warrant authorized by this section. Instead, he may, as in any other part of the state, simply arrest a person appearing to be mentally ill and conducting himself in a disorderly manner and arraign him for disorderly conduct.[8] The magistrate before whom the person is so arraigned then has power to commit him to a receiving hospital for observation under Section 870 of the Code of Criminal Procedure (criminal order) or, as noted above, under Section 81(2) of the Mental Hygiene Law (civil order). The criminal-order procedure is often used in New York City.

Still another statutory provision authorizes involuntary admissions; but this one, Section 82, has fallen into disuse. It

[6] Section 81(5), unlike Section 81(2), applies in areas where no receiving hospital exists as well as where they do exist. The arresting officer must immediately notify the director of community mental health services or, except in New York City or in Albany or Erie counties, the health officer. The official thus notified is required to arrange for determination of the mental condition of the person and for his care and treatment pending transfer to a mental hospital.

[7] See below for discussion of the practice of admission under Section 81(5) before the issuance of a warrant by the court, and of the constitutionality of the statute as so applied.

[8] We were informed that in Rochester an old city ordinance permitting arrest for public intoxication had been extensively used to hospitalize patients for observation.

authorizes the detention, or removal to a receiving hospital, of a person who is dangerously ill mentally, who is either at large or being cared for improperly, and who has enough property to maintain himself, or whose family has enough, but for whom no suitable place of confinement is provided. To apprehend such a person, the health or welfare officers mentioned in the section are to obtain a "precept" from a court and, holding this precept, "possess all the powers of a peace officer executing a warrant of arrest in a criminal proceeding." Section 82 has been carried down in the law from the Revised Statutes of 1829 (Ch. XX, Title III, Sec. 4), but is no longer used in practice.

In summary, then, a patient may be admitted to a receiving hospital for observation: (1) without legal process, under Section 81(2); (2) by a civil order of a court, either with or without the charge of an offense, under Section 81(2); (3) by a warrant procedure, in New York City and Erie County only, without charging any offense, under Section 81(5); (4) by a criminal order of admission, after charge of an offense, under Section 870 of the Code of Criminal Procedure; or (5) in law but not in practice by a court order under Section 82 in the case of a dangerous patient lacking a suitable place of confinement for whose care sufficient property exists but who is at large or improperly cared for.

These provisions are used for emergency admissions where immediate hospitalization is necessary; for short-term care to some extent; and for observation, screening, and channeling patients into state hospitals. The ways in which patients are sent from a receiving hospital to a state hospital, when this is necessary, will be described in Chapter V.

New York City Receiving Hospitals

Patients actually come to receiving hospitals in several ways. They may come voluntarily, or they may be brought by relatives. They may be referred by social service agencies or by the Veterans Administration. They may be brought in the ambulances of city receiving hospitals, or sent from other hospitals, from their homes or other places, or from courts, noncriminal or criminal, for observation.

About a fourth of all admissions to Bellevue and Kings County Hospital come of their own volition or with relatives; another fourth are referred by some social service agency or by the Veterans Administration; and the remaining one-half, approximately, are brought in the ambulances of the city receiving hospitals from one or another of the places mentioned. Jacobi Hospital in the Bronx rarely sends its ambulance for a patient who resists admission; such persons in that county are transported by the Bellevue ambulance to Bellevue Hospital. Elmhurst in Queens will send for a disturbed person only if he is in grave danger; otherwise, Kings County Hospital sends its ambulance for residents of Queens County and brings them to Kings County.

Before July 1960 the New York City police would aid, as a matter of routine, in transporting to the hospital persons who seemed to be mentally ill. Under a Police Department regulation, a police officer was even required to accompany every such person taken to the hospital in a public ambulance. Questions were raised, however, about the authority of the New York City Police Department to assist, simply on a statement of need by a physician, in the forcible removal of patients who were not disorderly. As a result of these questionings, the Police Department issued a new regulation in July 1960 providing that police officers should not aid in the removal of a person to a hospital unless the person is disorderly.

In an effort to meet this new situation, Section 81(2) was amended in 1961; [9] it now authorizes the director of a psycho-

[9] N.Y. Sess. Laws 1961, ch. 677, § 1, eff. April 17, 1961; Police Department, City of New York, Restraint and Forcible Removal of Persons Alleged to Be Mentally Ill, General Orders 46, §§ 6–10 (July 27, 1961).

pathic hospital in New York City to direct the removal of a person in need of immediate care and treatment or observation on a written statement of such need by any physician. This change was presumably designed to remove doubts about the authority of such a hospital and to authorize the police to remove by force a person who, while showing signs of mental illness and perhaps resisting arrest, is not in a true sense disorderly. The doctor's letter is all that is needed. The amendment applies only to hospitals operated by the city of New York.

A practical problem may arise in the operation of the new provision because of the requirement that the physician must notify the hospital in writing. In the large areas served by a city hospital, this requirement will entail serious delay and inconvenience. In emergencies this may be serious. One hospital director suggested that a verified telephone call from a physician would have been quicker and sufficiently safe.

Today, then, in New York City psychopathic hospitals a doctor's letter suffices to authorize the hospital's ambulance to bring the person to the hospital and to enlist the aid of the police if needed. But, as already noted, this is not the only way. Both in New York City and elsewhere Section 81(2)(a) provides for a report of apparent mental illness to be made by

> any person with whom such alleged mentally ill person may reside, or at whose house he may be, or by the father, mother, husband, wife, brother, sister, or child of any such person, or next of kin available, or by any duly licensed physician, or by any peace officer, or by any health officer, or by a representative of an incorporated society doing charitable or philanthropic work.

This report having been made, the following procedure is then authorized for bringing the person to the hospital:

> When the officer or officers directing any such institution are thus informed of an apparently mentally ill person, residing within the territory served by such institution, it shall be their duty to send a nurse or an examining physician, attached to the psychopathic wards of their respective institutions, or both, to the place where

the alleged mentally ill person resides or is to be found. If, in the judgment of the chief resident alienist of the respective psychopathic hospital or ward or of the examining physician thus sent, the person is in immediate need of care and treatment or observation for the purpose of ascertaining his mental condition, he shall be removed to such psychopathic hospital or ward.

If the examining physician goes with the ambulance, he makes the decision on whether to remove the person to the receiving hospital. If only a nurse goes with the ambulance, the statute does not explicitly impose on the nurse any duty or power to decide this question, but this duty and power may be implied; otherwise the provision for sending the nurse would be futile. The statute places a duty of deciding this same question, alternatively, upon "the chief resident alienist" of the receiving hospital, but it is hard to see how he can decide for or against the patient's removal unless he too is sent out with the ambulance.

In actual practice, neither a nurse nor an examining physician goes out with the ambulance to bring in persons reported to be mentally ill. The ambulance, manned by a driver and an attendant, picks up such persons after they are reported, in most cases, by a physician or, in the case of a veteran, by the Veterans Administration. If any of the other persons named in the statute report the illness, it is the general practice of the psychiatric hospitals in New York City to require referral from a doctor before removing the patient. If, however, the person is overtly dangerous, the hospital generally refers the family to the police or to the City Magistrates' Court for a summons.

Once past the door of the receiving hospital in the admitting ward, the patient is seen by a physician on the staff of the hospital who makes a clinical judgment as to whether the person is in immediate need of care and treatment or observation for the purpose of ascertaining his mental condition. If so, he is received and retained. The physician does not execute any certificate, however, because compulsory admission to a receiving hospital requires neither a medical certificate nor a petition.

The efficacy of a system by which a receiving hospital screens those patients who need no more than short-term care—if they need care at all—from those who need long-term hospitalization is evidenced by the large percentage of patients discharged from these receiving hospitals. As we have seen, from a half to two-thirds are never transferred to state hospitals or other institutions but are released to live and work in the community.

Nevertheless, it is a matter of grave concern that a patient may spend two to three weeks in a receiving hospital before being sent to a state hospital or discharged. With the overcrowded facilities and shortage of staff that plague the largest of these receiving hospitals, many of their patients fail to receive any real treatment during these two or three weeks. Such delays, in the cases of the multitude of patients who need prompt treatment, may imperil the chances of recovery. Psychiatric personnel are occupied with sorting, rather than treating, patients.

Receiving Hospitals outside New York City

Just as there are many ways in which patients come to receiving hospitals in New York City, so also are there many ways in which they come outside New York City. In Westchester County, for example, a panel of psychiatrists scattered throughout the county screens patients for admission to Grasslands. If one of these psychiatrists recommends observation in Grasslands, the hospital ambulance picks up the patient. In Monroe County (Rochester), a telephone call to the Monroe County Infirmary that a person is in need of observation leads the psychiatrists on the staff of the Monroe County Infirmary to get in touch with the person's relatives or family doctor. If he needs to be hospitalized, an ambulance goes to his house, with a nurse, to fetch him. When the patient has no relatives and no family doctor, a doctor from the Infirmary generally goes with the ambulance. Mosher Memorial in Albany has no ambulance service; there patients must come by themselves or be brought by their families.

Outside New York City, police may assist in removing a patient who resists hospitalization, but they are often reluctant to do so. For this reason Grasslands Hospital sometimes suggests that the relatives of a mentally ill person, who will not go peaceably in its ambulance, lodge a criminal complaint so that the police will be authorized to intervene.

In Erie County patients are usually admitted to Meyer Memorial Hospital, under Section 81(2), on a letter from a doctor. If the patient cannot come by himself, the Meyer Memorial ambulance fetches him, provided the family has furnished the hospital with a letter from a private doctor. If a patient comes into the hospital without a letter of referral, the admitting physician on duty may write such a letter for the patient if he thinks that he ought to be admitted. If the person resists being taken to the hospital, however, the family is advised to call the police, since the hospital is not authorized by Section 81(2) to remove patients against their will unless an examining physician from the hospital has first determined the patient's need for observation. (Section 81(2)(b), the 1961 amendment allowing the police to transport on a letter from any doctor, does not apply outside New York City.) Since examining physicians are not usually sent from Meyer Memorial to make an examination, the only alternative is a criminal complaint.

Removals by the police in Buffalo take place under the warrant provision of Section 81(5). This section, as already noted, requires the issuance of a warrant to bring the person before a court, an arraignment before a magistrate, and a certification by him to a receiving hospital for observation for up to sixty days. In some urgent cases, however, the patient is brought directly to the hospital without any warrant but with a request that he be brought to the City Court as soon as possible. In these cases, however, the patients are usually too sick to be brought to the court very promptly.

The practice of admitting the patient without a warrant and bringing him later before a City Court judge for arraignment has caused some anxiety as to its legality. If the person who appears to be mentally ill is not conducting himself in a disorderly manner, there seems to be no statutory authority for his forcible removal unless an examining physician from the Meyer Memorial Hospital has examined him and directed his removal, or unless a warrant has been issued under Section 81(5). An analogous situation in New York City, and a similar anxiety, prompted the 1961 amendment to Section 81(2), which authorizes a receiving hospital there to direct the removal of a person appearing to be mentally ill on a letter from a physician.

The usual length of stay in the receiving hospitals outside New York City is twelve days or less, with the exception of the Monroe County Infirmary, where patients may stay as long as three to four weeks.[10] As in New York City, many of the patients admitted to these receiving hospitals outside the city never need to be transferred to state hospitals and are discharged, instead, to the community after a short treatment. Table 4 (Appendix) shows the disposition in 1960 of patients admitted to the various receiving hospitals outside New York City.

Evaluation

Admissions to receiving hospitals in practice are more or less satisfactory adjustments to the wordings of old statutes enacted from time to time to meet problems when conditions were very

[10] The usual lengths of hospital stays in the other receiving hospitals outside New York City are as follows: Grasslands, 10–12 days; Meadowbrook, 5–6 days; E. J. Meyer Memorial, 10 days; Mosher Memorial, 9 days.

different from those of today. Sections 81 and 82 do not spell out clearly the authority of receiving hospitals to remove and detain persons who appear to be mentally ill, nor do they adequately reflect actual practice. Furthermore, the powers of receiving hospitals in specified geographic areas under Section 81(2) are confused with other powers, operative statewide, conferred by Section 81(5). The obsolete Section 82 remains on the statute books although it is never used.

In cases where a person is neither overtly dangerous nor disorderly, there is much to be said for the wisdom of the practice which prevails in New York City of restricting the persons permitted by the generous listing of Section 81(2) to set in motion the machinery for sending a person to a receiving hospital. This restrictive practice is in harmony with the new Section 81(2)(b) of 1961, which in New York City calls for a letter from a doctor before forcible transportation by the police may be undertaken. There seems to be no reason, with the number of doctors available there or in any other large city, for permitting any one of the many persons specified in the statute to report that a person should go to a receiving hospital. The provision of Section 81(2)(b) should be made applicable to all receiving hospitals throughout the state. If it were, a medical approval would doubtless be required to initiate every involuntary admission of a patient not overtly dangerous and not disorderly.

In cases where the person is overtly dangerous or where the person is conducting himself in a manner which in a sane person would be disorderly, the police should continue to have authority to bring a patient directly to a receiving hospital without prior medical approval. If a person who appears to be mentally ill is arraigned before a magistrate on a minor criminal charge, a civil order for his admission to a receiving hospital should be issued rather than a criminal order under Section 870 of the Code of Criminal Procedure.

Although Section 81(2) provides a speedy and efficient method of admission in most cases, it fails to give sufficient protection to an unwilling patient. Since no petition or medical certificate is required, such a patient may be admitted on the oral opinion of a single doctor on the staff of the receiving hospital. In a busy hospital with a large number of admissions, this does not provide sufficient safeguards.

This, however, is not the only defect of Section 81(2). Another serious defect is that it permits a patient to be legally detained for as long as two months with no judicial scrutiny of the propriety of his detention. During his stay he fails, in some of the larger receiving hospitals, to get the psychiatric treatment which is his due if he is sick—or the prompt release which is his due if he is not sick.

Vast differences exist, however, among receiving hospitals in their performance of their dual roles of screening patients for admission to other hospitals and of giving short-term treatment. Some receiving hospitals, as we have seen, devote the greater part of their time and effort to the process of screening and preparing cases and can, therefore, give therapy in only a few cases. Others are able to give short-term treatment to most patients, and they certify to other hospitals only those who require long-term care. This difference is probably related to differences in the availability and integration of health services in the community. Where health services are inadequate, it is likely that receiving hospitals will be overcrowded and overworked. Yet just here it is most crucial that all hospitals be able not only to observe and diagnose, but also to treat.

The recent proposal by the State Commissioner of Mental Hygiene to establish mental health districts in New York City which would integrate the psychiatric services now provided by the state and the city would go far toward meeting some of the medical and administrative problems of the receiving hospitals. Dr. Hoch said:

According to this plan each district will be served by a state hospital, a city hospital or a voluntary hospital which will take care of both inpatient and outpatient needs. The psychiatric services of the city hospitals will be converted to treatment facilities providing emergency care, clinic service, and short-term hospitalization. Patients received initially in the general hospitals who require long-term treatment will of course be transferred to state hospitals. Within each district other community services will be coordinated with those of the hospital in an integrated program of care.

When this plan is fully in operation, all receiving hospitals will provide treatment for patients in their home communities, and differences in the function of receiving hospitals and state hospitals will be minimized.

In sum, the solution in our opinion is not to eliminate receiving hospitals but rather to make them more rapid, more effective, and more comfortable centers for screening those cases which have to be sent elsewhere; to enable them to give real short-term treatment to those of their patients who need it; and to provide the same legal safeguards for all patients in psychiatric receiving hospitals as for patients in state mental hospitals.

DIRECT ADMISSION TO STATE HOSPITALS AND PRIVATE INSTITUTIONS

Apart from admission through psychiatric receiving hospitals, a nonvoluntary patient may enter a state mental hospital or a licensed private institution directly from his home or from a general hospital in the community. Such direct admission may occur in any one of five ways. The basic method is under Section 74 on a petition, the written recommendation of two doctors, and a court order. In an emergency two methods of admission are available which have less stringent requirements than Section 74: the health-officer admission (Section 72) and the incomplete court order (Section 75). In addition, two other nonemergency procedures exist: admission on the written recommendation of two doctors without court order (Section 73-a) and admission of nonobjecting patients on the certificate of a single physician (Section 73). Under each of these methods the patient may, in theory, be retained in the hospital without further process for a limited time only—never more than sixty days. In practice, however, the first, Section 74, and the last, Section 73, usually amount, for different reasons, to admission for an unlimited time. Here we shall discuss each of these nonvoluntary methods of initial admission to state hospitals and private institutions. In Chapter V we shall describe how a patient admitted initially for a limited time by one of these methods is retained for longer treatment when that is necessary.

The fundamental question in nonvoluntary admissions is, of course, in what cases society should interfere with liberty: what criteria should test the propriety of its doing so? Part One of this report refers to the New York criteria, especially those for admissions unlimited in time: that the person be mentally ill to an extent which warrants care and treatment and that he be in need of such care and treatment in a mental hospital. Other criteria appear in the patchwork of New York statutes, especially in the descriptions of other kinds of admissions, but those just given are the basic New York criteria.

Before describing initial admissions to state hospitals and licensed private institutions, we shall present the views of some New York State judges on how these criteria operate. In a questionnaire addressed to these judges, our staff asked how well or ill the judges think the patient's civil rights are protected by the New York criteria. Of the 58 judges who answered this question, 55 said that the statute was satisfactory; only 3 said that it was unsatisfactory. Of these judges, 51 also thought that in general the present procedures for court-ordered admission under Section 74 work "satisfactorily," and only 4 judges felt that they did not. But the accompanying comments reflected less satisfaction with the operation of these criteria than the 51 favorable "votes" might indicate. Several judges said that the standards for hospitalization are satisfactory, but, as one put it, that the real issue is the thoroughness with which the facts of each case are examined or, as another put it, that it is the "implementation which needs watching." Several judges think that the criteria are inappropriate for aged and withdrawn persons, a problem discussed in Section 4 of this chapter.

1. Admission by Two Physicians with Court Order

Under Section 74 the certificate of two doctors with a petition and a court order authorizes the admission of a patient to a state hospital or a licensed private institution. He may then be retained in that hospital for up to sixty days without further process. This is the theory. But because that further process is a rather routine act of filing a further certificate by the hospital, in practice a Section 74 admission is usually unlimited in time.

Although Section 74 contemplates notice to the patient and a hearing before the court order for the original admission, in practice, again, notice is usually not given and a hearing is held in only a minority of the cases. The judge usually signs this order of certification on the petition and the medical certificate without seeing the patient, his relatives or friends, or any doctor, and without investigating the facts of the case.

Admission under Section 74 is important not only because it is the basic method of initial admission in nonemergency cases in areas where receiving hospitals do not exist but also, as we shall see, because it is the principal method today by which patients in receiving hospitals are transferred to state hospitals and private institutions. Moreover, all the other methods of initial admission to state hospitals and private institutions are modeled on it. We turn, therefore, to detailed consideration of its provisions and procedures.

The Petition

Outside New York City in areas where receiving hospitals do not exist, the first legal step in sending an unwilling patient to a mental hospital for an indefinite period is generally a petition for a court order certifying that the person is in need of care and treatment in a hospital. Section 74 provides that the petition must contain a statement of the facts which show the mental illness alleged. In practice, before a petition is filed, there has usually been a consultation with a doctor. If he thinks that hospitalization is needed and if the patient will not go voluntarily, the physician will ask a relative or other proper person to sign a petition. As we have noted, the physician who is consulted is sometimes unaware of the possibility of a voluntary admission and will recommend a Section 74 admission even though it is not necessary.

This petition may be signed by any person with whom the patient resides or at whose house he may be, by any one of certain specified relatives [11] or "the nearest relative or friend available," by a committee of the patient, by "an officer of any well-recognized charitable institution or agency or home," by any one of certain specified welfare or service officers, or by a director of community mental health services in the city or county where the patient is (Section 74(2)). Although the statute has been amended so that it no longer requires the petition to be verified, two judges, in Westchester and Schenectady counties, still insist on verified petitions.[12]

[11] Section 74(2) specifies a parent, spouse, brother or sister, or child. The commissioner of welfare may sign the petition for an indigent person without relatives.

[12] Matter of Neisloss, 8 Misc. 2d 912, 171 N.Y.S. 2d 875 (Westchester Co. Ct., Garrity, J., 1957); information from replies to committee's questionaire addressed to New York State judges. The requirement of a

The statute does not require that the petition be signed within any specified period before the granting of the order, though it does require that the doctors' certificate be signed within the last ten days. The petition may have been signed at any time, even six months or a year before the admission. Yet the facts which evidence an alleged mental illness will differ, of course, depending on the time when a petition is executed. It may not be so essential that the petition recount recent events, to be sure, as it is that the medical certificate describe the patient's condition just before admission. And latitude as to when a petition was executed is an administrative convenience. But even conceding all this, the function of the petition—to bring to the attention of the court the facts thought to require hospitalization of the patient [13]—must be less well performed by a stale document recounting old facts than by a fresh one. The British Act, by contrast, specifies that no application for the admission of a patient shall be made by any person unless that person has seen the patient personally within fourteen days of the application [14] or, in the case of an emergency application, within three days.[15]

Generally, a relative signs the petition. In one upstate county, the records of the 110 cases of certification in the eleven-year period from 1947 through 1957 show that the spouse of the person thought to be mentally ill had signed the petition most frequently (in 40 per cent of the cases); next in frequency had been a public welfare official (17 per cent); then a child (10 per cent); then a parent (8 per cent) or a brother or sister (8 per cent); then a hospital director (6 per cent); then a nephew, niece, uncle, or aunt (4 per cent); and even more

verified petition was eliminated by N.Y. Sess. Laws 1955, ch. 794, *infra* note 20.

[13] People *ex rel.* Senecal v. Keill, 7 Misc. 2d 942, 166 N.Y.S. 2d 636 (Seneca Co. Ct., Bodine, J., 1957).

[14] British Mental Health Act, 7 & 8 Eliz. 2, ch. 72, § 27(3) (1959).

[15] British Mental Health Act, 7 & 8 Eliz. 2, ch. 72, § 29(4) (1959).

rarely a person described as a next friend, as the person with whom the patient was living, or as an officer of a private charitable institution. Thus in 70 per cent of the cases the petition was signed by a spouse or close relative; in 23 per cent by a public or private official; and in 7 per cent by other persons. A sampling of 71 cases of certification before 1947 in the same county and a comparison of these with the 1947–1957 cases showed that the proportion of petitions signed by members of the family in the later period had increased by about 10 per cent and that the proportion of petitions signed by public and private officials had decreased correspondingly.

Hospital directors were asked whether in their opinion any additional persons should be authorized to sign a petition, particularly doctors or police officers. In general, they thought not. Doctors examine the patient, and police officers sometimes help to transport him. But hospital directors generally think that it is better for the family to initiate the proceedings; when the patient has no relatives to petition, the statute authorizes a wide enough range of other impartial but concerned persons to do so.[16]

Examining Physicians

An examining physician is defined as any reputable physician licensed to practice in New York State who has been in practice for at least three years.[17] No examining physician may be a rela-

[16] The British Mental Health Act (Section 27) authorizes only the nearest relative or the mental welfare officer to make an application for admission. The Royal Commission on the Law Relating to Mental Illness and Mental Deficiency did not consider it appropriate that a friend, neighbor, or other private individual not related in kinship to the patient be authorized to make an application. Royal Commission's Report, para. 402.

[17] Mental Hygiene Law, § 2(18). In 1955 the requirement of "certified examiners" was abolished, because certification by the Department of Mental Hygiene did not appreciably increase the protection for pa-

tive of the petitioner or the patient or may be connected with the institution to which it is proposed to admit the patient.[18] The two physicians are required to make the examination jointly or separately, and within ten days before the order.[19] If separate examinations are made, the ten-day period is measured from the date of the first examination. The certificate must set out the facts and circumstances upon which the judgment of the examiners is based and must conclude that the person's condition is such as to require care and treatment in a mental hospital (Section 70(4)). The certificate of the examining physicans need not now be verified.[20]

---

tients and because physicians could and did avoid this function by failing to apply for certification. See N.Y. Sess. Laws 1955, ch. 794, § 3, eff. April 28, 1955.

[18] Mental Hygiene Law, § 70(3) provides that no examining physician shall be a manager, trustee, visitor, director, proprietor, officer, or stockholder of the institution to which it is proposed to admit the patient, or have any pecuniary interest in it, directly or indirectly, or be one of its resident physicians.

[19] N.Y. Sess. Laws 1961, ch. 504, § 1, eff. April 11, 1961, repealed the requirement that the two examining physicians conduct the examination jointly. The statute now permits the examinations to be conducted either jointly or separately. The Attorney General has ruled, under language similar to that now in effect, that if the order of certification is not issued within ten days of the medical certificate, a reexamination of the person should be made and the order should be obtained within ten days thereafter. N.Y. Ops. Atty. Gen. 323, 324 (1941).

[20] This change in the law was made in 1955 by an amendment designed to simplify the preparation of the papers, and thereby to facilitate admission. N.Y. Sess. Laws 1955, ch. 794, § 5, eff. April 28, 1955. It has been held constitutional by some decisions and unconstitutional by others. People *ex rel.* Senecal v. Keill, *supra* note 13 (constitutional); Matter of Allen, 207 Misc. 1036, 142 N.Y.S. 2d 547 (Schenectady Co. Ct., Liddle, J., 1955) (unconstitutional; but if constitutional, other statutes required the oaths); and Matter of Kenny and Matter of Paponja, 2 Misc. 2d 620 (Paponja), 154 N.Y.S. 2d 55 (Kenny), 57 (Paponja) (Jefferson Co. Ct. 1956) (identical opinions by Wiltse, J., agreeing on both points above with Liddle, J., in Allen case), appeal dismissed in Paponja on ground that order sought to be appealed was ex parte and not appealable, 6 App. Div. 2d 770, 174 N.Y.S. 2d 462 (4th Dept. 1958).

Examination by two physicians is intended to safeguard the patient against improper hospitalization on the theory that such an examination gives more protection than an examination by one alone. A majority of the judges and physicians questioned on this point agreed that the two-physician examination is important as a protection. Many hospital directors said, moreover, that examination by two physicians guards against slipshod examinations, reassures the patient and his family as to the need for the hospitalization, and lets the doctors share the responsibility for ordering it.[21] The recent amendment permitting the two examinations to be made separately saves the time of busy doctors and speeds admissions where time is of the essence.

In one respect the law concerning examining physicians seems unduly restrictive. The provision in Section 70(3) that no examining physician may be a resident physician in the hospital to which it is proposed to admit a patient was intended,

[21] In Guzy v. Guzy, 16 Misc. 2d 975, 184 N.Y.S. 2d 161 (S. Ct. Queens Co., Pittoni, J., 1959), aff'd 11 App. Div. 2d 1047, 206 N.Y.S. 2d 355 (2d Dept. 1960), the court dismissed an action by plaintiff against his wife and the two examining physicians who signed the certificate on which plaintiff was committed to a state hospital and hospitalized for 115 days. The court held that the plaintiff failed to make out a cause of action for false imprisonment, malicious prosecution, or malicious abuse of process.

"The gist of an action for false imprisonment is unlawful detention. . . . So that imprisonment which is authorized by process regular on its face and which is issued by a court of competent jurisdiction is lawful, and cannot give rise to a cause of action for false imprisonment, even though the process was erroneously or improvidently issued. It protects those securing the order resulting in the arrest or confinement and those who participated in the proceeding. . . . In short, where the court authorizes an arrest or confinement it is the act of the court and not of the complainant, and there can be no charge against him for a false imprisonment. . . ." (16 Misc. 2d at 976–77; 184 N.Y.S. 2d at 164.)

Nevertheless, numerous doctors expressed concern to our staff about the dangers of their being sued for false imprisonment.

no doubt, to guard against the possibility that an examining physician might have a personal or financial interest in hospitalizing any other person. But this sweeping prohibition disqualifies every psychiatrist of every state mental hospital as an examining physician for an admission to his own hospital. Although the prohibition may be proper with respect to licensed private institutions, where a physician on the staff might conceivably stand to gain from an admission, in a public hospital the staff can have no personal interest in increasing admissions; on the contrary, present emphasis everywhere throughout the state hospital system is upon prompt discharge of patients, and the administrative organization of each hospital is designed to achieve this objective.

This prohibition may often operate to deprive persons of examination by the very physicians best qualified to determine their need for treatment; this is particularly true in rural areas where state hospital psychiatrists are likely to be the only psychiatrists in many miles. Today, as state hospitals are beginning to reach out into the community with out-patient services and as community mental health services are being integrated with state hospitals, the legal disqualification of state hospital psychiatrists from participating in the admission of patients whom they may be treating on an out-patient basis becomes even more unreasonable and inefficient.[22]

[22] See discussion of this problem by Forstenzer, Problems in Relating Community Programs to State Hospitals, 51 Amer. J. Pub. Health 1152, 1154 (copyright 1961 by the American Public Health Association):

"In New York and in many other states, state hospital personnel are legally excluded from the decision making process in connection with hospitalization. By training and experience, hospital personnel are best equipped for work with psychotic patients, but by law they may not participate in deciding whether the patient will benefit most from hospitalization or from an alternative method of treatment in the community. The legal restrictions constitute a major deterrent to the effective use of hospital personnel in a consultative role to community agencies and to the psychiatric staff in community agencies. The latter lose a

Hospital directors mentioned this disqualification as aggravating their difficulties in securing eligible physicians for the certification of patients originally admitted by a health officer, a problem discussed in Chapter V. In one city where excellent psychiatric services are provided and where resources for psychiatric care are well coordinated, state hospital psychiatrists absent themselves from staff conferences on the disposition of patients in a receiving hospital. The state hospital director interprets the ban on participation by state hospital psychiatrists in admissions as prohibiting this activity as well. The loss of their skilled and informed judgment from the consideration of such cases seems unfortunate.

In support of the disqualification, however, some doctors urge that the patient's natural antagonism to the doctors who examine him for admission may continue if they proceed to handle his case and may indeed carry over to other hospital psychiatrists responsible for his treatment. Thus it may prejudice his progress. One hospital director told our staff that he finds it helpful to be able to lay the responsibility for the initial examination at the door of physicians who are not on his staff. Another hospital director, however, said that it is usually possible to direct any antagonism against the admitting doctor alone, while at the same time fostering a cooperative attitude toward the doctor responsible for the treatment.

England faced this problem in a more extreme form when it transferred the authority for detention of patients from the courts to the hospitals themselves. The General Secretary of the Medical Practitioners Union in England said: "Many doctors feel that the basis of trust on which all psychiatric treat-

---

valuable opportunity to familiarize themselves with the problems of psychotic patients. Frequently, the legal barrier against hospital staff involvement in the process of obtaining hospital care serves as an excuse for not encouraging and even for prohibiting the joint use of personnel by hospital and community services."

ment must rest will suffer as a result of their having to assume administrative or executive functions."[23] But this argument did not prevail, and the British Mental Health Act now permits one of the required medical recommendations to be given by a doctor on the staff of the hospital itself unless that hospital is a private institution.[24]

Notice

Notice of the application must be served personally on the person alleged to be mentally ill, at least one day before the application is made, unless the judge, in his discretion, dispenses with such notice on the ground that it would be ineffective or detrimental to the person. The judge *must* dispense with the notice if the examining physicians state in writing that it would be detrimental. (Section 74(3).)[25]

If the petition has been signed by anyone other than a spouse, parent, or other nearest relative, notice of the application must be served (even in a case where service on the patient is dispensed with) upon the spouse, parent, or relative if any such person be known to be within the county. If not, this notice must be served on the person with whom the patient resides, or at whose home he may be, or, in the absence of such a person, on a friend. Service shall be dispensed with in writing if none of the persons described in the statute are available to receive it. (Section 74(3).)

[23] Times (London), Feb. 17, 1959, quoted by Dr. A. D. D. Broughton in H.C. Deb., May 6, 1959, col. 417.

[24] British Mental Health Act, 7 & 8 Eliz. 2, ch. 72, § 28(3); Royal Commission's Report, para. 413.

[25] Commitment without personal notice to the patient appears to have been held to be constitutional in this state for at least sixty years. See discussion, and cases cited, on this point in Matter of Coates, 14 Misc. 2d 89, 91, 181 N.Y.S. 2d 599, 602 (1958), aff'd 8 App. Div. 2d 444, 188 N.Y.S. 2d 400 (4th Dept. 1959), aff'd 9 N.Y. 2d 242, 173 N.E. 2d 797 (1961).

In practice, in direct admissions to mental hospitals by two physicians with a court order written notice of an application for certification is, in fact, served on the patient only rarely. In most instances when the patient becomes acutely ill while at home, the examining physicians certify, rather routinely, that notice would be ineffective or detrimental. Their main object is to get the patient to the hospital as quickly as possible for treatment, without aggravating the illness and without precipitating flight or other untoward actions on his part. Instead of giving a formal written notice, the doctor usually explains to the patient, in rather guarded terms, that he is ill and needs help.

Service of notice on relatives or others close to the patient, of course, involves no traumatic or detrimental effects for the patient, and the statute requires such service wherever possible. Our staff found careful compliance with this provision. If there is any problem in connection with the service of notice on relatives, it lies in the difficulty of locating the relatives rather than in the requirements of the statute.

Hearing

On a demand by any relative or "near friend in behalf of" the patient, the judge must order a hearing to be held within five days from the order. Even in the absence of such a demand for a hearing, the judge may order it on his own motion. A copy of an order for a hearing must be served on the interested parties and on any others whom the judge may specify. If the judge cannot hear the application himself, he may appoint a referee to hear and report. At the hearing the judge, or his referee, hears the testimony introduced by the parties and examines the patient "if deemed advisable, in or out of court . . ." (Section 74(5)). If the judge then decides that the patient needs observation and treatment, he orders him admitted to the jurisdiction of the Department of Mental Hygiene.[26] If the judge refuses to certify the patient, he must state his reasons in writing.

If no request is made for a hearing and the judge does not order one, but if he is satisfied from the papers that the person *may* need treatment, the judge may order hospitalization for up to sixty days for observation and treatment (Section 74(4)).

In contrast to its provisions about notice for the patient, the statute does not require the judge to dispense with a hearing even if the examining physicians certify that such a hearing would be ineffective or detrimental. But since without notice the patient is unlikely to know about his right to a hearing, omitting that notice usually eliminates any demand by him for a hearing. Even if the relatives, who of course have notice, do request a hearing, an examination of the patient in court or out of court has to take place only "if [it is] deemed advisable." Although a doctor has no legal power to prevent a hearing, few judges will hold one if the doctor advises against it.

Outside New York City hearings are rarely held.[27] Generally,

[26] Prior to 1961 the statute required the judge to name in his order the specific state hospital to which the patient was certified. This procedure resulted in problems when the hospital named in the order was full and could not accept more patients. To meet this problem and to increase the flexibility in assigning patients to various hospitals, Sections 70 and 74 of the Mental Hygiene Law were amended to provide for certification of patients to the jurisdiction of the Department of Mental Hygiene. N.Y. Sess. Laws 1961, ch. 504, eff. April 11, 1961. Some justices in New York City object strenuously to the new law and procedure on the ground that it is an important part of the function of a judge who certifies a patient to a hospital to decide to what particular hospital he shall go.

[27] The first questionnaire which the committee addressed to New York State judges asked: "About how often in your court is a hearing with the patient present held before a court order for admission?" Only 1 upstate judge replied that hearings with the patient present are held regularly; 2 said that hearings with the patient present are held sometimes; and the majority, 33, said that hearings with the patient present are held rarely.

the petition and medical certificate, and an unsigned order of certification, are simply sent over to the judge for his signature. The judge sees neither the patient nor the patient's relatives. In one upstate county, as noted previously, no hearing has been held in the past ten years. Sometimes the judge sees the relatives in his chambers, particularly, in one city, relatives of indigent patients transferred from the county home to the state mental hospital or, in another city, relatives of patients initially hospitalized in a general hospital or, anywhere, relatives who are uncertain and fearful about hospitalization and who seek an interview with the judge.[28]

Court Order

The order must have been signed not more than ten days before the patient's admission to the hospital (Section 74(8)). Copies of the petition, the certificate, and the order and of certain other papers must be furnished immediately to the hospital. If the hospital is a licensed private institution, a copy of the papers must also be filed with the Department of Mental Hygiene and in the office of the clerk of the county where the patient resides. The judge must order all such papers filed in the county clerk's office to be sealed and exhibited only to the parties to the proceedings, or someone properly interested, upon order of the court. (Section 74(5)(6).)[29]

[28] The replies of New York State judges to the committee's first questionnaire, *supra* note 27, indicated that 9 upstate judges regularly hold hearings with relatives, 11 sometimes hold them, and 19 hold them rarely.

[29] Formerly all certification papers in cases of hospitalization in both state and private institutions had to be filed with the Department and sealed copies of all of them placed in the county clerk's office. N.Y. Sess. Laws 1954, ch. 167, § 1, eff. March 23, 1954, dispensed with the certified copy for the Department of Mental Hygiene and N.Y. Sess. Laws 1960, ch. 511, § 4, eff. April 14, 1960, dispensed with filing in the county clerk's office except, under both amendments, in cases of hos-

Admission of a certified patient is not automatic. The director or person in charge of the hospital may refuse admission if the papers required to be presented are not in order or if in his judgment the person is not mentally ill within the meaning of the statute. (Section 74(8).) The hospital sometimes exercises this right. Moreover, it also has discretion to discharge the patient at any time after admission and may do so immediately if it finds the patient not mentally ill.

The procedure for retaining the patient beyond the sixty-day period if he is in need of further treatment is described in Chapter V.

Evaluation

The theory of initial admission by two physicians with court order is that the patient, as well as his family, has a right to contest the admission before it occurs. If the patient is not informed of the application for admission, this right is illusory. In practice, written notice is rarely served on the patient, and the oral notice may be inadequate.

All physicians agree that the doctor should explain to a patient that he needs hospitalization and should tell him of the plans for hospital care. But physicians divide as to the deleterious effects of the service of a written notice. Those who oppose

---

pitalization in a licensed private institution. These changes were made because the filing of these papers, with two to ten pages for each case, was creating a problem of space in the offices of the Department and of the county clerks, particularly since the papers often do not microfilm well. The filing was felt to be unnecessary, since the Department receives from all state hospitals a weekly statistical report of all admissions, and since the certificate of the hospital director of need for care beyond the initial sixty days must still be filed in the county clerk's office. Memorandum of Department of Mental Hygiene in support of A. Int. 795, Pr. 4878, ch. 511, L. 1960, New York State Legislative Annual 255–56 (1960).

it comment, variously, that it puts an added burden on the patient, that it is brutal in that it confuses and antagonizes the patient and his family by injecting a note of formal accusation into the procedure, and that it may induce the patient to run away.[30] Those who favor written notice say that it does not at all involve the same trauma for the patient as does a hearing, or that while it may cause a temporary emotional upset it does no permanent damage except perhaps in the case of an extremely paranoid patient, or that it does not really hurt the patient so much as it hurts the doctor who does not want to be frank with his patient.[31]

One hospital director said that notice is dispensed with too often—that many doctors dispense with it in the same spirit in which they certify indiscriminately that a patient is dangerous to himself or others. He said that the failure to give the patient notice may embitter him and so may prejudice the success of his treatment. Along similar lines one upstate judge commented:

> Notice to the patient is dispensed with in too perfunctory a manner. It is entirely too easy for physicians to note that "it would upset the patient or be detrimental to his health." With the patient absent, the court can only rely on the medical certificate and important facts stated therein on the question of notice. It is a legal right which should not be lightly dispensed with.

Questionnaires sent both to judges and to physicians asked how important each respondent thought certain specified procedures to be in protecting the civil rights of patients in view of the special medical problems involved. Assuming, for example, that service of notice of an application for a court order on a patient would not in fact be detrimental to health, how important is such a service in protecting his civil rights? Table 5 (Appendix) gives the percentages of judges and physicians

[30] Comments of physicians in replies to the committee's questionnaire.

[31] *Ibid.* and comments from hospital directors in interviews with the staff of our committee.

who considered notice likely to be an important protection in such cases.

It is noteworthy that 86 per cent of all the judges answering this question thought notice important in such cases, whereas only 39 per cent of all the doctors thought so. In New York City, where notice and hearings are more common than upstate, a much higher proportion of judges (100 per cent in New York City, 72 per cent elsewhere) considered notice to the patient important. The same was true of the doctors (57 per cent in New York City, 34 per cent upstate).

Underlying the judges' stress on the importance of notice is doubtless the fact that their training and their approach to legal problems all assume notice and an opportunity to contest any deprivation of freedom as a fundamental constitutional right. The Supreme Court of the United States has spelled out these requirements as essential elements of due process in the commitment of the mentally ill.[32] But despite the importance attached by the judges to service of notice on the patient, none of them suggested a statutory change that would take away the doctors' power to decide that in certain cases notice would be ineffective or detrimental.

In upstate New York where no receiving hospitals exist, the judge's signing of the order has come to be quite generally treated as a form and a routine. Since, with a few outstanding exceptions, notice to the patient of an application is generally dispensed with and a hearing is rarely held, the judge's signa-

[32] Simon v. Craft, 182 U.S. 427 (1901); see Minnesota *ex rel.* Pearson v. Probate Court, 309 U.S. 271, 276–77 (1939):

"We fully recognize the danger of a deprivation of due process in proceedings dealing with persons charged with insanity or, as here, with a psychopathic personality as defined in the statute, and the special importance of maintaining the basic interests of liberty in a class of cases where the law though 'fair on its face and impartial in appearance' may be open to serious abuses in administration and courts may be imposed upon if the substantial rights of the persons charged are not adequately safeguarded at every stage of the proceedings."

ture is little more than a stamp of approval, an imprimatur, placed upon the certificate of the examining physicians. If we face the facts, the conclusion is inescapable that initial admission under Section 74 fails in most of these areas to live up to its pretension of being a judicial admission and has become in substance, although not in form, a medical admission.

2. *Emergency Admissions*

Persons who need immediate hospitalization in an emergency are admitted to psychiatric receiving hospitals, where these exist, pursuant to Section 81, as described at the beginning of this chapter. Elsewhere such emergency patients are often admitted directly to state mental hospitals or licensed private institutions by procedures which have to be less rigorous and less time consuming than admission by two physicians with a court order, described in the preceding section. The New York statute provides two methods for emergency admissions to state hospitals and licensed private institutions—a health-officer admission under Section 72 for up to sixty days or an admission on an incomplete court order under Section 75 for ten days.

Section 72 authorizes the director of a state hospital or a licensed private institution to accept as a patient a person who is dangerous to himself or others and who needs immediate care and treatment on the written request of a county commissioner of health, a health officer, or a director of community mental health services, or on that of an examining physician designated by any of these. The written request must be based on a personal examination of the person in question. (Sec. 72(1)(a)(b).)[33]

[33] Warner v. State of New York, 297 N.Y. 395, 79 N.E. 2d 459 (1948) held the state liable to a plaintiff admitted on a health-officer admission when the health officer failed to make a personal examination of the patient but relied, instead, on statements of the patient's wife. Damages were limited to the period before a later court certification,

The same officials are authorized to take the patient into custody, to detain him, to provide temporary care for him, and to transport him. Local peace officers are required to provide help on the written request of such an official, and reasonable expenses incurred are a charge upon the county from which the

---

however, since the valid court order, which extended the hospitalization beyond the initial sixty days, absolved the state from further liability for detention. Judge Fuld wrote in the majority opinion:

"Where personal freedom is at stake, insistence upon strict and literal compliance with statutory provisions is not only reasonable but essential. The State has a legitimate and vital interest in protecting its citizens from harm at the hands of potentially dangerous mental cases, but that is not the only interest to be served. The liberty of an individual, not yet adjudged insane, is too precious to allow it to be invaded in any fashion, by any procedure, other than that explicitly prescribed by law. Particularly is that true here, where the statute's demands are easily met and satisfied. Undoubtedly mindful of both the welfare of the patient and the necessities of emergency situations, the Legislature has provided a simple and swift admission procedure, especially for subjects who are 'dangerous' or in need of 'immediate care and treatment.' . . ." (297 N.Y. at 404, 79 N.E. 2d at 464.)

The dissenting opinion of Judge Desmond, in which two other judges joined, was based on the common-law powers of the state and of private persons to take custody of the insane, and on the finding by qualified physicians that the patient in the case at bar was a dangerous paranoiac. The Mental Hygiene Law nowhere states that its procedures are exclusive. Judge Desmond wrote:

"Given symptoms of paranoia, the decision as to whether a peculiar [*sic*] paranoiac is or is not dangerous is for qualified physicians to make. The courts cannot close their eyes to modern medical learning, or act as their own experts on psychiatric problems." (297 N.Y. at 408; 79 N.E. 2d at 466.)

In a more recent case, Brecka v. State of New York, 14 Misc. 2d 317, 179 N.Y.S. 2d 469 (Ct. Claims, Del Giorno, J., 1958), the Court of Claims dismissed a claim for false imprisonment because the health officer's certificate was found valid on its face. Although the certificate did not allege that the person was dangerous to herself or others, a charge of arson and a statement that she was mentally ill and in need of immediate care and treatment were held sufficient compliance with Section 72. Nevertheless, the court stated it was "not happy that it took forty-nine days to find out that the patient was not actually one who

patient was admitted. (Sec. 72(2)(3).) Under this form of admission the patient may be detained for up to sixty days without further process.

Section 75 provides for the admission and detention of a patient for not more than ten days on a petition and the certificate of two examining physicians but without any judge's signature if the patient needs immediate care and treatment, or if there is no other proper place available for his care and treatment, or if he is dangerous to the public safety. The director or other person in charge of the hospital may refuse to admit such a patient if he finds the reasons stated in the certificate to be insufficient, or if he finds the patient's condition not to necessitate immediate treatment. Admission on an incomplete court order is thus intended to permit the patient to be brought quickly to the hospital after an examination by two doctors; it postpones for ten days the need to obtain the court order. When the order is obtained, it permits the patient to be retained for sixty days from the date of the order before final certification, a total of seventy days.

Extent of Use of the Emergency Forms

Where no receiving hospitals exist, these two methods of admission, and especially the health-officer admission, are used for a significant portion of all admissions. In the year ended March 31, 1960, 1,763 patients, or 17.3 per cent of the 10,188 admissions to state hospitals serving the upstate area, were admitted on a health officer's certificate. About half that num-

---

would be dangerous to herself or others. Condemnation of the apparently lackadaisical manner of completing the medical inquiry would be but a speculative gesture on the part of the court. What other remedies, if any, are available to her against those who took claimant into custody and certified her condition as herein indicated, is a question upon which another tribunal must pass." (14 Misc. 2d at 322, 179 N.Y.S. 2d at 473.)

ber, 910 patients, or 8.9 per cent of the admissions in that year to hospitals serving the upstate area, were on an incomplete court order.[34] The two forms together thus accounted for 26.2 per cent, or more than one-fourth.

In the New York City area, however, patients may be admitted quickly to a psychiatric receiving hospital under Section 81. Only 197 patients, or 1.2 per cent of the 16,324 admissions to the state hospitals serving the New York City area in the year ended March 31, 1960, were on a health-officer's certificate; and only 517 patients, or 3.2 per cent, were on an incomplete court order. In the state hospitals serving Rochester and Buffalo, cities where facilities for admission under Section 81 also exist, health-officer admissions in 1959 were 4 per cent, and 2 per cent, respectively, of total admissions. Thus it is clear that Sections 72 and 75 are used as alternatives to Section 81 in areas where there are no receiving hospitals.

Not only does the extent of the use of these emergency methods vary between New York City and upstate; it varies also among the individual hospitals (Table 6, Appendix). In Suffolk County on Long Island, for instance, the health-officer admission is not used; the incomplete court order takes its place. In several upstate hospitals, however, health-officer admissions constitute one-fifth of total admissions and in one hospital more than one-quarter of all admissions.

Health-Officer Admissions

Inquiry among health officers showed that the health-officer admission is used mainly in emergencies when, as the statute requires, the patient needs immediate care and treatment or is dangerous to himself or others.[35] It is also used, however, as a

[34] Statistics from the New York State Department of Mental Hygiene, Division of Statistical Services.

[35] Replies to a questionnaire, circulated by our committee, from 78

convenient and easy admission when the patient is not at all dangerous.[36] A health-officer admission requires examination by only one physician and he a public servant. In rural areas where physicians are not readily available, it is often easy to turn to the health officer for a quick admission. Sometimes the health-officer admission is used, furthermore, because its use followed by a court order under Section 74 (which order can remain tentative for 60 days) extends from 60 to 120 days the time during which a patient may be retained in a hospital without incurring the stigma involved in a final order of certification.

---

county commissioners of health, health officers, and their designees. A majority of the 78 respondents (55) said that the statutory justification for using the health-officer admission—that the patient is dangerous to himself or others—is a frequent factor in the use of the health-officer admission; 42 said that a frequent factor is a need for assistance from the sheriff or police to restrain or transport the patient. Two health officers stated affirmatively that they do not use the health-officer admission unless there is a true emergency involving danger. (Directors of community mental health services were not included in this mailing, since they have been authorized to act under Section 72 only since 1959. N.Y. Sess. Laws 1959, ch. 782, § 3, eff. April 23, 1959. The views of these directors were sought through a questionnaire from the committee addressed to physicians.)

[36] Questionnaire to health officers, *supra* note 35. A significant minority of the respondents (17) said that dangerousness is infrequently the reason for using Section 72; 29 said that the need for assistance in transportation is infrequently the reason.

A significant number of respondents checked other reasons as frequent motivating factors for using a health-officer admission, as follows: 31, the difficulty or inconvenience of arranging examination by two physicians; 27, conduct which in a sane person would be disorderly conduct; 17, the unavailability of the judge to sign the order; and 13, the unwillingness of relatives to sign a petition. One or two respondents mentioned other reasons as frequent causes for the use of the health-officer admission, such as the following: that a person is in a state of acute alcoholism; that a person is wandering, confused, and senile; that the police request a health-officer admission; that a general hospital is unable to care for a patient long enough to secure certification under Section 74; or that relatives at a distance are unable to sign the petition.

Today many patients who respond well to therapy can be discharged within 120 days.

Taking and transporting patients. Taking and transporting an unwilling patient who may be violent or dangerous often has its difficulties. In New York City, as we have seen, a receiving hospital is now authorized to send its ambulance to pick up a patient on a written statement of a doctor. And throughout the state, under a 1956 amendment to Section 72,[37] local peace officers, on the written request of a health officer or of other persons authorized to effect admission under Section 72, are required to take the patient into custody as so directed. Of course, patients to be admitted on a health officer's certificate may also be transported to the hospital in ways other than by a police car or a sheriff's car—by their families, by the ambulance of a general hospital, by a volunteer ambulance squad, by the Welfare Department, or by an ambulance of the state hospital if the particular hospital follows the practice, as some do, of picking up all patients within the area it serves, regardless of method of admission.

In a questionnaire directed to health officers, we inquired about possible trauma to a patient arising from transportation in a police car and from assistance by peace officers in seizing and restraining him. A majority of the 78 respondents (49) considered transportation in a marked police car not traumatic, since many patients admitted on a health-officer admission are disoriented and not in contact with reality. Help from the police in seizing, restraining, and transporting patients was said by 42

[37] N.Y. Sess. Laws 1956, ch. 72, § 1, eff. March 10, 1956. This amendment was recommended by the New York State Interdepartmental Committee on Laws Governing Hospitalization of the Mentally Ill in its Report, p. 1 (unpublished, dated June 10, 1954, and made available to our committee by the New York State Department of Mental Hygiene), after the committee (of which Dr. Robert C. Hunt was chairman) found that health officers do not have sufficient power or authority to command assistance in seizing, restraining, and transporting patients whose hospitalization they have a duty to effect.

respondents not to be traumatic and by 30 to be traumatic to some degree.[38] The opinion of this majority was borne out by the former mental patients questioned in the Fountain House survey.[39] Police were involved in the admission of fifteen of these persons; a majority of these fifteen said that they did not think that the presence of the police did any harm.[40]

Hospital directors were divided in their views on the advisability of using marked police cars and police in uniform to transport patients. A few directors expressed the belief that marked cars and uniforms are salutary as symbols of authority. More directors, however, think that these devices are traumatic to the patient and his family and that transportation can best be handled by trained transfer agents and the ambulance of the state hospital, or at least by police cars which are unmarked and policemen who are not in uniform.

A majority of the health officers who replied to the committee's questionnaire believe that they now have enough authority and facilities to carry out their responsibility under Section 72 with respect to the transportation of patients. But some criticism was leveled at the limited resources available to health officers. A majority said that places for temporary lodging of patients and funds to meet the costs of health-officer admissions are not adequate.[41]

[38] Replies to health-officer questionnaire, *supra* note 35.

[39] See note 3 to Chapter III, *supra*.

[40] *Id.* None of the fifteen patients in whose admission the police were involved thought that the police were there because they had done something wrong. The predominant feeling with regard to the presence of the police was not anxiety but rather resentment toward relatives who had called them in. In the two cases in which anxiety was mentioned, it was alleviated by friendly conversation with the police.

[41] A majority of the 78 respondents to the health-officer questionnaire, *supra* note 35, considered the following resources adequate: power of health officer to apprehend and restrain (60); cooperation from peace officers (66); appropriate means of transportation (61); and number of designees (54). A majority of the respondents (47) considered inadequate the places available for temporary detention of persons to be ad-

Adequacy of single examination by health officer. Since a health-officer admission requires examination by only one physician, who may be either in clinical medicine or in public health, it is important to consider whether health officers are well enough qualified to decide on the need for hospitalization. Some of the persons questioned said that the statute imposes too great a responsibility on health officers, many of whom do not feel qualified to meet it. Others said, however, that health officers do not need to make a refined psychiatric diagnosis but merely a decision on whether observation in a hospital is indicated. This decision is made only in an emergency, when the patient may be dangerous to himself or others, and is always reviewed by the hospital's admitting psychiatrist. Finally, if the health officer does not feel qualified, he is permitted by the statute to call on a designee, who is likely to be a clinician in private practice, or on the director of community mental health services, who is usually a psychiatrist.[42]

Examination by just one doctor in a health-officer admission presents not only the medical question of the competency of a health officer to decide on the need for hospitalization, but also the legal question of the adequacy of a single examination as a safeguard for the patient. Is detention for up to sixty days justified by the finding of a health officer that a patient is dangerous, together with the hospital's approval of the admission?

An expeditious method of emergency admission is necessary,

---

mitted under Section 72 and the financial resources available to pay for transportation.

[42] Answering a questionnaire addressed to county commissioners of health, district and regional health officers, and city health officers, a majority of the twenty-two respondents thought that health officers are adequately qualified to determine the need for hospitalization, since borderline cases are not usually admitted by this method. Despite this general satisfaction with the ability of the health officer to perform the duties imposed on him by Section 72, a majority of these same respondents also said that too much responsibility is placed on the health officer, and that it should be shared by many doctors.

of course, and some protection is afforded by lodging the responsibility with a doctor who is a public official. This may not justify the use of the health-officer admission in many nonemergency situations. And even in emergency cases it may not justify a full two-month period of detention without opportunity (except by habeas corpus) to contest such detention in court.

Admission on Incomplete Court Order

Admission on an incomplete court order was designed for use when a judge is not readily available, and it is often used for this purpose. But it is also used, in practice, when a health officer refuses to handle emergency admissions or when any other method of admission is inconvenient for some reason.

Notice to the patient of the application for admission is usually dispensed with on the ground that notice would be ineffective or detrimental to the patient (Section 74(3), discussed in the preceding section of this chapter), and a hearing is rarely held. Two sets of papers containing the petition and medical certificate must be prepared, since one set of these papers must be sent with the patient to the hospital and the other to the court for the judge to sign within ten days. One hospital director requests that both sets of papers be delivered to the hospital, so that the hospital can make sure that the papers are sent to the judge. Another hospital director complained that when the judge is at a distance it sometimes takes great effort to get his signature within ten days. In many places the incomplete court order is never used, partly, we are told, because of the inconvenience involved in furnishing the two sets of papers.

The complexity of this method has been contrasted with the simplicity of emergency admissions to receiving hospitals, described at the beginning of this chapter. Although use of the incomplete court order saves the time otherwise needed before the admission to get the judge's signature, it does not save any of the time needed to get a petition and an examination by two physicians.

Evaluation

In all nonvoluntary admissions the patient's need for prompt medical care must be balanced against his right to legal safeguards. In an emergency admission the scales tip first toward prompt admission, but adequate safeguards surrounding the retention of the patient in the hospital must be provided. The longer he can be detained under such an emergency admission, the more rigorous should be the safeguards of his liberty in order to be adequate.

In considering the two methods of emergency admission to state mental hospitals and licensed private institutions, we found the health-officer admission a sound and workable method of emergency admission. Hospitalization is effected promptly. If it is limited—as Section 72 does limit it—to emergency cases in which the patient is dangerous to himself or others, authorizing a health officer or a director of community mental health services, or a designee of either of them, to effect admission is sound both from the point of view of the patient and from that of the public. Moreover, the apprehension which some health officers seem to feel about their duty and responsibility under Section 72 as the sole examining physician seems to be groundless if their functions are properly executed pursuant to statute.

Although health officers now have authority to command help from local police and sheriffs' departments in taking a patient to a hospital, the functioning of the health-officer admission could be improved by providing adequate places to lodge persons who are to be admitted on a health-officer admission and by making allowance in the budgets of health officers for the costs of these admissions.

Since a health-officer admission permits a patient to be admitted on the certificate of a single physician without notice to the patient or an opportunity for a hearing, the crucial question is whether adequate safeguards surround the retention of such a patient in the hospital. This question is discussed in Chapter V.

The admission on incomplete court order provides a method of emergency admission in cases when a judge is unavailable or the health officer refuses to act. But the time saved in getting the patient to the hospital by postponing the signature by the judge seems relatively unimportant, and administratively this method of admission is a complicated way of meeting an emergency. The judge's signature, without notice to the patient and an opportunity for a hearing, adds little protection for the patient. Thus the incomplete court order seems to offer little advantage as an efficient method of providing prompt care, and its legal safeguards are more a matter of form than of substance.

Both these methods of emergency admission permit retention of the patient in the hospital for considerable periods of time. Under the health-officer admission this period is sixty days under that admission itself, plus sixty days under the Section 74 order of certification that is likely to follow before that order can become final, or in practice 120 days. Under the incomplete court order the period is ten days, plus a similar sixty days under Section 74, which in this case is even more automatic than after a health-officer admission, or in practice an assured seventy days. Unlike many states, New York does not have a method of emergency admission that permits detention for only two or three days.[43]

With these provisions in mind, we asked health officers and

[43] See American Bar Foundation, The Mentally Disabled and the Law 39 and Table II-M (1961).

other physicians what the proper initial detention period in an emergency should be. The answers varied,[44] but all the respondents specified periods of time which they thought sufficient to permit diagnosis and evaluation of a case. Significantly, however, those who specified thirty days or more looked on the initial detention period in an emergency admission as a means not only of effecting immediate hospitalization but also as a means of giving treatment in the hope often of releasing the patient without having to certify him. From this inquiry it appeared that the proper initial detention period in an emergency admission is a medical and an administrative matter, to be determined in the light of the assumed function of such an admission. If the function is simply to bring the patient under treatment quickly, then a short period is indicated, in which case some short cuts in procedure may be justified. If the function is also treatment, a longer detention period is needed, in which case greater procedural safeguards may be essential to fairness and due process.

In the light of this evaluation of the two methods of emergency admission to state hospitals and licensed private institutions, it would seem advisable, if adequate safeguards can surround the patient's retention in the hospital, to abolish the admission on incomplete court order in favor of the health-officer admission.

[44] An overwhelming majority of the 78 respondents thought that the initial detention period in an emergency admission should be less than sixty days; more than two-thirds of the respondents thought that it should be less than thirty days; and just over one-third of the respondents thought that it should be less than fourteen days. The same question was asked in the questionnaire addressed to psychiatrists and other doctors with experience in admissions. Of the 149 respondents to this question, the largest number (51) favored a short initial detention period of less than two weeks, but 41 favored a period of from thirty-one to sixty days, and 25 favored a period of from twenty-two to thirty days.

3. *Admission by Two Physicians without Court Order*

In 1960 the New York Legislature fashioned yet another form of initial admission to state mental hospitals and licensed private institutions.[45] This is Section 73-a. Originally a proposal by the New York State Department of Mental Hygiene, its final version had the benefit of revision by leading representatives of both bench and bar.[46]

Section 73-a provides for compulsory admission for up to sixty days on: *first,* a petition by a relative or any other person who could ask a court order under Section 74(2); *second,* certification by two physicians, one of these being a qualified psychiatrist; and, *third,* an examination of the patient and concurrence on the need for admission by the hospital's own psychiatrist. After these three steps have been taken, and without any prior notice, the patient goes to the hospital. But within three days after the admission the hospital must serve a written notice of the application on the patient setting forth the patient's rights, under the statute, to seek his own discharge. This notice to the patient will be dispensed with if the doctors state,

[45] Mental Hygiene Law, § 73-a; N.Y. Sess. Laws 1960, ch. 854, § 1, eff. April 21, 1960.

[46] A conference was held on March 12, 1959, at the Appellate Division, First Judicial Department, to consider the proposal. In attendance were the presiding justice of that court, the presiding justice of the Appellate Division for the Second Judicial Department, the Commissioner of Mental Hygiene and the Associate Counsel for the Department of Mental Hygiene, the Chairman of the Committee on Mental Hygiene of the New York State Bar Association, and a representative of the Legal Aid Committee of The Association of the Bar of the City of New York. Report for 1959 of Committee on Mental Hygiene, New York State Bar Association Reports 139, 141 (1960). For more facts about the enactment of Section 73-a, see Willcox, Some Comments on "Commitment Procedures and the Non-mentally Ill," 33 N.Y. State Bar J. 316 (1961).

in writing, that it would be useless or hurtful. But in every case the notice must be served on the nearest relative.

If the patient, or someone on his behalf, in turn gives a written notice to the hospital of the patient's desire to leave, he will be discharged unless the hospital initiates a judicial admission within five days after the notice or within ten days after the admission, whichever of these two days may be the later. Even if there is no such notice from the patient, judicial admission is required in order to retain him for more than sixty days unless the patient will stay voluntarily under Section 71 or as a nonobjecting patient under Section 73.

This enactment of yet another method of initial admission on top of all the statutory methods already in existence was undertaken in the effort to provide a method of admission that would facilitate prompt care and treatment, with the least traumatic effect upon the patient, and that would permit regular direct admissions to state hospitals without judicial processing of patients through receiving hospitals.[47] The provisions for a judicial proceeding after admission were intended to provide full protection for the patient's legal rights.

Experience under Section 73-a has been limited. The Department tells us that it has distributed 73-a forms for three hundred patients a month, all to admission hospitals in the metropolitan area of New York City. But only a few patients have been sent to state hospitals by the use of these forms. Up to August 1961 no admissions under Section 73-a have occurred in upstate New York or from the two eastern counties of Long Island. The gradual introduction of Section 73-a procedures is intended to limit their use to those areas where the judges indicate their willingness to complete 73-a admissions by court certifications when these may become necessary.

[47] See Memorandum of Department of Mental Hygiene in support of A. Int. 4540, Pr. 5014, ch. 854, L. 1960, New York State Legislative Annual 255, 257–58 (1960).

Evaluation

Despite the limited use of Section 73-a thus far, many hospital directors are enthusiastic about it. They feel that with it New York has at last a frankly medical, rather than a legal, admission for nonemergency cases. With hospitals becoming more and more open, and patients thus having more and more freedom, these directors think that the safeguards contained in this new procedure are sufficient protection against improper hospitalization: a petition by a relative; an examination by three physicians, two of whom must be psychiatrists; and an opportunity for judicial hearing soon after admission.

Section 73-a may ultimately permit many patients to enter a mental hospital, be treated, and be discharged without the need for any court certification. If more than sixty days are needed for treatment, some of these 73-a patients may agree to stay voluntarily, instead of being certified.

The psychiatrists in general hospitals in New York City welcome 73-a warmly because it makes possible the sending of patients directly to state hospitals, from wherever they are, without having to send them first to a crowded city receiving hospital, to be moved again in a fortnight or so to a state hospital.

Three objections to the new procedure have been suggested. One is that in vast areas of the state not enough psychiatrists are available to serve as examining physicians. This difficulty will be accentuated by the provision of present law, discussed in Section 1 of this chapter, which bars an admitting hospital's psychiatrists from examining for admissions to their own hospitals. This potential difficulty has not become an actual one because, as we have seen, the use of 73-a has been limited to hospitals in New York City, where psychiatrists are most readily available.

The second difficulty, which again has not yet arisen, relates to the place of the hearings which may be demanded by patients. Section 73-a(3) incorporates by reference the procedural provisions of Section 74; it thus appears to provide for hearings before "a court of record of the city or county, or a justice of the supreme court of the judicial district in which the alleged mentally ill person resides or may be." The problem is that the statute does not expressly provide a procedure for a change of venue. If hearings must be held in the county of the patient's residence when demanded, injury to the patient's health and administrative trouble and expense may be caused by carrying a patient back to his own county for a hearing.

The third objection is by far the most serious. It is that a patient taken without notice and against his will to a hospital may well be too ignorant, too confused, or too despondent to avail himself of the rights to judicial review so carefully tendered by Section 73-a. This is part of the broader question whether well-meant legal safeguards are in reality sufficient for patients who are without expert and devoted advisers to inform them and to champion their rights.

4. Admission of Nonobjecting Patients

One method by which a patient may enter a mental hospital has some of the features both of a voluntary and of a compulsory admission. Section 73 gives authority to the hospital to receive and retain any person suitable for care and treatment who does not object thereto on a petition and on the certificate of a single examining physician. Although the petition may be signed by any of the persons authorized to sign a petition under Section 74,[48] the Department of Mental Hygiene prefers that the petitioner for an admission under Section 73 be a member of

[48] See Section 1 of this chapter.

the family.[49] In most cases the patient's family has the greatest concern for his welfare. But this is not always true and, as we shall see, some New York judges are deeply concerned to protect patients against families who seek to slough off responsibility for aged and troublesome members. This concern is one expression of the effort of our society to grapple with the increasingly serious problem of care of the aged.

The medical examination by one physician must precede the admission by not more than ten days. Thus the results of the examination must be based on the patient's condition as it was just before the admission. The single physician who acts under Section 73 need not be a psychiatrist nor be specially qualified otherwise.

Admission to a mental hospital under this section can be likened to a voluntary admission in that the patient does not object, that no order is made by any court before the admission, and that no such order may be needed at any time. None will be needed if neither the patient nor anyone on his behalf ever objects to his being kept in the hospital. If the patient is truly nonobjecting and if he truly understands the implications of what he is doing (which may not be the same thing at all), it matters little whether he signifies his consent by signing an application for a voluntary admission or by submitting passively.

[49] State of New York, Department of Mental Hygiene, Policy Manual, § 404(c), Aug. 1, 1960:

"Although under the statute, the petitioner on a one physician's certificate may be any one of the several persons who can petition for a judicial certification, it is the opinion of the Department that it is preferable that the petitioner in such cases be a member of the prospective patient's family.

"Under the statute, this member could be the mother or father, the husband or wife, the brother or sister, the child, or the nearest relative.

"The foregoing does not preclude the admission of patients on papers with any of the petitioners permitted under the law."

The important question is, however, whether the patient admitted in this way is truly nonobjecting. The question looms large because this method is so commonly used for senile patients, who are often confused and disoriented and frequently despondent or withdrawn.[50] These are dependent persons in need of protective care; as such they are entitled to procedures that will guarantee their rights meticulously. Their very illness may prevent them from understanding hospitalization or objecting to it. Since this method of admission often results, in practice, in the patient's staying in the hospital for the rest of his life, it is treated in this report as the involuntary admission which it so often is, and it is therefore subjected to the same scrutiny as other methods of involuntary admission.[51]

Use of this method of admission has increased markedly in recent years, as Chart 2 indicates. In the state as a whole it has risen from nearly 1.5 per cent of all admissions in 1949 to nearly 10 per cent in 1959, with a slight decline in 1960. This increase is especially marked in the hospitals serving the New York metropolitan area.

As with other methods of admission, the extent of its use varies considerably among different hospitals and among different areas. According to Chart 2, in 1959 nearly 15 per cent of the admissions to state hospitals serving the New York metropolitan area were by this method (more than 17 per cent in 1958), whereas fewer than 2 per cent were so in state hospitals serving the upstate area. (Table 3 in the Appendix gives the number of admissions by county in 1960 under Section 73.)

Since this method is so useful and so much used for older

[50] Section 73 is used for other passive patients too; it is thought to be well adapted, for example, to the case of the young mother in postpartum delirium, who after a few days of hospitalization will probably be willing to stay voluntarily.

[51] The American Bar Foundation in its comprehensive report, The Mentally Disabled and the Law 22 (1961), likewise classifies the nonprotested admission as an involuntary admission.

CHART 2. Trends in admission of nonobjecting mental patients in ew York State on a single physician's certificate: Percentages of ɔtal admissions under Section 73 of the Mental Hygiene Law, se- ɛcted state mental hospitals, New York State, 1949–1960

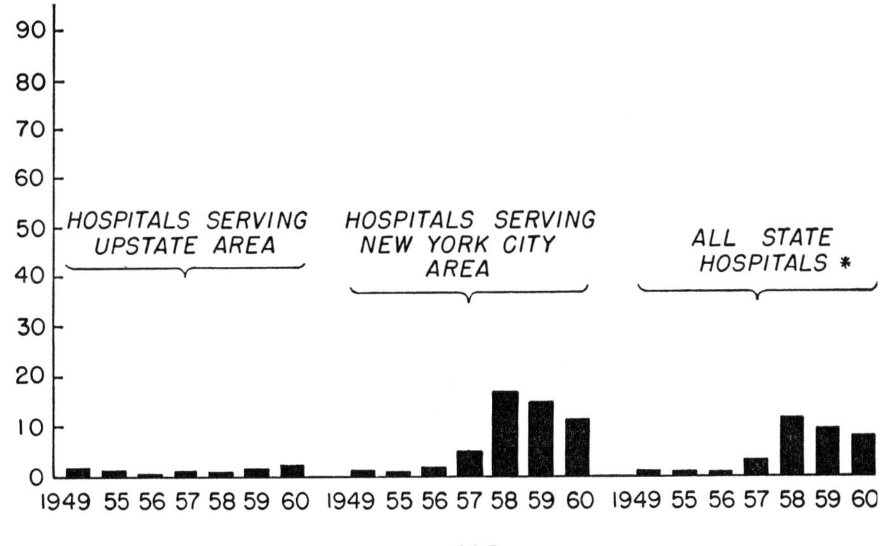

ource: New York State Department of Mental Hygiene, Division of Statistical Serv- :. (See Table 7, Appendix, for supporting data.)

* The Psychiatric Institute is omitted because, with its special role, almost all its ients enter voluntarily.

patients, it should be noted that persons over sixty-five account for an increasing proportion of first admissions and that diseases associated with senility are becoming more and more common.[52] In 1960 in New York State 6,927 admissions, or about

[52] See Health Information Foundation, Progress in Health Services, vol. IX, no. 8, Hospitalized Mental Illness in the U.S. 4, for data showing that, for the nation as a whole, persons aged 65 and over accounted for about 1 in 8 of all first admissions to public mental hospitals in 1922 (12.9 per cent) but by 1957 their proportion of the total had risen to more than 1 in 4 (26.8 per cent). See Table 1, p. 7, of that publication for increasing rates per 100,000 civilian population of first admissions

26 per cent of all admissions (26,783), involved patients sixty-five years of age or over.[53] A similar picture emerges from the figures on admission classified according to diagnosis. After schizophrenia, which accounted for the largest group of first admissions in New York State in 1960, the next largest group of first admissions—6,566 or 24 per cent—were patients with diseases of senility.[54] The problem of senile patients is clearly becoming more important.

Even though the use of nonobjecting admissions is increasing, the vast majority of patients over sixty-five and the vast majority of patients with diseases of senility are still admitted by two physicians with a court order under Section 74. Only 15 per cent of each of these two groups were admitted on a one-physician certificate in 1960. Although the use of the one-physician certificate is on the rise, therefore, it has by no means become the prevailing way of admitting senile patients.

In practice, the single physician of the statute is usually the family doctor. He probably knows both the patient and his family. He can therefore make the examination with the least possible expenditure of time and money, and also with the least possible disturbance to the patient. He is likely to be in a good position to determine whether going to a mental hospital is the best course for his patient, although it cannot be denied that in some cases he will probably look at the case from the family's point of view rather than from the point of view exclusively of the welfare of his patient. Neither the statute nor the regulations require, however, that the single physician shall have had

---

with senile psychoses and psychoses associated with arteriosclerosis. See also Cohen, Mental Illness among Older Americans, Report Prepared for Consideration by the Special Committee on Aging, U.S. Senate, p. 1 (1961).

[53] Statistics from the New York State Department of Mental Hygiene, Division of Statistical Services.

[54] *Ibid.*

previous acquaintance with the patient, as the new British act does.[55]

The essential characteristic of an admission under Section 73, as already noted, is the patient's lack of objection.[56] If the patient objects, he must be rejected as unsuitable for this form of admission. The patient may object at any time: at the time of his medical examination, for example, or during his transit to the hospital. In fact, transfer agents of state hospitals who take patients in hospital ambulances are expressly instructed to reject any patient to be admitted under Section 73 who objects during transit.[57] A patient may also object, of course, at the time of admission when informed of the character of the institution and the reason for his being there.[58]

If the patient fails to object at any of these stages, he may then be kept for up to sixty days and even thereafter until fifteen days after written notice of his desire to leave. In that event, the director must either discharge the patient or, if he thinks further hospitalization needed, must initiate proceedings for a judicial order, as explained in Chapter V. The necessity for a court order authorizing continued detention rarely arises, however, since these patients, withdrawn, passive, and often elderly, almost never take the initiative to give a written notice of desire to leave.

[55] British Mental Health Act, 7 & 8 Eliz. 2, ch. 72, § 28(2).

[56] Section 73; N.Y. Ops. Atty. Gen. 265 (1946). If the person to be admitted under Section 73 has been adjudicated incompetent and is therefore incapable of objecting, the consent of his committee stands in place of his own consent. People *ex rel.* Stavies v. Loughlin, 195 N.Y.S. 2d 364, 370 (Sup. Ct. Bronx Co., Chimera, J., 1959) (not officially reported), aff'd 11 App. Div. 2d 646, 201 N.Y.S. 2d 150 (1st Dept. 1960).

[57] Department of Mental Hygiene, Policy Manual, *op. cit. supra* note 49, at § 404(b).

[58] Department of Mental Hygiene, Policy Manual, *op. cit. supra* note 49, at § 404(a), discussed in Chapter III, *supra.*

Evaluation

In evaluating the operation of Section 73, the staff has been particularly concerned with the safeguards provided for these patients who do not have enough insight to sign a voluntary admission but who do accept hospitalization without affirmative objection. Although this method makes available the advantages of a noncompulsory admission to persons unable to apply voluntarily, and although it has the virtue of administrative simplicity, it may work some grave injustice by failing to accord to many nonobjecting patients any real opportunity to object. In addition, it raises large questions of medical and social policy in the care of the aged, questions which are the subject of extensive study by groups specially qualified in the field of geriatrics.[59]

No better statement of the objection to admission of senile patients under Section 73 exists than that expressed by Mr. Justice Brenner in 1958 in *Matter of "Jones."*[60] The case involved an application for certification under Section 74 of a ninety-six-year old man, but the court took the occasion to condemn Section 73, by contrast to 74, as a technique "increasingly used by the Department of Mental Hygiene" which

> effectively shunts seniles into involuntary confinement without awareness by them of their plight and without their actual approval or judicial surveillance. These unwanted seniles may not even hope to escape factually involuntary confinement because the possibility of private care, often provided at a judicial hearing, is

[59] E.g., White House Conference on Aging, February 1961; Subcommittee on Problems of the Aged and Aging of the Committee on Labor and Public Welfare, United States Senate; Joint Commission on Mental Illness and Health; The National Council on Aging; New York State Department of Mental Hygiene, Dr. Alvin I. Goldfarb, Consultant on Services for the Aged.

[60] 9 Misc. 2d 1084, 1085–86, 172 N.Y.S. 2d 869, 870–71 (Sup. Ct. Kings Co. 1958).

denied to them and, of course, they cannot thereafter effect their own release.

Moreover, the denial of judicial hearing or sanction is based on a statute of questionable constitutionality because it is grounded on a fictitious consent given by one who concededly is confused and disoriented. Even if *positive objection* is not required by the Mental Hygiene Department, the consent thus extracted is dubious because the senile is not likely to understand that the admitting institution is a mental institution, even if he be told that it is. Often he is chagrined and humiliated following family rejection and has neither the will nor the capacity to object even if he be carefully advised. That he is aware of his right to object or of the significance of his failure to object is doubtful. In short, the pink sheet procedure [referring to the form used until recently for admissions under Section 73], in my view, is little less than a ruse designed to circumvent the need for judicial consideration or review of the transfer of the senile to a mental institution. Thus unknowingly certified, without opportunity to secure private custodial care, we have assembly line incarceration, depriving the aged of their liberty of person and, as was said by Judge Garrity (*Matter of Neisloss,* 8 Misc. 2d 912, 913): "No matter how sweetly disguised or delicate the language, involuntary confinement is a loss of freedom." [Emphasis is in original.]

Justice Brenner is not alone in his criticism of the admission of senile patients under Section 73. Supreme Court justices in New York City who met with our committee agreed; they emphasized the need to differentiate between aged persons who are unable to care for themselves and aged persons who are mentally ill. This distinction, however, cannot always be made with clarity. Aged persons may be on a continuum ranging from severe mental dysfunction to mild disorientation, and their condition may change from time to time. Studies of psychiatric services for the aged have shown that patients in old-age homes, nursing homes, and state hospitals could properly be cared for in one or another institutional setting depending on factors other than the patient's condition.[61]

[61] Goldfarb, Review of a Pilot Study on Psychiatric Services in New

Other judges have also spoken on this subject. In March 1960 various Supreme Court justices presented their views on the commitment of aged persons to the Joint Legislative Committee on Problems of the Aged of the New York State Legislature. Their statements stressed the lack of facilities for the care of the aged, particularly those on the borderline of mental illness who are without relatives or resources.[62] Rather than use Section 73, some of these justices would prefer to hospitalize the aged by means of a court order after a hearing.

It has been urged that the aged should be certified to mental hospitals as "helplessly aged" or as "helpless due to old age." [63] This would be less stigmatizing than a certification as "mentally ill." Our staff considered this suggestion seriously, but doubted the constitutionality under the state constitution [64] of conferring on the Department of Mental Hygiene duties relating to persons who are merely aged but who are not mentally ill. Moreover, according to the Commissioner of Mental Hygiene, the state hospitals could not accommodate all who are merely aged without doubling their size.

York State (1958); Cohen, Mental Illness among Older Americans, *op. cit. supra* note 52, at 2.

[62] On this same point Justice Miles F. McDonald of the Supreme Court, Kings County, wrote our committee:

"The real difficulty in the present situation lies principally in the fact that there are no adequate facilities to handle the senile who, though technically mentally ill because of old age, are not really insane in the generally accepted meaning of the term. Many conscientious judges object to committing patients as mentally ill merely to afford them the care that is required by their feebleness and their years, as these judges believe that imposes a stigma not only upon the elderly person but upon their children."

[63] See opinion of Justice Brenner in Matter of "Anonymous #1" to "Anonymous #12," Alleged Mentally Ill Persons, 206 Misc. 909, 138 N.Y.S. 2d 30 (Sup. Ct. Kings Co. 1954) deploring the necessity of certifying elderly persons in order to provide care for them. A bill to permit certification as a helpless aged person, A. Int. 434, Pr. 434, was introduced in the 1961 legislature but failed to pass.

[64] N.Y. Const. art. 17, § 4.

In an effort to learn the views of doctors, we included in our questionnaire to physicians a question which, after noting the increase in admissions under Section 73, particularly for senile patients, asked the doctors their opinions of this method. Table 8 (Appendix) shows the responses from doctors in New York City, from doctors in upstate New York, and from directors of community mental health services in all parts of the state. A majority of the physicians in each group, and 69 per cent of all respondents, consider this method of admission satisfactory. The only significant disapproval came from 39 per cent of the upstate physicians.

Comments favorable to this method said that it is less traumatic and less stigmatizing than a court proceeding; that it lets the patient be admitted to care with privacy and dignity; that it helps relatives who feel some guilt about hospitalizing their ill or aged relatives; that it saves time, work, and money; and that it is more like an admission to a general hospital for a physical illness, while yet protecting the patient's rights through the hospital's examination at admission, through the sixty-day period of observation, through the periodic medical review, and through the right to leave on fifteen days' notice. The answers from New York City pointed out one particular advantage of this kind of admission in that city: that it obviates the need to send a patient to a receiving hospital before sending him to a state hospital. For older people, who are apt to be deeply disturbed by changes in routine, moving from one hospital to another can be gravely harmful.

Some physicians commented that this method would be all right if certain precautions were taken, viz., if the single doctor were a psychiatrist; if the method were used for emergencies only; if the nearest relative were to agree to the admission in writing; if the method were not used where relatives disagree about the need for hospitalization; if it were not used where an estate is involved; if controls were set up to protect the patient's property; and if the method were used only for admission to a state hospital, not to a private one. Mental hospital administrators say, also in qualified approval of the method, that all these aged patients were mentally ill and in need of psychiatric care when they came into the hospital, although some may now be sufficiently recovered to leave the hospital if ways to take care of them outside could be found.

Those doctors who thought the method unsatisfactory commented that examination by two physicians is a valuable protection both for the patient and for the doctor; a single physician may wonder whether he is not being too strongly influenced by the family. If a patient is truly nonobjecting, one physician said, he ought to be admitted as a voluntary. Some doctors expressed the same concern voiced by many of the judges—that this method of admission may not adequately protect patients against improper hospitalization.

Consideration of all these opinions, the work of other groups on this problem, and our own studies convinced us of the need for an enormous increase in good facilities for care of the aged in varied kinds of institutions and in the community.[65] Until more geriatric facilities of these kinds are available, the state mental hospitals have to continue to be our main resource. These aged patients must have protective care—medical care for their physical disabilities, psychiatric care for their mental and emotional problems, and custodial care to ensure their safety. The efforts of several New York State hospitals to develop separate geriatric wings is a recognition of the special problems involved. These efforts, and the changing public attitude toward mental hospitals as they become more open and

[65] In addition to institutions of various kinds, Cohen, Mental Illness among Older Americans, *op. cit. supra* note 52, at 8–12, discusses the need for community evaluation centers, day-care centers, foster home or family care, and part-time hospital programs to care for the aged in the community. For an illuminating historical discussion of the aged, see Rosen, Cross-cultural and Historical Approaches, in Hoch and Zubin (eds.), Psychopathology of Aging (1961).

more therapeutically oriented, should do much to lessen the stigma involved in caring for aged patients in mental hospitals.

These remarks on the complex problem of care for the aged are presented in order to set in proper perspective the lesser problem of how best to admit these patients to mental hospitals. The difficulties that judges meet daily in certification of aged patients or that hospitals meet in the admission of nonobjecting senile patients are real, but they cannot be overcome short of a vast expansion in adequate facilities for taking care of geriatric patients. Our staff shares the view of a majority of the doctors that this medical method of admission can be made satisfactory for passive patients, including those who are senile, but has serious reservations about the safeguards now provided by Section 73. Certain modifications in it are therefore desirable. But it must be recognized that solution of the entire problem, as noted above, calls for more and better facilities for taking care of older persons.

CONCLUSION

These then are the ways in which nonvoluntary patients may first enter a mental hospital. As we have seen, all methods of initial admission are, in practice, effected by doctors. The one method which requires the certification of a court before admission (Section 74) is, in practice, also effected by doctors, since the signature of a judge has become a routine formality in a large majority of the actual cases. This is likewise true of the emergency admission on incomplete court order (Section 75), where a judge's signature must be added within ten days after admission.

Chapter V will describe the ways in which each of these initial methods may be extended by court certification into an indefinite hospital stay.

V

Retention of Nonvoluntary Patients for an Indeterminate Period

Mental hospitals are not prisons, but they do, by force on body or mind, deprive patients of some freedom.

Any person hospitalized against his will is entitled to watchful protection of his rights, because he is a citizen first and a mental patient second.

AN essential part of our recommendations for initial medical admission is the protection provided by the following recommendations concerning retention of patients in state hospitals, licensed private institutions, or receiving hospitals:

Recommendation No. 1 (Mental Health Review Service). A new state-wide agency, called provisionally the Mental Health Review Service, shall be established as an agency independent of the hospitals and of the Department of Mental Hygiene and shall be responsible to the courts handling mental hospital admissions.

The Mental Health Review Service will have the duty of studying and reviewing the admission and retention of every nonvoluntary patient. It shall have two aims: (1) to explain to the patient and his family the procedures under which a patient enters and is retained in a mental hospital, and to inform them of the patient's right to a hearing before a judge, his right to be represented by a lawyer, and his right to seek an independent medical opinion, if desired; and (2) to provide the court with information on the patient's case to establish the need for his care and treatment in the hospital or his right to discharge. The Service will also recommend to the court, in all cases where the Service sees the need, the desirability of the patient's having legal representation or of his being examined by another psychiatrist.

Staffed by persons trained for this work, the Mental Health Review Service will have a primary duty to guarantee that patients know their rights and that the court has before it the facts necessary for deciding the question of the propriety of a patient's retention.

The Mental Health Review Service shall be available in state hospitals, in licensed private institutions, and in psychiatric receiving hospitals—in short, in all mental hospitals which any patients enter against their will.

Although the primary functions of the Service will relate to nonvoluntary patients, it will also have the duty of explaining to voluntary patients their status and rights and will be available to aid voluntary patients who ask for its help.

Recommendation No. 4 (*Notice*). Within five working days after a patient's admission, the hospital shall be required to serve written notice on the patient and his relatives of their right to request a judicial hearing on the need for care and treatment of the patient in a mental hospital and of the right to obtain representation by a lawyer at the hearing. The patient shall be authorized to designate up to three persons, in addition to those now specified in Section 74(3) of the Mental Hygiene Law, on whom the notice should also be served. The Mental Health Review Service will make certain that notice has been served under this recommendation and that the patient has been informed of his rights.

Recommendation No. 5 (*Court Review with Judicial Hearing*). If the patient or other interested person requests a hearing, or if the Mental Health Review Service recommends a hearing, a judicial hearing shall be held promptly. No time limit shall be placed on the right to demand a hearing; the right shall remain open at all times during the first sixty days of hospitalization. The person requesting the hearing shall be allowed to choose whether it will be held in the county of the patient's residence, the county from which he was admitted, or the county where the hospital is located. Any interested party, including the hospital, may apply to change the place of hearing to any other county in order to serve the convenience of the parties or the condition of the patient. Before the hearing the Mental Health Review Service shall investigate the patient's case and report its findings to the judge.

Recommendation No. 6 (*Hospitalization after Hearing*). After hearing, the judge shall either order discharge of the patient or make an order authorizing the hospital to retain the patient for care and treatment for a period not to exceed six months. In appropriate cases, the order may authorize transfer of the patient from the hospital of admission (which may be a psychiatric receiving hospital) to any state hospital or to a licensed private institution.

Recommendation No. 7 (*Court Review without Hearing*). If, after service of the notice proposed in Recommendation No. 4, no hearing is requested by the patient or his relatives within the first sixty days of hospitalization and no hearing is recommended by the Mental Health Review Service, and if the patient does not agree to remain in the hospital as a voluntary patient; then, upon an application for authority to retain the patient and upon a certificate of the hospital director that further care and treatment of the patient is necessary, presented to a judge before the expiration of the first sixty days of hospitalization, the judge may make an order authorizing the hospital to retain the patient for care and treatment for a period not to exceed six months.

Notice of this application for authority to retain shall be served on the patient and his relatives by the hospital and explained to them by the Mental Health Review Service, and relevant information about the case shall be furnished by the Mental Health Review Service to the judge, all in the same way as the notice and review proposed in Recommendations No. 4 and No. 5.

Recommendation No. 8 (Renewal of Authority to Retain). The judicial authorization for the retention of a patient for care and treatment in a hospital shall be renewed periodically. Before the expiration of any period of retention, the hospital may apply for renewed authority to retain the patient, and notice of such application shall be served on the patient in the same way as the notice proposed in Recommendation No. 4. The Mental Health Review Service shall also make a further investigation of the patient's case. Within fifteen days of the notice of application, the patient and his relatives shall be given an opportunity for a full hearing.

After the initial six-month judicial authorization, an order may be made authorizing retention of the patient for an additional year; after the additional year, an order may be made from time to time authorizing retention of the patient for a period not to exceed two years.

The time periods are intended as maximums, and the judge should have full authority to shorten the time periods. The time periods should be applied so that minor errors or delays will not subject the hospital to liability for false imprisonment.

If the hospital makes an application for renewal of authority to retain before expiration of the prior period, the existing authority shall continue until judicial action on the application.

Recommendation No. 15 (Transfer from Receiving Hospitals to State Hospitals). If, at any time after admission to a psychiatric receiving hospital under the proposals contained in Recommendations No. 2, No. 3, or No. 14, no hearing has been requested or recommended by the patient or someone on his behalf, a patient may be transferred without judicial order from a psychiatric receiving hospital to a state mental hospital, and the sixty-day period of the initial admission shall run from the time of admission to the transferring hospital. Notice of the proposed transfer shall be given to the Mental Health Review Service and to the persons notified of initial admission as proposed in Recommendation No. 4.

Recommendation No. 17 (Medical Release). The present provisions for release and discharge of patients on the certificate of the director of a state hospital or the person in charge of a licensed private institution shall be continued.

Recommendation No. 18 (Judicial Release). Present provisions for release of mental patients by the courts shall be implemented with the assistance of the Mental Health Review Service. These provisions include (1) the right to a writ of habeas corpus, (2) the right to review of the admission by a judge acting on the verdict of a jury as provided in Section 76 of the Mental Hygiene Law, and (3) judicial review of the decision of a hospital director against release, and provisions allowing release by the Commissioner of Mental Hygiene, pursuant to Section 87 of the Mental Hygiene Law. An application under any of these provisions may be made in the county of the patient's residence, the county from which he was admitted, or the county where the hospital is located. Any interested party, including the hospital, may apply to change the place of hearing the application to any other county in order to serve the convenience of the parties or the condition of the patient. There shall be no filing fee in any judicial proceeding involving the personal liberty of any person found or alleged to be mentally ill.

Recommendation No. 23 (Voting Rights). Section 152(6) of the Election Law shall be amended to eliminate the statutory disqualification from voting of persons "committed to an institution for the care and treatment of the mentally ill." However, appropriate provisions shall continue to allow disqualification from voting of persons adjudged incompetent or persons committed to an institution for the care and treatment of the mentally defective.

In Chapter IV we surveyed the six legal roads by which nonvoluntary patients may first reach a mental hospital and be detained there for limited periods of time. One of these ways to a state hospital or licensed private institution, as already shown, is by means of a certificate of two physicians with court order under Section 74. Section 74 also provides the sole procedure for converting any one of these initial admissions to any mental hospital into an indeterminate detention in a state hospital or licensed private institution.

To retain a patient for an indeterminate period of time, Section 74 requires a judicial order of certification, tentative at first and limited at that stage to sixty days, but becoming indeterminate on the filing of a certificate by the hospital director. In theory, it also requires that notice of the application for his tentative certification be given to the patient and to his nearest relative and that a hearing be held on the demand of any relative or near friend in behalf of the patient or on motion of the judge. But notice to the patient may be dispensed with if it would be ineffective or detrimental to him. Nor is a hearing required.

The court's order may direct the patient's admission to an institution of the Department of Mental Hygiene for the care and treatment of the mentally ill. If the patient continues to need care and treatment for more than sixty days after the judge's order, the hospital director may simply file a certificate to that effect in the county clerk's office. On the filing of this certificate the judge's order becomes, in the language of Section 74(7), a "final order."

In this chapter we shall describe the steps in converting each kind of initial admission, including the tentative court-ordered certification for not more than sixty days, into a court-ordered indeterminate detention. We shall also examine to see how far practice accords with theory in providing court consideration of every case before a final certification for an indeterminate time.

MOVEMENT OF PATIENTS FROM RECEIVING HOSPITALS TO A STATE HOSPITAL OR PRIVATE INSTITUTION

In New York City

In New York City most patients certified to state hospitals or licensed private institutions are originally admitted to psychiatric receiving hospitals, as we have seen, under Section 81(2), for examination and screening. But some of them are in other hospitals in the city first. And—incredible though this may seem—a patient in any other hospital in New York City whose doctors decide that he needs treatment in a state hospital and who does not enter the state hospital voluntarily or as a nonobjecting patient must normally be sent first to a city receiving hospital. Certification is then undertaken there after a new and largely independent restudy of his case. This extra stay in another hospital delays the patient's treatment, which is often needed at once. It compels him to adjust himself to a new environment for some two weeks. It strains facilities that are already overcrowded. It greatly increases the cost of getting the patient to a state hospital.

Attempts to avoid this detour have been made by sending such a patient, with an attendant from the general hospital, to appear before the court at Bellevue, or by having the judges sit at hospitals other than the city receiving hospitals. Neither effort has worked out well. The practice of funneling all patients who have to be certified through a city receiving hospital has become firmly fixed. Dissatisfaction with this practice is widespread and vehement.

Patients in New York City receiving hospitals who are found to need long-term care in a state hospital or licensed private institution are transferred in several ways. Some few go, as we have seen in Chapter III, as voluntary patients. Others are admitted to state hospitals under Section 73 as nonobjecting patients on a petition and the certificate of a single physician. In 1960 approximately three-quarters of the patients transferred to state hospitals from Jacobi Hospital in Bronx County or from Elmhurst Hospital in Queens County were admitted in this way. A few patients in New York City were transferred in 1960, under the new Section 73-a, on a petition and the certificate of two physicians, one a psychiatrist. The vast majority of patients from Bellevue and Kings County Hospitals, however, were and are transferred under Section 74 by the order of a court.

Although several courts are thus authorized to certify, in practice a Special Term of the New York Supreme Court handles all the certifications in New York City. The justices sit in rotation, two days a week at Bellevue Hospital in New York County and two days a week at Kings County Hospital in Kings. Justices of the Supreme Court for Bronx and Queens counties also sit in rotation at Jacobi and Elmhurst Hospitals, respectively.

The cases come before the court on a petition, usually signed by an administrator of the receiving hospital—only occasionally by a relative. The examining physicians are psychiatrists on the receiving hospital's staff.

Notice of an application for certification is served personally on every patient over thirteen years of age except on rare occasions. Since serving a notice on a patient who is already in a hospital is less likely to do harm or to cause flight than serving one on a patient who is still in the community, the practice of dispensing with notice, so common in initial admissions from the community under Section 74, is not common here. Service in the hospital is usually made by the attending psychiatrist the day before the court sits [1] by distributing a batch of formal notices to several patients at a time, often when they are all together. On every notice to a patient some form of explanation similar to this is added: "This is not a summons. If you are willing to go to a state hospital, you need not appear. If you do object, contact your doctor immediately." [2]

Our staff heard many complaints about the way in which notice is served on the patient. One was that many patients do

[1] An opinion of the Attorney General stated that the requirement of one day's notice under an earlier but similar statute was met by service at any hour of the day preceding the day of the court's certification. N.Y. Ops. Atty. Gen. 354 (1923).

[2] The wording of the notice differs slightly in different hospitals.

not understand the meaning of the notice or the procedure and that no explanation is given to them. For example, some few patients who can afford to pay do not know that they can elect to go to a private hospital. Our staff was told that some doctors, in giving the patients their notices, say casually, "Here, put this in your pocket." Thus, while service of notice on patients is rarely dispensed with in receiving hospitals in New York City, the way in which it is served is often so perfunctory, and the information it conveys so meager, that it does not fulfill its function.

One case was reported to us of a seventy-year-old man who had been living alone in New York City. He had been seen at his home by a psychiatrist from the Welfare Department. Taken thereafter to a New York City receiving hospital, he was about to be transferred to a state hospital without any hearing because he did not seem to object. Through the intervention of a sympathetic social worker of the Welfare Department, a hearing was requested for this old man. The mere request stimulated the hospital, now aware that someone was interested in him, to release him into the custody of the social worker. But for the social worker's intervention, the patient's objection would never have been known. We cannot say that such things happen often, though we may of course suspect that they do. That such a case can happen once, however, shows that the system badly needs improving. Although it makes more work for everybody at the receiving hospital, objections from patients ought to be facilitated by efforts to have patients understand their rights.

Another criticism is that the short time allowed between the service of a notice and the hearing often does not allow the patient to reach his family or others to discuss his transfer to a state hospital.

At Bellevue the same formal notice which the patient receives is mailed to his nearest relative, with a statement added to it, similar to that added to the notice to the patient, saying that no appearance at the hearing is necessary if the person served is willing to have the patient go to a state hospital. This notice to the relative is mailed five days before the petition is presented to the court, or seven days if sent outside the state. Notice to relatives is given with scrupulous care in New York City, and judges are strict in enforcing this requirement. Two judges in Kings County delete the statement about nonappearance usually added to the form because they insist on the attendance of relatives at all hearings. Our staff observed that hearings were adjourned because the judge suspected that notice had been mailed to a wrong address. And judges often adjourn hearings if the relatives are not present, even though they may have been served with notice, in the hope that a second service will bring them to the hearing. Our staff found the practice in the service of notice on relatives to be exemplary.

Although hearings on an application for a court certification are much more common in New York City than upstate, they occur, even in New York City, in less than one-sixth of the cases. Of the 5,097 patients in the psychiatric ward of Bellevue in 1960 for whom certification to state hospitals was sought, 834—or 16 per cent of the patients—had hearings at which the patient appeared. In Kings County Hospital such hearings are held in a larger proportion of the cases because the judges there make it a practice to see every patient possible. Even in Kings County, however, about 30 per cent of the patients recommended for certification are reported to the court to be too ill or too disturbed to attend a hearing. Thus in 1960 about 70 per cent of the 4,645 patients certified from Kings County were seen by a judge. A judge sitting at Kings County Hospital sees an average of sixty patients, and often as many as eighty or a hundred, in a single morning.

At Jacobi Hospital four of the justices of the Supreme Court for Bronx County likewise make it their practice to see every patient possible before signing an order of certification. The other justices do not; they come to the hospital only if hearings are scheduled.[3] When hearings are not to be held, the commitment clerk delivers the papers to the Bronx County Court House for signature by the justice in chambers. Of the 96 patients certified to state hospitals from Jacobi in 1960, only 30 had hearings. (As mentioned in Chapter III, many patients from Jacobi are transferred to state hospitals under Section 73 as nonobjecting patients.)

At the psychiatric division of the City Hospital at Elmhurst the justices of the Supreme Court for Queens County also see all patients possible before signing orders for certification. Few patients are actually certified to state hospitals (38 in 1960) at Elmhurst, however, because that hospital follows the same policy as Jacobi in transferring nonobjecting patients to state hospitals on a single physician's certificate. Of those who do not go as volunteers, about 10 per cent object and have to be certified.

The physical setting in which hearings are held at Bellevue has been vividly described by Justice Bernard Botein, Presiding Justice of the Appellate Division, First Department:

> Bellevue Hospital sprawls over several square blocks in lower Manhattan. If a visitor were to stroll through the halls of the seventh floor, on the Thirtieth Street side of the hospital, he would come upon a small courtroom. It probably appears as incongruous in its setting as a hospital ward would seem in the County Courthouse.
>
> In this courtroom hearings are held upon petition of the superintendent of the hospital to commit allegedly mentally ill persons to state institutions. It is about one-half the size of the courtrooms in the County Courthouse. It has an elevated bench, a railed enclosure beneath the bench, which contains a few chairs and a table,

[3] If only one hearing is scheduled at Jacobi Hospital when one of these justices is sitting, and if the staff feels that the patient should be certified immediately, the patient is taken in an ambulance to the justice's chambers at the Bronx County Court House.

and a desk for the court stenographer. There is no jury box and no elevated witness stand. The proceedings are informal, but a complete record is made by an official court stenographer. Hearings are held every Tuesday and Friday throughout the year.[4]

Kings County Hospital, in contrast with Bellevue, has no special court facilities. Instead a large conference room is used, and the judge, a clerk, a nurse, and a psychiatrist all sit behind a long table facing the patient on the other side of the table.

At both Bellevue and Kings County the patients to be certified are brought, before the court convenes, to a small waiting room next to the courtroom. Each patient waits his turn for his case to be called, and at Bellevue (where there are fewer cases than at Kings County) the relatives may visit with the patients while they are waiting.

Our staff was concerned by one feature of the hearings which must be extremely disturbing to the patients and their relatives. When defendants in criminal cases are to be certified, they are brought to this waiting room handcuffed and in the custody of two or more armed, uniformed officers of the City Correction Department. There they too wait their turn, along with the other patients. In these circumstances the noncriminal patients and their relatives probably do not understand that these heavily guarded men are in confinement under a criminal court order; in all likelihood they assume that they are simply other patients like themselves. It seems unnecessary to introduce this atmosphere of a criminal court. The defendants could be

[4] Botein, Trial Judge 253 (copyright 1952 by Bernard Botein; used by permission of Simon and Schuster, Inc.). In 1944 the special commission appointed by Governor Dewey under the Moreland Act concluded that it was a mistake to have the hearing room set up as a courtroom, as is done at Bellevue Hospital; it recommended that the proceedings be informal and conducted with the atmosphere of a medical conference rather than with that of a court. Report of New York State Commission to Investigate the Management and Affairs of the Department of Mental Hygiene of the State of New York and the Institutions Operated by It, The Care of the Mentally Ill in the State of New York 95 (1944).

brought to the courtroom from the prison wards after the call of the regular calendar and after the other patients and their relatives have left.

Hearings vary greatly both in length and in depth. At Kings County the practice of seeing every patient, except those who are too violent or too ill, was begun when the hospital was small and a judge could see all patients with ease. Today, with the huge growth in the number of patients, this practice prevents careful attention to each individual unless the calendar happens to be short. On an average day when the judge must "hear" sixty patients in one morning, he cannot possibly give a hearing. What a patient actually receives in the few minutes allotted him, it has been well said, is a "seeing." At Bellevue, by contrast, because of the practice of holding hearings there only on the cases in which patients or relatives object to certification, the hearings are sometimes much more adequate. The average hearing there lasts from fifteen to thirty minutes; occasionally one lasts for two, three, or four hours.

The typical Bellevue hearing opens with the testimony of the psychiatrist, who may or may not be sworn as a witness, depending on which Supreme Court judge is presiding. The psychiatrist reads to the court the data contained in the hospital record, including statements of relatives and others, statements made by the patient to the doctor, the diagnosis, and sometimes the prognosis.

Most Bellevue psychiatrists say that this testimony by the doctor in the patient's presence is traumatic. The patient hears the doctor reveal to the court things which he may have told the doctor in confidence or things which he may now wish to deny or rebut. The doctor necessarily appears in the role of the patient's antagonist. The judge may question the doctor concerning symptoms, diagnosis, and the need for treatment. He always gives a full opportunity to the patient and his relatives to make statements in rebuttal of the doctor's presentation.

Except in rare cases, the statements of all participants are taken without regard to legal rules of evidence.

At Kings County Hospital the same staff psychiatrist sits next to the judge throughout the calendar. This psychiatrist identifies the hospital record and then, without more, states for the record that the patient has been examined and is in need of further hospitalization. Sometimes he gives the diagnosis, but rarely the facts on which the diagnosis and recommendation are based.

We heard criticism of the legality of the procedure in these hospitals on the ground that the law requires that one of the examining physicians be called and sworn; in some cases the staff psychiatrist who sits next to the judge is one of the examining physicians, but in many cases at Kings County Hospital the psychiatrist who appears has had nothing to do with the patient. Another criticism is that in many cases the patient is sent out of the room while the judge asks the relatives whether they have anything to say and is therefore not present while the doctor and his relatives discuss his case with the court. The efficacy of the judicial investigation is also criticized on the ground that, although the judges often try, in the short time available, to explore with patient and relatives alternative plans for care and treatment, this questioning is without benefit of any social worker or any social worker's report.

If the patient has counsel, counsel of course participates in the hearing and cross-examination. But such representation is extremely rare. If a patient asks for an attorney, the judge usually decides whether one is needed. Because no working system has ever been established for providing counsel, it is most unusual for counsel to be assigned, even when requested. At Jacobi Hospital, if the patient asks for a lawyer and cannot afford to engage one, it is the practice for the court to hear the case and then decide whether counsel is needed, expecting, if so, to adjourn and notify the Legal Aid Society. But such an adjournment has occurred at Jacobi only once—in 1959. The Legal Aid Society has offered to provide representation for patients and has notified the judges in the First Judicial District that a panel of lawyers is available, but the Society has been called on only occasionally.

Only on rare occasions also does a private psychiatrist testify in opposition to certification. If a private psychiatrist is willing to undertake care and treatment of the patient on an out-patient basis, the receiving hospital will almost always release the patient to him. Although a panel of private psychiatrists has been made available in New York County to make supplementary examinations at the court's request, their advice has been sought by the court in very few cases.

Sometimes a judge, after hearing all the parties, will say from the bench that he is sending the patient to a state hospital for observation for sixty days. He hopes by such a mode of expression to make the court's decision less painful for the patient. A judge may say, for instance, "The hospital will keep you only about three weeks," or "I'm sending you to Blank State Hospital for only sixty days," or "They will keep you there for sixty days; if you don't improve at the end of sixty days, you will be transferred to another hospital." Sometimes, however, a judge will deliver his determination in the language of criminal law, saying "I'm afraid I'll have to send you away," or "The place you are going to is just up the river."

Some judges, as already noted, send the patient out of the courtroom and explain the decision to the relatives, reassuring them that hospital care is really necessary. In some cases the judges purport, disingenuously, to take the matter under advisement, saying to the patient that they will think the case over. Then when the patient has been certified, the medical staff is left to explain to the patient what has happened. One reason, among others, why a judge may do this is that occasionally a patient becomes violent on hearing the decision. Recently an extreme case of this occurred; a patient on hearing the judge's decision fractured the skull of a psychiatrist.

Judges seldom deny the application for certification. At Bellevue in 1960, 79 petitions out of 5,097, or about 1.5 per cent, were denied. (The 79 petitions denied constituted nearly 10 per cent of the 834 contested cases.) At Kings County in 1960, 159 petitions out of 4,842, or about 3 per cent, were denied.[5] At Jacobi in 1960, 10 petitions out of 106, or a little more than 10 per cent, were denied. One judge denied 8 of these 10; 5 of the 8 patients thus released were readmitted to Jacobi within two months and certified by another judge.[6] At Elmhurst in 1960, 8 petitions out of 46, or about 17 per cent, were denied.[7]

These judicial denials, overriding the psychiatrists' recommendations in even a small proportion of the cases, are of crucial importance to our study. If the judges are right in these cases and the doctors are wrong, then the intervention of the court is an important protection for individual freedom. If, however, the judges are wrong and the doctors are right, then the court's intervention injures both the patient and society.

To this crucial question we can offer no satisfying answer. The few facts which we have been able to glean can be interpreted to support each reader's predilection, either for medi-

[5] Exact figures are not available on the number of contested cases at Kings County Hospital, although, as noted in the text, a judge sees about 70 per cent of the patients to be certified. It is interesting to note that in Kings County Hospital two of the sixteen judges together denied 105 of the 159 petitions which were denied in 1960, and three of the sixteen judges denied 125 of the 159.

[6] Doctors told our staff that some judges in New York City are known as "committers" and some as "releasers" and that adjournment is sometimes requested to avoid a particular judge with a particular penchant.

[7] Denial of a petition for certification at Elmhurst does not mean discharge from Elmhurst unless the court expressly orders it. If the patient consents to stay, Elmhurst Hospital continues treatment. One patient remained at Elmhurst for six months after denial of a petition for certification.

cal admission or for judicial admission. This subject deserves intensive research which the limitations of our own work did not permit. The following at least suggests what might be undertaken.

Information furnished us by the Department of Mental Hygiene shows that approximately one-third of the patients discharged by judges in 1957 from Bellevue and from Kings County Hospital were subsequently admitted to state hospitals or licensed private institutions. A substantial number of the patients whom the judges considered able to function in the community appear from this sketchy information to have been able to do so. But what happened to them and how well or badly they functioned are not yet known. The story of the two-thirds discharged from Bellevue and from Kings County Hospital who were not readmitted remains to be written.

Outside New York City

The problem that plagues New York City—the funneling of all patients to be certified through a city receiving hospital—does not exist in the other areas which have receiving hospitals. In these areas, where the county courts handle certifications, there are numerous direct admissions to state hospitals without any prior admission into a receiving hospital.

In those cases outside New York City where patients do enter state hospitals from receiving hospitals, notice is rarely served on them. (One receiving hospital is an exception in that it always serves such notice.) The administrators prefer, in general, to explain to the patient, orally and gently, his need for further hospitalization rather than to serve a formal notice containing the words "mentally ill" and announcing a court proceeding. They believe that the patient should feel that he is going to a state hospital on "doctor's orders" rather than on "judge's orders," as one administrator put it. In the case of litigious paranoid patients, however, the notice may be served on the patient as a protection to the hospital.

The hospitals which have this strong policy against serving notice on the patient are meticulous in serving notices on relatives. In one county a deputy sheriff, not in uniform, serves them. In another county notice to all relatives who might conceivably be concerned has become such a preoccupation that admission is often delayed while all those in outlying areas are being served. In one receiving hospital, however, notice is not served on relatives who have signed a form consenting to the patient's going to a state hospital.

In the receiving hospitals outside New York City, hearings with the patient present are rarely held. Occasionally when a relative objects to having the patient sent to a state hospital, the judge will meet with the relatives to discuss it. The hospital psychiatrist is usually present, and sometimes a social worker from the hospital. One receiving hospital with more than a thousand transfers to state hospitals a year told us that hearings with the patient present almost never occur, and that hearings with relatives present take place in about two dozen cases a year, or less than 2.5 per cent of the number of cases heard.

The usual procedure in receiving hospitals upstate is for all the papers to be sent to the judge of the county court for signature. The judge's signature has come to be mainly a form, with little real meaning, since he generally signs the order on the basis of the certificate of the examining physicians without seeking an opportunity to examine the case on its merits. One psychiatrist in a receiving hospital remarked that although the judge's signature may make the persons involved feel more comfortable it is nevertheless true that somebody must be protesting before the role of the judge can be really meaningful.

Thus far we have discussed court-ordered transfer to state hospitals or private institutions of patients initially admitted to receiving hospitals under Section 81(2). We turn, now, to examine the process by which patients initially admitted to state hospitals or licensed private institutions may be detained there for long-term treatment.

RETENTION OF PATIENTS INITIALLY ADMITTED TO A STATE HOSPITAL OR PRIVATE INSTITUTION

Initial admission to state hospitals or licensed private institutions by two physicians and a court order may be accomplished under Section 74. As we have seen in considering the operation of this section in the receiving hospitals, it embodies and expresses the concept that every order of certification should be tentative at first, for observation and treatment for sixty days. During this time many patients can be treated and discharged without becoming subject to any final order of certification. The Court of Appeals in the *Coates* case has described the effect of this initial order as one of "tentative finality." [8]

If a patient first admitted to a state hospital or licensed private institution under Section 74 is deemed to need care beyond sixty days, the proper official of the hospital (the director or the physician in charge, or the medical officer designated by either of them) may, as we have seen, simply file a certificate to that effect in the office of the county clerk. This he may do at any time within the sixty-day period. On this filing the judge's tentative order of certification "shall become a final order," indeterminate, so that the patient may be detained until discharge (Section 74(7)).[9]

[8] 9 N.Y. 2d 242, at 254, 173 N.E. 2d 797, at 804, *supra* note 25, Chapter IV.

[9] It is interesting to note that the procedure of Section 74(7) for making the court order final by the filing of the director's certificate applies equally to an order made after a demand for a hearing (Section 74(5)) and to an order where there has been no such demand (Section 74(4)). Yet Section 74(4) permits the order, whenever the patient *may*

In practice this certificate is often filed routinely, probably by an assistant director of the hospital; and this is usually done without any notice to the patient or his relatives.[10] In one hospital, at least, preparation of the certificate is started soon after the patient is admitted, and it is filed at once so as to be on the safe side. Thus a final and definitive certification occurs which might never have been necessary if the full time available had been allowed to elapse before a decision. Failure by any hospital to file the certificate within the sixty-day period makes the state liable for false imprisonment for any detention, even of a single day, thereafter; and a writ of habeas corpus will be granted.[11]

---

require care and treatment, for admission for observation and treatment "for a period not exceeding sixty days," whereas Section 74(5) requires a judicial finding that the patient *is* in need of observation and treatment and imposes no explicit limitation, in this particular subsection itself, upon the period of the admission. The reason for this seeming anomaly is doubtless historical: Section 74 before its revision in 1944 provided both for tentative admissions and for final commitments. In that year all certifications were made, in intendment at least, tentative for up to sixty days.

[10] This was confirmed by Miss Curtis' study of individual cases in three upstate hospitals. (See note 5 to Chapter III.) Miss Curtis found a general tendency in the hospitals to withhold from patients information about the consequences of particular admission methods and about changes in legal status. This may be because of unwillingness to face an unpleasant issue or because such a policy is thought to be in the best interests of the patient's health.

[11] See People *ex. rel.* Granskofski v. Whitehead, 10 App. Div. 2d 801, 198 N.Y.S. 2d 204 (4th Dept. 1960), aff'd 8 N.Y. 2d 962, 168 N.E. 2d 854 (1960). See also Matter of Coates, *supra* note 8 and discussed fully *infra* note 18. Because of concern about liability on the part of the state if a hospital fails to file the certificate within the sixty-day period but detains the patient longer, a bill, S. Int. 741, Pr. 741; A. Int. 986, Pr. 986, was introduced in the 1961 legislature to make the judge's order final from the beginning, rather than interlocutory. The bill would have preserved, however, the medical review of each case, which the present law, by making mandatory the filing of the certificate if the patient needs further care, intended to require as a preliminary to any indeterminate

Moreover, the direction in the order to observe and treat "for a period not exceeding sixty days" tends to become "sixty days," and patients who may not need to stay in the hospital for all that time may nevertheless be kept routinely. For such reasons one hospital director suggested that the initial period of detention should be flexible.

This procedure will be evaluated after the provisions for review, under Section 76, of a judge's final order have been described. It suffices to say here that the procedure for making the order final simply by the filing of the hospital's certificate has been criticized as never giving the patient an opportunity to contest his detention.

---

commitment. The Department's position, as set forth in its memorandum in support of that bill, was as follows:

"The Department believes that the judge's order of certification should be final when made rather than interlocutory. No useful purpose has been accomplished during the past 15 or 16 years since orders of certification were made interlocutory in the first instance by operation of law with a condition attached that they would become final upon the filing by the director or physician in charge of the institution prior to the expiration of sixty days from the date of the order of his certificate to the effect that the patient was in need of continued care and treatment beyond the first sixty days. On the contrary, some problems have arisen by reason of the fact that inadvertently, the director's certificate has not been filed on or before the sixtieth day which has resulted in the order of certification terminating by operation of law and thereafter the patient has been held contrary to the law until such time as a new admission was had upon proper papers. It is proposed to retain the provision that the director file the so-called sixty day certificate to carry out what was believed to be the original intent of this provision, namely, that it will assure that the patient will not be forgotten in a large institution and his case will be objectively reviewed on or before the sixtieth day and a conscious determination made by the director as to whether further hospitalization of the patient is needed. However, the validity of the continued further hospitalization of the patient after the sixtieth day will no longer be determined by the fact that the certificate has been filed on or before the sixtieth day."

The bill did not come out of committee before the 1961 legislature adjourned.

RETENTION OF PATIENTS ADMITTED BY EMERGENCY METHODS

Health-Officer Admissions

If hospital care is needed for longer than the sixty-day period authorized under Section 72 and if the patient does not agree to remain voluntarily,[12] the statute specifies that the health officer (or other person authorized to effect admission under Section 72), on the hospital director's recommending continued hospital treatment in writing, shall secure the requisite petition and cause the patient to be examined by physicians. If the patient is found to be mentally ill, he then is to be "admitted" under Section 73 if he does not object, or under Section 74 if he does. If he is found not mentally ill, the patient is, of course, to be discharged.

These statutory commands for extending a health-officer admission are ignored more often than they are obeyed. Forty-two health officers in replying to a questionnaire said that an extension is seldom or never obtained by the health officer's procuring the petition and arranging for two medical examinations, as the statute requires, whereas only twenty-two said that the statutory procedure is always, often, or sometimes followed. Under this procedure, when it is followed, the hospital director notifies the health officer of the patient's need, and the health officer comes to the hospital with another examining physician to make the examination. In three counties—Herkimer, Steuben, and Tompkins—the petition is often secured at the time of the health officer's initial examination of the patient or at the

[12] Experiences differ with respect to conversion of health-officer admissions into voluntary admissions. In one hospital, our staff was told, half the health-officer admissions become voluntary patients; in another, we were told, it is rare for a patient admitted by a health officer to become a voluntary patient because he usually lacks the necessary insight into his own needs.

time of the admission to the hospital, so that certification under Section 74 can be initiated simultaneously with or shortly after the health-officer admission. (It will be recalled that the statute contains no legal requirement that a petition be fresh.)

In most places the hospital finds it more convenient to arrange for examination of the patient by two examining physicians from outside the hospital and to obtain the petition from a relative at some time when he visits the patient. When the hospital thus arranges for the extension, the health officer has no responsibility after the patient's initial admission except, perhaps, to see that the fees of the examining physicians are paid if the patient cannot pay. An overwhelming majority of the health officers who responded to the committee's questionnaire favored giving this responsibility to the hospital in law as well as in fact.[13] One respondent was concerned that it might be too heavy a burden for the hospital to arrange the extensions, but even he felt that the health officer should have no responsibility after the original admission. That most hospitals do in practice arrange for the extensions without help from the health officer indicates, perhaps, that the task is not too burdensome. Only one hospital director expressed a strong opinion in favor of keeping the responsibility for the extension on the health officer.

Patients are not usually served with a notice when their health-officer admission is to be extended by a court order, nor are they informed that they are to be certified. Relatives, on the other hand, are usually notified. Our study of individual patients in three upstate hospitals revealed that the first inkling many patients receive of an extension of their hospitalization results from the arrival of two examining physicians. Many

[13] Sixty-five respondent health officers said that the state mental hospital should be responsible for extension of a health-officer admission; 8 said the health officer should be; 3 said the state hospital and the health officer should be; and 1 said the person initiating the original hospitalization should be.

patients fail, in fact, to understand the significance of this examination; they receive no explanation of it. The doctors usually certify that notice to the patient would be ineffective or detrimental, and the judge does not then require a notice. He has, in fact, no power under the statute to do so.

Hearings before a judge with the patient present, as provided by Section 74, are almost never held in certification proceedings following upon a health-officer admission; [14] a majority of the health officers and their designees responding to the committee's questionnaire thought that a hearing with the patient present should, in general, not be held.[15] Their reasons for opposing such a hearing are that it is detrimental to the patient in most cases, that the patient would not understand the procedure, and that decision about the need for further hospital care is a medical matter. A few comments specified that a hearing with the patient present should be held in special cases only, or when the patient demands it. Thus these health officers favored the present practice of extending a health-officer admission without a hearing.

When the judge has signed an order certifying a patient originally admitted on a health-officer admission, the patient is then in the position of one admitted initially under Section 74: he may be detained for sixty days for observation and treat-

[14] Sixty-two respondent health officers said that a hearing with the patient present before certification is held seldom or never; only 1 respondent said that such a hearing is held sometimes. Similarly, hearings with relatives or friends present, but with the patient absent, are rarely held. Fifty-eight respondents said that this kind of hearing is never or seldom held; only 2 respondents said that it is sometimes held. The only situation in which a hearing is held with relatives alone present, one respondent commented, is when a welfare commissioner has signed a petition and relatives are served with notice. The 63 respondents all agreed that the patient is seldom or never represented by an attorney in these proceedings.

[15] Fifty-three respondent health officers were opposed to a hearing with the patient present before certification; 11 favored it; and 3 had no opinion.

ment, and the order becomes final and the detention indeterminate on the filing of the director's certificate before the end of that sixty-day period. Thus, as already noted, a patient originally admitted by a health officer, may be detained for 120 days before his order of certification can become final.

Incomplete Court Order

The judge's signature on one set of the papers containing the petition and the medical certificates within ten days after the patient's admission under Section 75 completes the court order. Section 75 seems to disregard the fact that the medical certificates here could be as much as twenty days old. (The apparent inconsistency of this with Section 70(4) is noted below in the discussion of retention under Section 73, which involves a similar difficulty but one even more serious.) By the completion of the order the patient is put in the same position as a patient originally admitted under Section 74: he may be detained for sixty days for observation and treatment, and the order will become final and the detention indeterminate upon the filing of the director's certificate before the end of that period. Thus a patient originally admitted on an incomplete court order may be detained for seventy days before an order of certification becomes final.

As in the case of an initial admission by two physicians and a court order, under Section 74, so here, on the court's completion of an incomplete court order, notice to the patient is usually dispensed with, and a hearing, either with or without the presence of the patient, is rarely held. The judge's signature is thus a pure form, for the judge relies on the medical certificate and the hospital's confirmation of the need for hospitalization.

If this procedure is questionable for patients not yet in a hospital, *a fortiori* it is questionable where the patient is already hospitalized. There seems to be little or no justification here for dispensing with notice. Without the notice and the opportunity for a hearing which it tends to afford, the judge's signature can add little or no protection for the patient. And injury from the notice is much less likely to a patient who is already in a hospital than to one who is not. When the patient is there already, the notice cannot induce flight, nor does it carry any threat of confinement but, if anything, some hope of freedom.

RETENTION OF PATIENTS ADMITTED BY TWO PHYSICIANS WITHOUT COURT ORDER

Under Section 73-a a patient admitted on a petition and the certificate of two doctors (at least one a psychiatrist) must be given notice of his rights within three days after admission. This notice to the patient may be dispensed with if it would be ineffective or detrimental to him, but notice must in all cases be given to his relatives. And at any time before certification the patient or someone on his behalf may serve written notice of his intention to leave. If the hospital decides that the patient needs further care, then within five days from receipt of the notice (or ten days from the admission, if that is a later day) the hospital director or physician in charge must apply for court certification under Section 74. The application is made on the certificate of the director that the patient needs further care and on the original petition and medical certificates. The provisions of Section 74 apply except that the medical certificates could be as much as seventy days old instead of ten. (The apparent inconsistency of this with Section 70(4) is noted below in the discussion of retention under Section 73, which involves a similar but even more serious difficulty.)

If no such notice is served, the patient may, within the first sixty days of his hospital stay, sign an application for voluntary admission under Section 71 or he may be admitted as a nonobjecting patient under Section 73. If neither is done within that time and if the hospital decides that care and treatment beyond the sixty days are needed, the hospital must, within that time, apply as above for court certification.

Experience with admissions under this section is too limited to generalize about the notice and hearing. Conversion of this form of admission into a judicial admission requires the execution of a court order, much as Section 75 requires the completion of one. In addition, the statute explicitly requires three medical certificates before that court order. When the order is made, the patient may be detained for an additional sixty days—or 120 days in all—before the order can become final in the usual manner upon the filing of the director's certificate.

RETENTION OF NONOBJECTING PATIENTS

All the forms of admission for limited periods discussed thus far must be converted into judicial admissions to retain the patient beyond the initial detention period. This is not true of admission under Section 73 for nonobjecting patients. This need never be converted into a judicial admission unless there is notice that the patient objects. Section 73 permits the detention of a nonobjecting patient, admitted on a petition and the certificate of a single physician, for not more than sixty days. Thereafter he may be detained until fifteen days after written notice from the patient, or from someone on his behalf, of his intention or desire to leave the hospital. If, on receipt of such a notice, the hospital believes that further detention is needed, its director certifies that fact to a judge of a court of record (after notice of this application has either been given or dispensed with as provided in Section 74(3)). The judge in his discretion may then issue an order certifying the patient, pursuant to Section 74.

This procedure, which is rarely used, is inconsistent with another provision in the present law. Section 70(4) requires that a medical certificate be dated within ten days before the "admission." The physician's certificate, which was the basis for the original nonobjecting admission, may also be used for the certification of such a patient who has given notice of his intention to leave. When it is used in this way, it is more than ten days old and describes the patient's condition before his initial admission. We have noted that Section 75 similarly permits certification on medical certificates up to twenty days old, and Section 73-a permits it on certificates as much as seventy days old. For patients originally nonobjecting, there is, for one of the two required certificates, actually no limit at all. The certificate for the nonobjecting admission would never be dated within ten days prior to the certification, and it might be older by months or even years. If Section 70(4) could be read to mean ten days before the original admission, use of an old certificate would not technically violate that; but if the purpose of Section 70(4) is, as one presumes, to ensure that certification will be based on the patient's condition at the time of the decision, then Section 70(4) is contradicted by all these other provisions.

Moreover, instead of an examination by a second "examining physician" (normally required by Section 74(1)), the director of the hospital certifies the need for further confinement of a nonobjecting patient. The director or a member of his staff has, of course, examined the patient in order to make this determination. But if this examination takes the place of a second medical certificate, then the procedure is inconsistent with Section 70(3), discussed in Section 1 of Chapter IV, which prohibits doctors from serving as examining physicians in admissions to their own hospitals.

If no notice of desire to leave is ever received, the patient may be kept, without any further proceedings, until he is ready for discharge or until he dies.

In considering these matters realistically, it must be borne in mind that the discharge of many an aged patient has to be deferred until appropriate arrangements can be made for his care outside the hospital. Patients whose medical condition warrants discharge often cannot be released because they have no suitable place to go. Entrance into a mental hospital and release from a mental hospital are not simple medical problems; they are mixed questions of medicine and sociology, of health and welfare.

REVIEW OF ORDER OF HOSPITALIZATION

Section 76 gives the right to a patient, or to any relative or friend on his behalf, dissatisfied with a final order of certification to petition, within thirty days, a justice of the supreme court other than the justice who made the order to rehear and review the certification. A jury will be summoned and the case will be conducted in the same manner as a determination of incompetency by a judge and jury.[16]

This provision in the law is rarely used.[17] Hospital directors could recall few instances in which such a review had been sought; all the forty-two judges who answered a question on the frequency of its use said that it is used seldom or never.

Despite this the Court of Appeals has held that Section 76

[16] If the verdict of the jury is that the person is sane, the justice is required to discharge him. If the verdict is that the person is mentally ill, the justice is required to certify to that fact and to make an order of recertification. This same procedure of rehearing and review under Section 76 is available also to any person aggrieved by the decision of a judge or justice refusing to certify a mentally ill person proved dangerous to himself or others. There are provisions concerning appeals and the like. See full text of Section 76.

[17] Our staff's inquiries, in fact, found nobody familiar with any actual case under Section 76—nothing but some quite vague recollections. McKinney's annotations show some litigation under it, notably the use of Section 76 to obtain discharge of the patient who was involved in Warner v. State, 297 N.Y. 395, 79 N.E. 2d 459 (1948); and, more recently, the *Coates* case discussed below.

saves the constitutionality of Section 74. In the recent *Coates* case,[18] the issue of due process in a compulsory hospitalization under Section 74 was before the court. The court held that the confinement, beyond the temporary sixty-day period and on the

[18] Matter of Coates, 9 N.Y. 2d 242, 173 N.E. 2d 797 (1961). Doris Coates was admitted to Rochester State Hospital "for observation and treatment for a period not exceeding 60 days" on an order by the County Court of Monroe County, dated April 17, 1957, pursuant to Section 74(4) of the Mental Hygiene Law. Personal service of the application for this order had been dispensed with pursuant to Section 74(3) by reason of the following statement in the certificate of the examining physicians: "Personal service of notice would be aggravating and detrimental to patient in her present mental state." There had been no demand for any hearing as allowed by Section 74(5). The order provided that it should become final on the hospital's filing a certificate stating the need for further care in the office of the county clerk, as provided in Section 74(7). Two weeks after the admission, on May 2, 1957, such a statement was filed. No notice of this was given to the patient. Eleven days later, on May 13, 1957, the patient was released by the hospital to the care and custody of her mother, with a requirement that she report to the hospital once a month.

Two months after the admission, on June 17, 1957, the patient petitioned, pursuant to Section 76, for a jury trial of the issue of her mental illness. This petition was denied as untimely by order of September 11, 1957, because it had not been made within thirty days after May 2, 1957, when the certificate of need for further care had been filed.

On February 3, 1958, the patient filed a notice of a motion to vacate the original order of certification of April 17, 1957, on the ground that the statute was unconstitutional. This was denied by order of March 28, 1958, and the original certification and related proceedings were thereby ratified. Matter of Coates, 14 Misc. 2d 89, 181 N.Y.S. 2d 599 (Sup. Ct. Monroe Co., Brasser, J., 1958). From this order the patient sought to appeal directly to the Court of Appeals on the constitutional question. The Court of Appeals dismissed this appeal, without costs, on the ground that no direct appeal of a constitutional question lies if its resolution involves a question of statutory construction. Matter of Coates, 5 N.Y. 2d 917, 918, 156 N.E. 2d 722 (1959).

The appeal thus reverted to the Appellate Division, Fourth Department, where it was heard together with an appeal from the earlier order of September 11, 1957, that had denied review under Section 76. That court reversed the order denying a jury trial under Section 76 but affirmed the order denying the motion to vacate the original order of

simple filing of the hospital's certificate without notice of that event to the patient, is constitutional because the patient has a right to a prompt and complete review *ab initio* under Section 76. The thirty-day period within which such a review must be sought does not begin to run until an actual notice of the filing is given to the patient. This reading of the two sections makes Section 74 constitutional.

The Court of Appeals also said in the *Coates* case that a patient who has not been served with notice of the filing of the certificate does not automatically lose his right to seek review ninety days after the initial order under Section 74, as the Appellate Division had indicated. The patient has the right, instead, to challenge the Section 74 order under Section 76 until thirty days after he has received a notice of the filing of the certificate. If he has never received it, his right to challenge continues forever.

This means that many thousands of patients, hospitalized

---

certification. Matter of Coates, 8 App. Div. 2d 444, 451, 188 N.Y.S. 2d 400, 407 (4th Dept. 1959). It said that Section 74 should be construed in such a way as to permit notice of the filing with the county clerk of a certificate of need for further care (making an order of certification final) to be served on the patient at any time within thirty days after the end of the sixty-day tentative period, when no notice of the filing of this certificate had previously been given to the patient. But that court thought that the Department of Mental Hygiene could set the thirty-day period of Section 76 running by serving a notice of the filing during the sixty-day period; in that case the period for a petition under Section 76 would expire thirty days after such service.

From this decision a further appeal was taken to the Court of Appeals. The only issue raised in that court was the validity of the original order of certification. In affirming the order denying the motion to vacate, the court held, in brief, that Section 74 is constitutional because, and only because, of the availability of review under Section 76. It disagreed with the Appellate Division, however, on the issue of the construction of Section 76 and laid down the rule that a petition under Section 76 was never foreclosed unless and until a notice had been served personally on a patient and more than thirty days had passed thereafter.

under Section 74 and never served with a notice of the filing of the director's certificate, now have a continuing right to seek review under Section 76 even though they may have been in the hospital for many years. The Department of Mental Hygiene does not plan to give notice of the prior filing to this large group of patients and is content, according to the Department's counsel, to permit the Section 76 remedy to remain open to all certified patients at all times, just as the remedy of habeas corpus is always open to them. Although the Department's position removes any time limitation on the right of patients to avail themselves of this remedy, in practice patients are not benefited if they do not know about it.

DISCHARGE

The import of an involuntary admission for an indeterminate period cannot be accurately assessed without considering the right to discharge and the actual practices with respect to it. The hospital's power to discharge, effectively and conscientiously exercised, is a primary safeguard against wrongful hospitalization. All judges questioned regarding periodic medical review as a safeguard of patients' rights ranked it as important. The seriousness of the wrong done to a person improperly kept in a hospital depends to a large extent upon the possibility or probability that the detention might continue indefinitely, without reconsideration of whether the patient ever needed hospitalization or of whether he continues to need it.

The most common method of discharge by far is a medical discharge by the hospital. Section 87 authorizes the director of the hospital, by certificate filed with the Department, to discharge a patient (not held upon an order of a criminal court) who, in his judgment, is recovered; or a patient who, in his opinion, is not mentally ill; or a patient who is not recovered but whose discharge will not be detrimental to the public welfare if the director is satisfied that friends or relatives of the patient are willing and financially able to care for the patient after discharge.[19]

The policy of discharging patients, wherever possible, to convalescent care, with treatment continued in after-care clinics where drugs are supplied without cost, has permitted the discharge of many patients who would formerly have stayed in the hospital for a long time. Patients admitted on court order are almost always discharged to convalescent care rather than discharged absolutely. This is done so that if a patient should break down during his convalescent care he may be rehospitalized without the necessity of a new proceeding. One hospital director commented that absolute discharges are used only for those patients who are completely recovered or who are in civil service or other employment in which discharge to convalescent care could embarrass them and impede their rehabilitation.

Decisions by the doctors to discharge patients are affected not only by the increased number of cases of discharge to convalescent care but also by the philosophy, now growing among modern psychiatrists and hospital directors, that their job is to treat mental illness—not to act as jailers and not to guarantee the ability of every released patient to live in the community with complete safety to himself and others. One indication of

[19] See page 185, *infra,* for amendment of Section 87 in 1961. General Order 42 of the Regulations of the Department of Mental Hygiene requires the establishment in each institution of a special release committee of three experienced psychiatrists to review problem cases being considered for release (patients who are, or who are likely to become, dangerous to themselves or others; patients with a significant record of arrests or convictions or both; patients with a significant history of sex offenses or of fire setting; or patients who have hallucinations). The committee presents its written recommendations on release to the director, who makes the final determination. In private institutions the procedures are required to conform as closely as practicable to these requirements. Special release officers, experienced psychiatrists, function in each hospital; and inspectors from the Department of Mental Hygiene provide an additional check on releases.

the safety of liberal release policies is the extraordinarily low incidence of crime among released mental patients. In 1954 the New York State Mental Hygiene Council reported, on the basis of a study of 10,247 male patients released from state mental hospitals in 1947 and followed for 5.6 years, that the annual arrest rate for released mental patients was four times less than that for the general population.[20] Experience with the open hospital and the effects of drug therapy have combined with more tolerant public attitudes toward mental illness to induce more liberal policies on the release of patients.

The actual effectiveness of this more liberal policy is impeded, however, by the shortage of psychiatrists. In New York State civil hospitals, there is one doctor for every 116 patients.[21] With such a ratio as this, it is understandable that discharges must often be delayed and that patients whose conditions warrant discharge may often be overlooked. Nevertheless, the New York State Mental Hygiene Council found after its study in 1954 that, "in general, . . . the over-all plan of releasing patients is fundamentally sound and conscientiously administered." [22]

Practices in the review of cases differ in the various hospitals. The director of one reported that in one half of his hospital the staff is in such close contact with the patients that no formal system of review is needed; in the other half every chronic patient is reviewed for possible discharge twice every year. In another hospital the director is planning to institute a system of periodic review whereby the staff would review each case

[20] New York State Mental Hygiene Council, Report on the Study of Release Procedures for Mental Patients in New York State 11 (unpublished MS, Dec. 7, 1954, lent to the committee by the Department of Mental Hygiene).

[21] National Committee against Mental Illness, Inc., What Are the Facts about Mental Illnesses in New York State 25 (1960).

[22] Report, *supra* note 20, at 8–9.

once every six months and would be required to defend continued hospitalization in each case.

One possible method of insuring periodic medical review is to require a periodic renewal of the authority to detain each patient. Under the British Mental Health Act, a patient compulsorily admitted for treatment may be detained for not more than one year. The authority for detention may be renewed for another year by the responsible medical officer of the hospital after an examination of the patient; thereafter, it may be renewed for periods of two years each in the same manner.[23] Similar suggestions have been made for New York State.

A serious obstacle to the release of many patients who are medically ready for discharge is the lack of a suitable place for them to go. Some families are unwilling or unable to take patients back. Since 1961 the unwillingness of relatives to receive and care for a harmlessly ill patient is no longer a legal obstacle to release (N.Y. Sess. Laws 1961, ch. 429, §3, eff. Sept. 1, 1961). For practical and humanitarian reasons this same factor often controls the patients in the other two categories of Section 87: patients recovered and patients not mentally ill.

Our study of individual cases in three upstate hospitals showed that more patients would be released if there were adequate homes or environments to which they could return. Patients may be discharged to local Welfare Departments, and these Departments give aid to patients once they are discharged. But a great need exists for increased aid from social services to provide homes for patients who are still in the hospital but who are medically ready for discharge.

In theory, a medical discharge is not the only method of release short of Section 76 or habeas corpus. The Commissioner of Mental Hygiene has legal power under Section 87(1)(e) to dis-

[23] British Mental Health Act, 7 & 8 Eliz. 2, ch. 72, § 43 (1959).

charge any patient who in his judgment is improperly detained. But no example of the use of this method has been found. In addition, a patient may apply to a court for discharge if the director of the hospital refuses to discharge him. A hearing must then be accorded to the director, and security must be furnished for the good behavior and the maintenance of the patient. The court thereupon may order the patient's discharge (Sec. 87(1)(d)). This procedure is used very infrequently.

Always available, in addition, is the right to petition for a writ of habeas corpus. Section 204 of the Mental Hygiene Law provides for it explicitly in mental cases, but it would exist in any event under fundamental law as codified by Article 77 of the Civil Practice Act. Hospital directors commented that they sometimes welcome the granting of a writ, such as, for example, one in favor of a patient who is in fairly good shape but may be dangerous when drinking. The hospital may be reluctant to court the legal hazards and the risk of criticism involved in releasing this patient. The judge who releases him is immune from suit and protects the hospital from all the risks of doing what it would itself like to do for the patient.

Several hospital directors commented on the financial obstacles to a patient's bringing a writ of habeas corpus, particularly the cost of retaining a psychiatrist, without whom he stands little chance against the doctors of the hospital. They also commented on the fact that few patients who petition for writs are able to be represented by an attorney.

EVALUATION

How well do courts perform the function of deciding whether an unwilling patient should be detained for an extended period of time in a mental hospital?

The Court of Appeals in the *Coates* case [24] recently examined

[24] Matter of Coates, *supra* note 18.

due process of law in judicial admissions. A hearing or an opportunity to be heard is essential. But the hearing may occur after admission or even after the issuance of a final order "so long as the patient has the right to a prompt and complete hearing or review of the determination *ab initio*." [25]

Actual notice of the right to a hearing is necessary before the order can be final in the sense that it precludes review under Section 76. Although Section 74(7) provides that on the filing of the director's certificate the tentative order of certification shall become final, the Court of Appeals said: "Inasmuch as the initial order is subject to the provisions of section 76, it cannot be final where review is invoked until after a determination by the court in the section 76 proceeding." [26] If actual notice is not given to the patient, the order never becomes final, in this sense, under the *Coates* holding. Nevertheless, the order, followed by the filing of the director's certificate, supplies sufficient authority to detain the patient beyond the sixty-day period.

Some flexibility is therefore permissible in the procedures leading to compulsory admission. With this in mind (but before the Court of Appeals had spoken) our staff asked judges and doctors how important they thought particular procedures to be for safeguarding the rights of patients, taking into account the patients' medical needs.

Hearings

Table 9 in the Appendix shows the percentages of judges and doctors who think hearings either with the patient present or with only the relatives present to be important in court-ordered admissions. Thirty-five per cent of the judges of upstate New York consider a hearing with the patient present to be important, although such hearings are rarely held there. An even

[25] *Id.* at 254, 173 N.E. 2d at 804.

[26] *Id.* at 254, 173 N.E. 2d at 804–05.

larger percentage of the upstate judges, 60 per cent, consider a hearing with only the relatives present to be an important safeguard. In New York City, where hearings are much more frequent, the percentages are much higher. Among the judges there, 94 per cent consider a hearing with the patient present to be important, and 79 per cent consider a hearing with relatives present to be important.

Seventy-three per cent of all doctors think a hearing with the patient present not important. As for a hearing with relatives alone, the doctors were almost evenly divided on its importance, 48 per cent considering it important and 52 per cent considering it unimportant.

One does not have to go as far as the doctor who called hearings "antiquated, inhumane, unwieldy, and complicated" to recognize that hearings are not desirable in all cases. When the doctors agree that the patient needs hospital care, when the family does not object, when the patient has been told of the plan for hospitalization and has raised no objection, and when there is no reason to suspect any overreaching, then the patient's interests may well be best served by a speedy admission without the delay and the formality of a hearing. It is wrong to make all patients go through a hearing that may be needed by only a fraction of them.

For a hearing to be meaningful, there must be an objection from some source. If this objection is to be made by the patient, clear, understandable, and full notice of the application must be given him. In no other way can the contested cases and the doubtful cases be isolated from the clear cases in which a hearing is not necessary. Yet the difficulty with this is, of course, that notice to a disturbed person that he will have to go into a mental hospital is deemed by many doctors to be detrimental. A balance of evils is involved.

In those doubtful cases where a hearing is needed, a real hearing—not a formality—is required. Although the judge is not trained in psychiatry, the judge has to evaluate technical medical testimony. He must often cope with difficulties of language with foreign-born patients, at times dealing with them through an interpreter. He must try to find out about possible alternative plans for the care of the patient, although no social service investigation may have been made. He must protect the patient's rights, although usually no attorney is there to help him do so.

Representation by Attorney

Table 10 in the Appendix shows the percentages of judges and doctors who think that representation by an attorney is important. The judges were almost evenly divided on the importance of representation, whereas a great majority of physicians considered representation by an attorney unimportant. Some judges qualified their statements on the importance of representation by adding "provided it would not be injurious to the patient." Others favored leaving the decision to the patient. Some judges pointed out that in certain kinds of cases close judicial scrutiny and perhaps representation by an attorney are advisable: in cases of hospitalization by the petition of a spouse when there is hostility between the two and in cases of hospitalization of aged patients whose families are eager to be rid of the burden of caring for them.

Upstate physicians were the only doctors who commented on representation by an attorney. Some pointed out that a lawyer can be helpful as he sees the examination of the patient develop, but others expressed the fear that a lawyer might conceive his role to be that of winning a case by preventing hospitalization. Concern was expressed by doctors (as well as by judges) that in many cases representation might be detrimental to the patient. Some said that a lawyer is not needed because the petitioner, two examining physicians, and the judge all have the patient's interests at heart. A typical reflection of these physicians' views was the comment by one of them that "representation should not be prevented, but it is not important." [27]

Seeking possible light on this problem, our staff investigated briefly the operation in the District of Columbia of a system in which the court appoints a guardian to represent the patient in each preliminary hearing before the Commission on Mental Health and in each final hearing before a court.[28] The guardian appointed is usually, but not necessarily, a lawyer. He is usually asked to take a batch of some half-dozen cases at one time. Little or no compensation is available for the guardian. Not

[27] Each questionnaire to judges asked what kind of representative the respondent would favor (lawyer, nonlegal representative, psychiatrist, or other physician) in various kinds of cases (contested cases, doubtful cases, all cases). A lawyer was the majority choice for contested cases. Doctors and lawyers received an almost equal number of votes for doubtful cases. Little support was expressed for a nonlegal representative in all cases.

The first questionnaire to judges also asked what method of appointment of representatives the judges would favor. The answers varied, but warrant the limited conclusion that most judges think lawyers ought, when possible, to be privately retained, but that they do not have a similar preference as to physicians. Their slight preference, in fact, was for doctors appointed by the court.

Concern was expressed lest a system of court-appointed lawyers might lead to heavy demands on the bar. One judge suggested that the county should pay the fee of the representative when the patient or his family cannot do so.

[28] In spite of the discretionary wording of the 1939 act, 21 D.C. Code, §§ 311–312 (1951), recent court decisions have held that an attorney or other guardian must be appointed in both kinds of hearing. Dooling v. Overholser, 100 U.S. App. D.C. 247, 243 F. 2d 825 (D.C. Cir. 1957). Lafferty v. District of Columbia, 107 U.S. App. D.C. 318, 277 F. 2d 348 (D.C. Cir. 1960), held that after a determination of insanity made by the Commission on Mental Health, the Commissioner must apply for a court hearing and serve the patient with a five-day notice of a hearing at which the patient may appear in person or by attorney, with a trial by jury if desired, to oppose a final order of commitment.

much time is allowed him for preparation, although he does interview each patient and submits a short report on each case to the Commission.

In practice, representation by guardians in Washington, D.C., seems to have become rather *pro forma*. At times the guardian has been prevented by the Commission from acting as a true attorney should, and he has been discouraged from cross-examining the doctors or examining the hospital records on which the medical opinions are based. Today the situation has probably improved in this respect. But in the judgment of a number of the lawyers in the District who are familiar with its system, the required representation in every case has become a routine formality which provides little or no added protection to a patient. It causes many jury trials and some delay and occupies an undue amount of the psychiatrists' time.[29]

Jury Trial

The judges were also questioned on the importance of jury trials in court-ordered admissions as a protection for the patient. All but one of these respondents said that such jury trials are unimportant. It was the safeguard which attracted the least support of any of those on which the judges were queried. The comments show that these judges think that jurors are not, in general, competent to decide the issue in this kind of case.[30] In certain special cases, however, some judges think that juries

[29] See, however, approval of the system in the District of Columbia expressed by Hugh S. McGee, Chairman, Mental Health Committee of the District of Columbia Bar Association in testimony before the Subcommittee on Constitutional Rights of the Senate Judiciary Committee, Hearings, *op. cit. supra* note 32 to Chapter III, at 55.

[30] See Weihofen and Overholser, Commitment of the Mentally Ill, 24 Texas L. Rev. 307, 345–46 (1946).

are important—where the patient or his relatives are contesting certification, where the patient appears rational, where an application is made for review of an order to hospitalize, and where the patient is a senile person.[31]

Procedures Used in Doubtful Cases

An effort was made to ascertain from the judges how often examination by a court-appointed psychiatrist and certain other procedures are used in doubtful cases. Table 11 (Appendix) shows the frequency with which these procedures are said to be used; it shows also that New York City judges tend to use all these procedures more frequently than do upstate judges.

In general, the judges made it clear that the most important evidence in deciding for or against a certification is that of the doctors. But a majority of the judges thought each kind of evidence listed was important. In order of importance after the medical evidence, they ranked statements of facts and circumstances in the petition, testimony of relatives and friends, testimony of the patient, report of a social service agency, the court's independent observation of the patient, and, lastly, the court's independent observation of the family.[32]

[31] None of the respondents mentioned the atmosphere of an adversary proceeding which a jury trial throws over what should be primarily a medical determination. See Curran, Hospitalization of the Mentally Ill, 31 N. Car. L. Rev. 274, 283 (1953).

[32] Limited importance only can be attached to these rankings. The method was to assign an arbitrary value to each answer, i.e., "very unimportant" was valued at 1; "fairly unimportant," at 2; "fairly important," at 3; and "very important," at 4. The results were then totaled for each kind of evidence. The higher the total score, the more important that kind of evidence was considered. The results provide a very rough comparison of the judges' opinions on the relative importance of various kinds of evidence, but the preferences stated are of course generalizations, not applicable to any individual case.

Judicial and Medical Roles

Finally, judges and doctors were asked what they thought the judicial and medical roles in admissions ought to be. Five formulations were offered ranging from a medical admission with a right to a hearing after admission to a purely judicial admission. Table 12 (Appendix) shows the preferences of the respondent judges and doctors for the various medical and legal roles. The medical admission was favored by the highest percentage of all the doctors, whereas the present system, item (d) on the table, was favored by the highest percentage of judges.

The reasons given by physicians for favoring a medical admission is that the problem is primarily medical and calls for a medical judgment. The patient's rights and legal interests can be adequately protected through procedures made available after the admission (rigorous proof of the need for detention, opportunity for a hearing, the right to habeas corpus, and the like) without delaying needed treatment. For example, two directors of community mental health services commented:

> I feel strongly that the determination of mental illness is a medical function. The patient's rights must be protected, of course, but it is my guess that few instances of commitment for nefarious purposes have occurred. It is my feeling that state hospital administrators demand the "protection" of the judge (against suit by the patient or his family) which leads to a continuation of the practice of making it difficult to get patients into hospital without tedious formalities which perpetuate and exaggerate fear of hospitalization in patients and families.

And:

> As long as this remains both a legal and a medical problem, with different points of view, patients must be easily admitted to treatment for medical reasons and through medical personnel. The legal

profession must assume responsibility for review, maintaining the rights of the individual and correcting any deprivation of liberty not warranted under the law.

The reason given by judges for wanting authority for the court is that hospitalization deprives a patient of his freedom and that a court provides the best protection of the rights of the patient. This preference of the judges is particularly interesting in view of the fact that in civil certifications by courts the most important decisions are really made by the doctors. By their certification that notice to the patient would be detrimental, the doctors decide what procedural rights he shall have—often deciding in fact, though not in form, that he is to have no hearing. By their expert testimony they control the decision on his hospitalization. Although the judges recognize these facts, they are loath to give the physicians a responsibility commensurate with the power which they do in fact exercise when such a delegation would cut down the discretionary powers of the court.

A few judges, however, agreed with the doctors that if proper safeguards could be provided the initial admission should be medical. A cogent expression of this view came from Justice Miles F. McDonald of the Supreme Court, Kings County:

> I submit the following: I have been fairly familiar with these procedures for a period of over twenty years as a practicing lawyer, assistant district attorney, district attorney and Supreme Court judge; and while I have definite views, I am not a crusader with respect thereto, although I firmly believe that much of the present procedure is unnecessary and could be avoided, and at the same time, I am convinced that certain safeguards should be maintained for the benefit of an alleged mentally ill person. In all my experience I have never seen any case where the physicians wilfully attempted to secure the adjudication for an ulterior purpose or were venal in any respect. I believe that in rare cases there have been errors; but that the errors are made not only in good faith but in an honest attempt to secure care for a person who would otherwise

be denied it if he were not declared mentally ill. I am of the opinion that in the first instance commitment could be made upon the certificate of a physician attached to a state mental institution without a hearing, provided that the person to be committed were notified that such commitment was to be made and that he was afforded a reasonable opportunity to object thereto. In connection with the phrase "reasonable opportunity" I mean that realistically, —that there should be some person or persons whose responsibility it should be to ascertain whether or not the alleged mentally ill person desired to oppose the commitment. From my experience it is rare that the patient has any objection. However, when there is an objection there should be a full scale hearing and all proceedings should be stayed until the hearing has been held. If the alleged mentally ill person is indigent he should have the right to have counsel assigned to him and should be afforded the opportunity of an examination by physicians not associated with the hospital where the proceedings were initiated. He should have the power to subpoena relatives and friends and other witnesses. This is particularly important where the commitment is based upon a history given by some person who might have an ulterior motive in exaggerating or falsifying the history.

. . . . .

Without exception, I have found that the doctors in the various institutions in which I have conducted hearings are capable, honest and well-meaning, and are doing their best in the interest of the patient.

As soon as some safeguards are provided so that the mentally ill patient can have an opportunity for a hearing, I would be pleased to leave these proceedings in the hands of the doctors in the first instance.[33]

[33] Letter dated October 27, 1960, addressed to the committee and quoted with the permission of Justice McDonald. Omitted before the last two paragraphs is a paragraph in which Justice McDonald comments on the problem of the admission of senile patients. It is quoted in Section 4 of Chapter IV, *supra*.

VI

Property and Business Interests of the Mentally Ill

IN this state, as in most states, legal protection is available for persons who are physically or mentally unable to care for their own business affairs and their own property. This protection safeguards also the interests of their creditors. When the protected person does not want to pay his debts or, more generally, when he does not want to use his property in the way others use it in his interest, the word "protection" becomes a two-edged sword. A court may "protect" a person from his own reckless acts, or from injurious acts by others; but it may also "protect" him from enjoying the use of his own property. The right to such use is enshrined in the Constitution and is generally thought to be almost as fundamental as the right to personal liberty. Any deprivation of it must be surrounded with proper safeguards if it is to accord due process.

The law recognizes that not every mentally ill person needs to be protected in this way. Some can handle business and property with understanding and even with acumen. But the law also recognizes that many do need such protection, either because of the illness itself or because their freedom of action is restricted by confinement in a hospital and necessary hospital rules. Patients in mental hospitals, furthermore, are always treated somewhat differently from other patients in respect to these matters. In addition, there are special regulations in our state hospitals applicable to their patients alone.

The general legal doctrines, applicable to all mental patients, are based on the concept of "incompetency." This concept should be distinguished sharply from that of "mental illness" or "certification to a mental hospital." "Incompetency" relates to legal capacity or status: incapacity in law to contract, to make a will, to own property, and to effectuate other acts relating to the management of one's property or affairs. "Certification to a mental hospital" because of "mental illness" does not relate to legal status or capacity such as this; it refers rather to the patient's need for involuntary hospitalization. The special statutory protections which apply only to patients in state mental hospitals are not based on the concept of "incompetency." They apply to every such patient whether he is "incompetent" or not.

The committee has not undertaken to study the vast legal area of incompetency except as it may affect admissions to mental hospitals.

New York law today provides four kinds of control over the property and business interests of persons who are mentally ill. The first is the body of law relating to the effect of mental illness in private litigation, absent a judicial finding of incompetency; the second is the statute authorizing the appointment of a guardian—termed a "committee"—for persons who are unable to care for their persons or for their property; [1] the third is the statute which empowers the Commissioner of Mental Hygiene to allow directors of state mental hospitals to "receive or obtain" certain kinds of personal property belonging to any patient and with it to set up a fund for the patient in the hospital; [2] and the fourth is General Order 10 of the Department of Mental Hygiene, which places restrictions on the legal acts of a patient in a state mental hospital.[3]

[1] N.Y. Civ. Prac. Act, art. 81, §§ 1356 et seq.

[2] Mental Hygiene Law, § 34(14).

[3] General Order 10, Regulations of the Department of Mental Hygiene, promulgated in October 1959.

The first and second are aspects of general law applicable to any person within the state and are grounded in the concept of incompetency. The third is a statute applicable to all patients in state mental hospitals, but to them alone. The fourth is a matter of present practice under the Mental Hygiene Law.

INCOMPETENCY IN EXISTING LAW

A judicial decision that a person was or is incompetent to manage his own affairs or that he was or is unable properly to carry out particular transactions may be made for a number of different reasons. He may be a chronic alcoholic. He may be physically incapacitated. He may be a mental defective, a senile person, or a person who is mentally ill. The basic doctrines under which courts act in all these cases are similar. But they have evolved somewhat different formulas for the different situations. Since we are primarily concerned with persons suffering from mental illnesses, we stress the judicial language applicable to those cases. This language, to a considerable extent, is also applicable to mental defectives and to senile persons.

Common-Law Power of a Court

We must note, first, the general body of law relating to the effect of mental illness or other mental incapacity on a person's control of his property when no judicial finding of incompetency has been made. The authority of a court to intervene in the business affairs of a person who is mentally ill rests on the established doctrine that it is the duty of the state to protect from the consequences of his own acts any person "not under the guidance of reason." [4] In the exercise of this power, for

[4] Although the holding was concerned with an incompetency proceeding, the general power of a court was expressed by Haight, J., in

instance, a contract will be declared voidable if one of the parties was unable "to form an intelligent purpose deliberately to execute the matter in question." [5] The protected party, or his legal representative, may accept or reject the contract as his best interests determine. Similarly, a marriage will be annulled if there is incapacity to consent "for want of understanding." [6] In order to uphold the will of a person alleged to have been mentally ill at the time of its execution, it is necessary to show that "the testator has sufficient capacity to comprehend perfectly the condition of his property, his relations to the persons who were, or should, or might have been the objects of his bounty, and the scope and bearing of the provisions of his will." [7]

In all these cases, before it extends its protection, the court must be persuaded that the incapacity alleged actually involves lack of comprehension of the act in question. In other words, a litigant who raises the issue of his lack of understanding must prove that he was unable intelligently to perform the act at issue. If he is attempting to avoid an act, the mental patient has an advantage. Proof that the person involved was a certified patient in a mental hospital during the time in question apparently has the effect of shifting the burden of proof to the person

---

Sporza v. German Savings Bank, 192 N.Y. 8, 14, 84 N.E. 406, 408 (1908) as follows:

"Jurisdiction is inherent in the state over unfortunate persons within its limits who are idiots or have been deprived of the use of their mental faculties. It is its duty to protect the community from the acts of those persons who are not under the guidance of reason, and also to protect them, their persons and property from their own disordered and insane acts."

[5] Morse v. Miller, 39 N.Y.S. 2d 815, 818 (Sup. Ct. Wayne Co., Van Voorhis, J., 1943), aff'd 267 App. Div. 801, 47 N.Y.S. 2d 288 (4th Dept. 1943).

[6] New York Domestic Relations Law, § 7(2).

[7] Delafield v. Parish, 25 N.Y. 2, 29 (1862).

who is claiming against the patient.[8] Mere presence in such a hospital would probably have the same effect even without the certification.

The difficulty with this kind of protection, however, is that it comes after the fact—sometimes long after it. In business affairs third parties must often be assured of the legal competence of the party with whom they are dealing at the time of the particular transaction. Furthermore, this kind of court protection cannot preserve the business position of a person confined in a mental hospital, who is as a consequence physically unable to handle his affairs. It was for these reasons that the concept of a legal guardian or, in New York State, a committee was evolved long ago.

Appointment of a Committee

Article 81 of the Civil Practice Act governs the appointment of committees for all persons. The elaborate provisions of this article extend the jurisdiction of the supreme court and county courts to cover "the custody of the person and the care of the property of a person incompetent to manage himself or his affairs in consequence of lunacy, idiocy, habitual drunkenness, or imbecility arising from old age or loss of memory and understanding, or other cause."[9]

A finding of incompetency, which must be made by a jury, establishes jurisdiction.[10] The court must then preserve from

[8] No cases were found directly on this point, but cases do hold that if a general mental illness is shown it is up to the opponent to prove "lucid intervals" in which the action was taken. Morse v. Miller, *supra* note 5; Aiken v. Roberts, 164 N.Y. Supp. 502 (Sup. Ct. Wayne Co., Rodenbeck, J., 1917). The showing of hospitalization with no rebuttal is probably enough to indicate mental illness.

[9] N.Y. Civ. Prac. Act, § 1356.

[10] N.Y. Civ. Prac. Act, §§ 1364 et seq.

waste or destruction the property of the incompetent person.[11] To do this it is directed to appoint an individual to act as a "committee" of the person of the incompetent, or of his property, or both.[12]

The committee's power is, for the most part, coextensive with the duty placed upon the court. The "commission," a written document from the court authorizing the committee to act, must in effect state "that possession, care and management of the personal estate, and care and management of the real estate has been granted, given and committed to said committee." [13] In addition, certain specific duties are laid upon the committee.[14] The only specific limitation on its power is that it "cannot alien, mortgage or otherwise dispose of real property, except to lease it for a term not exceeding five years, without the special direction of the court obtained upon proceedings taken for that purpose." [15]

The court is directed to keep strict watch over its representatives. Each committee of the property is required to file an inventory, account, and affidavit annually.[16] The presiding judge or justice of the appointing court is charged with the duty of inspecting these accounts and inventories or directing their inspection; in practice the actual examinations are done by "referees" appointed by the judge.[17]

If the court is dissatisfied with the work of a committee, there is discretion to suspend or remove it at any time.[18] When an incompetent regains his competency, or when he dies, the jurisdiction granted by Article 81 ends. The article provides for a

[11] N.Y. Civ. Prac. Act, § 1357. [12] N.Y. Civ. Prac. Act, § 1358.

[13] N.Y. Civ. Prac. Act, § 1358-a(5).

[14] See N.Y. Civ. Prac. Act, § 1377-a, Examination and inventory of safe deposit boxes and safes; and § 1377-b, Proceedings to discover property withheld.

[15] N.Y. Civ. Prac. Act, § 1377. [16] N.Y. Civ. Prac. Act, § 1378.

[17] N.Y. Civ. Prac. Act, § 1379. [18] N.Y. Civ. Prac. Act, § 1377.

restoration of the property and for a final accounting when competency is regained,[19] or for a final accounting when the incompetent dies.[20] The committee, then, is an integral part of the court; it provides that essentially passive institution with an active arm, necessary to protect an incompetent's property and business in a world where conditions constantly change.

This, in broad outline, is the scope of Article 81. It is applicable to all persons, whether or not they are mentally ill. But here, again, an exception is made for patients certified to a state mental hospital. In order to have a committee appointed for such a patient, it is not necessary to undertake the long and expensive procedures required for other appointments.

Section 1374 of the Civil Practice Act authorizes the appointment of a committee for a certified patient in a state mental hospital by means of a very summary proceeding. The director of the hospital, represented by the Assistant Attorney General in charge of the case, may present a petition to the court alleging that the patient has been duly certified and that he is still in the hospital. The statute indicates no need for more evidence of incompetency than that which may be provided by proof of these allegations. The court may even dispense with notice to the patient if "sufficient reasons" for doing so are alleged. The court, acting without a jury, is then required to determine whether the allegations are true and, if they are, may proceed immediately to appoint a committee.

Special notice must be taken of the fact that a committee may be appointed under Section 1374 without any finding, either by judge or jury, of actual incompetency. This distinguishes the provision markedly from the procedure for appointing a committee under the other provisions of Article 81, in which a jury finding of incompetency is a prerequisite to the appointment of a committee. Under 1374 a judge may appoint a committee simply on the ground that the person for whom a

[19] N.Y. Civ. Prac. Act, § 1382. [20] N.Y. Civ. Prac. Act, § 1383.

committee is sought "has been committed to a State institution." [21]

PROTECTION FOR CERTAIN MENTAL PATIENTS NOT BASED ON THEIR INCOMPETENCY

We have noted that mental patients receive certain protections of their property and business interests more easily than others. Those in state hospitals are also given certain protections which are not given to others at all.

Limited Committeeship

Section 34(14) of the Mental Hygiene Law, though it has never been recognized as providing for a limited committeeship, does just that in its actual effect. It provides, in pertinent part:

> Notwithstanding the provisions of section thirteen hundred fifty-six of the civil practice act, providing for jurisdiction over the person and property of an incompetent, the commissioner [of mental hygiene] may authorize the directors of state institutions in the de-

[21] See also Martello v. Cagliostro, 122 Misc. 306, 311, 202 N.Y. Supp. 703, 707–08 (Sup. Ct. Kings Co., Cropsey, J., 1924):

"There is no requirement that the incompetency of the person be either alleged or proved [in a Section 1374 proceeding], except as that is established by the fact of his commitment, and the commitment itself. The incompetency need not be found upon such an application. It is not an issue there. Seemingly it is deemed to have been established by the commitment and not to be open for further consideration. . . .

". . . The 'further proof' which may be taken . . . does not mean proof of incompetency. It may be the court would wish to know about the incompetent's property, or more about his relatives, with a view to determining who should be appointed a committee. . . ."

See also Matter of Walker, 57 App. Div. 1, 67 N.Y. Supp. 647 (4th Dept. 1900); Trust Co. of America v. State Deposit Co., 187 N.Y. 178, 79 N.E. 996 (1907), and McCabe v. State, 208 Misc. 485, 144 N.Y.S. 2d 488 (Ct. Cl. 1947).

partment to receive or obtain funds or other personal property excepting jewelry due or belonging to a patient who has no committee, up to an amount or value not exceeding two thousand five hundred dollars without taking proceedings for the appointment of a committee. . . . Such funds and the proceeds of the sale of other personal property so received shall be placed to the credit of the patients for whom received, and disbursed, on the order of the director, to provide luxuries, comforts and necessities for such patients. . . . The commissioner may authorize directors, on behalf of such patients to give receipts, execute releases and other documents required by law or court order, to endorse checks and drafts, and to convert personal property except jewelry into money by sale for adequate consideration. . . .

This provides a limited form of committeeship over "a patient who has no committee." Whether it gives authority to exercise such power only over patients who have been committed or who have been found to be incompetent or whether the power extends to all patients is not fully clear from the section and has never been judicially determined.

The more limited construction seems to be suggested by the section's opening phrase: "Notwithstanding the provisions of section thirteen hundred fifty-six of the civil practice act, providing for jurisdiction over the person and property of an incompetent." It may imply that the power is limited to cases in which a court would have jurisdiction to appoint a committee, i.e., to cases of persons found to be incompetent under the general provisions of Article 81 or of persons who have been committed and who therefore qualify under Section 1374. But on the other hand, the body of Section 34(14) provides that directors of state institutions may be authorized to "receive or obtain funds or other personal property . . . due or belonging to a patient who has no committee." This language suggests that the power extends to any patient "who has no committee," no matter how he was admitted and whether incompetent or not.

This is not the only ambiguity in the statute. The main limitations on the power of the director over the property of the patient seem to be that he may exercise no control over jewelry, or over real property, or over personal property in excess of $2,500. The last limitation is not clear. It might mean a single $2,500 for each patient, no matter how long he stayed. It might even mean a single $2,500 for each patient, no matter how many times he was readmitted. On the other hand, it might mean $2,500 a year or even $2,500 at any one time. This last reading would, of course, impose no limitation at all upon liquid cash assets. As the fund was diminished, it could be replenished from such assets to the extent of the patient's resources.

With regard to other personal property, it is not at all clear what the powers of the director are. The power of the Commissioner to allow a director, on a patient's behalf, to "execute . . . other documents required by law" may mean he can redeem bonds or sign stock proxies. Under this phrase he might even be able to sign a lease to real property on behalf of the patient, although he is not able to "obtain funds or other personal property" other than rents. The power to execute papers may perhaps be limited more closely by the use of the word "releases" and the principle of *ejusdem generis* to papers incidental to the obtaining of funds.

Nevertheless, under a broad construction there may be statutory authority for a director of a state hospital to exercise a fairly full committeeship over all the personal property (except jewelry) of all patients in his hospital. These powers can be initiated, under the authority of the Commissioner of Mental Hygiene, without any judicial authorization whatsoever.

Maintenance and Support

Another form of protection, or management, exists for a patient in a state mental hospital which is not based on any judicial declaration of incompetency. As noted at the beginning of this chapter, legal protection must include the payment of the patient's debts. One such debt is imposed by Section 24 of the Mental Hygiene Law, which provides that a patient shall be liable for the cost of his care, maintenance, and treatment in a state mental hospital.[22] A reimbursement rate is fixed administratively for all patients,[23] but the Commissioner may require payments from particular patients which are at, or less than, or greater than the reimbursement rate. He can thus adjust the payment to a particular patient's ability to pay. But the acceptance of a lesser amount does not release the patient from his responsibility for the remainder unless the Commissioner waives, as he may, the right to recovery.[24]

The patient is protected from the full force of this obligation by the legal provision that he is not liable for it alone. His committee, guardian, or trustee is, of course, liable to the extent of his property which any of them may control. In addition, however, "the husband, wife, father, mother and children of such patient, if such relatives are of sufficient ability, shall also be jointly and severally liable and responsible for such payments." [25]

The obligation of these relatives is made enforceable by Title 8-A of the Code of Criminal Procedure.[26] This title repeats the liability [27] and provides that "proceedings may be maintained pursuant to the provisions of this title to compel the support and maintenance of any patient or inmate in a state institution, or in family care, who is either unable or who refuses or neglects to pay for his support and maintenance therein." [28] The Department of Mental Hygiene may institute such an action.[29] Relatives served with notice are to be treated

[22] Mental Hygiene Law, § 24(1).
[23] Mental Hygiene Law, § 24(7).
[24] Mental Hygiene Law, § 24(1).
[25] Mental Hygiene Law, § 24(2).
[26] Code Cr. Proc., § 926-a-g.
[27] Code Cr. Proc., § 926-b.
[28] Code Cr. Proc., § 926-c(1).
[29] Code Cr. Proc., § 926-c(2).

as prima facie able to pay unless they prove the contrary. The court is given leeway to require the contribution of more than one relative if no one of them is able to meet the whole obligation,[30] and to modify its original order from time to time "as circumstances may require."[31] It also has broad discretion as to the form of its order. It may require security for the undertaking. It may even imprison the person liable for up to six months, until the security is furnished. The order operates to impose a lien on real estate belonging to the person liable.[32] If that person refuses to comply with the order, he is guilty of a misdemeanor and, in addition, may be punished for criminal contempt of court.[33]

The existing law on the protection, or management, of the property and business interests of mental patients may thus be divided into two parts: that which is available to mental patients who may be judicially determined to be incompetent for any purpose or for whom a committee is judicially appointed, and that which is not based on such a determination or appointment but which is available, probably, to all patients in state mental hospitals. The first part comprises the common-law powers of a court to protect a person in private litigation and its statutory powers to appoint a committee to act in his behalf. The second part includes the powers of the directors of state mental hospitals to act as limited committees for their patients and to require relatives of the patient to pay for his support and maintenance.

PRACTICE UNDER EXISTING LAW

In practice, the most important protections of the property and business interests of mental patients are those provided by Section 34(14) of the Mental Hygiene Law. The Department of Mental Hygiene has given this statute a broad inter-

[30] Code Cr. Proc., § 926-c(3).

[31] Code Cr. Proc., § 926-c(5).

[32] Code Cr. Proc., § 926-d.

[33] Code Cr. Proc., § 926-e.

pretation. The Commissioner assumes and exercises the power to authorize directors of state mental hospitals to act as committees for all patients, regardless of the method of their admission and regardless of whether they would be eligible to have a committee appointed under other provisions of law. The Department's interpretation, furthermore, makes of little effect the $2,500 limitation on the amount of a patient's funds which a director may control; it construes the phrase to mean $2,500 at any one time. In actual fact, a patient's fund often contains a good deal more than this amount.

Under this reading, a director's power is extensive. There is little personal property which he cannot reach. But the Department prefers that the power be used only as a last resort. It has codified this policy in General Order 10.[34] This regulation begins by prohibiting patients without a committee from signing any legal document unless ordered to do so by the Commissioner or by a court.[35] But it makes two broad exceptions to this. Instruments affecting the patient's personal rights and property may be signed, at the discretion of the hospital director, if the director certifies that the patient understands his act and is not coerced. This is thought to provide a healthy flexibility because capacity to sign a particular document may well exist along with certain kinds of mental illness.[36]

The other exception relates to checks. Any check, of any size, to the patient's order may be endorsed by him if it is to be deposited in the business office of the hospital for his use. The director has discretionary powers, too, to allow the patient to endorse or to draw any check, for any use whatever, if it is for less than one hundred dollars. The director, or one of his assistants, must be present at the time any patient signs or endorses any check or legal document.[37]

[34] General Order 10, Regulations of the Department of Mental Hygiene, promulgated October 1959.

[35] General Order 10, subd. b.

[36] General Order 10, subd. c.

[37] General Order 10, subd. b.

Hospital directors are well content with these regulations. They try to persuade patients to take as much responsibility for their financial affairs as they are capable of taking. Whenever possible, a patient will be asked to endorse checks for deposit to his account, to sign receipts for small withdrawals and for minor purchases from the hospital store, and to give written orders for payments by the hospital out of his account, even for payments of substantial debts and family remittances. Little trouble is usually encountered in handling these matters with voluntary patients; they tend to understand the need and are receptive. Even paranoid patients, who may be difficult to persuade, will often respond to strong efforts by the hospital staff to explain the problem and to enlist their cooperation.

Sometimes, however, it is not possible to get such cooperation. When this happens, there is no difficulty about minor purchases. The hospital store simply makes a note of them in the patient's account. Larger items pose greater difficulties. When the hospital finds that dependents or others are in dire need, it may override the patient's objections and make the payments nevertheless.

The hospitals and the Department prefer to use Section 34(14) rather than a more formal committeeship for obvious reasons. It avoids the need for even the relatively simple Section 1374 proceeding, and it allows the hospital almost full control of a patient's property.

In all but a small fraction of the cases, this form of limited committeeship provides all that is needed by way of protection for the property and business interests of patients in the state mental hospitals although it is exceedingly simple, lacks all formal controls, and depends on the probity of the hospital's staff. Though we made no intensive study of it, we formed the impression that it cares for the needs of the ordinary patient. It does not, however, suffice for all cases. Apart from the question of the extent of a hospital director's power, never precisely determined, he simply does not have the time, nor is he equipped, to provide the continuous care which is sometimes needed. Changing circumstances, which cause fluctuations of property and business values, mean that active care is necessary whenever substantial interests are involved. Furthermore, for persons who are mentally ill or need protection for other reasons but who are not patients in a state hospital, the simple and easy form of protection provided by Section 34(14) cannot, of course, be used.

Where the protection of this statute is not sufficient or where it cannot be invoked, the only safe recourse at present involves a judicial declaration of incompetency in some form. True, the business interests of a patient or other ill person may sometimes be managed by means of the continued honoring of a power of attorney given earlier to a spouse or some relative. Such powers appear to be honored and relied upon even when the third person dealing with the attorney knows of the hospitalization or other incapacity. But this method is hazardous and unsure; it depends largely on the willingness of the third party to take a "business risk." If the patient is later proved to have been incompetent, the power of attorney is voidable and any act under it unauthorized.

As has been noted, the protection flowing from a finding of incompetency may be in either of two forms: the power of a court to protect a person after finding that he did not understand an act which embroiled him in litigation and the power of a court to appoint a committee to care and act for him.

Our study did not include an analysis of the practical or legal effects of mental illness in private litigation. Presumably courts, when persuaded that a mentally ill person acted without understanding, will protect him insofar as they can without doing an injustice to the other party. After a committee has been appointed, the court will, of course, rely on the committee and will void any action of the incompetent which the committee could have done for him.

Most of the committees appointed for state hospital patients are authorized by Section 1374. The provisions of Article 81 require a costly and burdensome proceeding, so that appointments under them will be undertaken only if the need for the appointment is great, if the estate involved is substantial, and if the alleged incompetent has not been certified to a state mental hospital so as to make 1374 available. For these reasons, from 80 to 90 per cent of the committees now functioning in the First Department are committees appointed under Section 1374.

Even among the patients certified to a state mental hospital, only a tiny minority have had committees appointed. Between twelve and sixteen hundred committees are appointed each year under Section 1374. This compares with about fifteen thousand certifications each year. About seventy-five hundred such committees are now operating throughout the state. Most of them involve estates of less than $5,000, but some run up to $10,000, and occasionally one is found reaching as high as $60,000.

Section 1374 is used by hospital directors primarily in the cases in which it is impossible to reach the patient's funds in any other way and in which the funds are needed to reimburse the hospital or to provide for the patient's expenses.

In practice it is need, rather than any concept of legal incompetency, which in most cases impels a hospital director to ask for the appointment of a committee. He is likely to look to the patient's age, his predicted stay, the size of his estate, and other such factors to see whether such a need exists.

From the point of view of a hospital director, the need to have a committee appointed may arise in the case of a voluntary and nonobjecting patient as well as in the case of one certified under Section 74. When there has been a certification, the director can proceed immediately under Section 1374. But in these other cases he must first have the patient certified in order to be able to use the simple procedure. It is not realistic to expect a hospital to use the cumbersome and expensive procedures of Article 81. Under existing law, certification is the only way to avoid using them. Hospital directors are not happy about having to cause certifications for this reason. They told our staff that it is a "cruel" legal formality.

The impetus for an appointment under 1374 comes from the hospital usually, but not always. The families and relatives of patients in state mental hospitals prefer to use this section rather than the other procedures of Article 81. The stimulus will therefore come at times from them, even when the use of 1374 requires the certification of a previously uncertified patient. Once every two or three years, perhaps, the family of a person not yet in a state hospital—perhaps in a private mental institution—will have him certified and sent to a state hospital for the sole purpose of making possible the use of Section 1374. After an appointment has been made in such a case, the patient may be returned to the private institution.

When a family seeks the appointment of a Section 1374 committee, the hospital will normally send the necessary information and forms to the Attorney General's office, which then prepares the petition and presents it to the court.

EVALUATION

The property and business interests of mental patients in state mental hospitals are in the main protected sufficiently and reasonably well by powers delegated to the staffs of these hospitals. In a few cases proper protection calls for more active and constant care than the staff members can give. When a state hospital director determines that there is need for more protection, or for protection different from that which his staff can supply, he has to ask a court for the appointment of a committee. When the patient has been certified, the director can proceed immediately under the relatively easy provisions of Section 1374. But when a voluntary or nonobjecting patient is involved, the director must first have him certified.

Although Section 1374, as written, is restricted to use by state hospitals, it is so much simpler and less burdensome than a full incompetency proceeding under the provisions of Article 81 that relatives of patients and private mental institutions prefer to use it when they can. In order to do so, however, a patient not already certified in a state mental hospital must be both certified to such a hospital and sent there physically. The petition for the appointment of a committee must then be signed by the director of that hospital. State hospital officials rarely object to this use of their time and facilities. Although unnecessary certification, and sometimes even transportation, may well be injurious to a mentally ill person, it is likely to be less traumatic for him, and much less expensive for him and his family, than a full-fledged incompetency proceeding under the procedures of Article 81.

The committee takes the view that the present laws in this field are, in general, adequate in practice. But they are so, to a considerable extent, in spite of the statutory provisions rather than because of them.

The language of Section 34(14) of the Mental Hygiene Law, for instance, might be supposed to limit that statute's application to property worth $2,500 for each certified patient. The interpretation of the Department of Mental Hygiene has minimized the effect of this restrictive language. It is important that there be a way in which a hospital can routinely provide adequate protection for the property and business interests of most of its patients to the extent that such protection is needed.

The committee is also of the opinion that a flexible, nontraumatic, and inexpensive method should be available by which a committee can be appointed for those persons whose property cannot be properly protected under Section 34(14).

Section 1374 of Article 81 of the Civil Practice Act provides a partial answer at present. But it has serious defects. From the medical point of view, the limitation of its use to certified patients in state mental hospitals means that some patients have to be put through an unnecessary and often harmful process in order to qualify. This greatly detracts from its usefulness. From the legal point of view, the lack of a requirement for a finding of incompetency at the time of the appointment of a committee means that the court's role is merely ministerial. There is no decision to be made, but only an administrative act of appointment.

The committee is of the opinion that no amendment of Section 1374 would be sufficient to meet these objections. We therefore recommend that New York State enact a statute which would authorize the appointment of a "conservator" for hospitalized mental patients who are unable to care for themselves or for their property by reason of advanced age, mental illness, or weakness. This recommendation is based on studies of cases of hospitalized mentally ill persons and is therefore limited to this class of persons. We have no reason to suppose, however, that our recommendation could not, at some later date, be extended to cover those who are mentally ill but not hospitalized as well as mental defectives and senile persons, since the problems these people face are virtually indistinguishable from those which we have studied. Support for this view, it should be noted, has been expressed to our staff by persons who are examining the problems of senility.

We believe there are three basic goals which the legislation we propose should attempt to achieve. The first is to make a single simple appointment procedure available, at least for all hospitalized mentally ill patients, whether their hospitalization was nonvoluntary or voluntary. The second is to allow courts as much discretion as possible in the disposition of individual cases. And the third is to provide procedural due process for any person who feels unjustly caught in the web of intricate procedure. With these broad aims in mind, the committee was impressed by the California Conservatorship Act,[38] a statute designed at first as an alternative to, and eventually as a replacement for, the guardian and ward chapter of the California Probate Code.[39]

The California act was passed in 1957 as a result of fifteen years of effort on the part of a series of committees, composed of judges and lawyers of differing legal viewpoints and belonging to different legal organizations throughout the state of California. They were concerned about the way in which stigma had become attached to incompetency proceedings. Many elderly people and their relatives shunned the appointment of the usual guardian, even when one was needed, because a finding of incompetency would necessarily be involved. In an attempt to exorcise this stigma, new terminology was adopted: a "conservator" takes the place of a "guardian"; a "conservatee" that of a "ward"; and "conservatorship" that of "incompetency," as the title of the proceeding.[40]

We accept these new terms, although perhaps we are not so sanguine as were the California drafters about the effect of the change on the amount of stigma attached to the proceeding. Furthermore, we also recommend that New York follow the example of California and adopt a new statute as an alternative to, rather than as an immediate replacement of, Article 81. New terminology, whatever its effect may be as to stigma, will be necessary to distinguish an appointment under the new scheme from an appointment under the old.

The California statute provides for the appointment of a conservator by a court if it is "satisfied by sufficient evidence of

[38] Cal. Prob. Code Division 5. [39] Cal. Prob. Code Division 4.

[40] For a general discussion of the aims of the drafters, see Lord, Conservatorship vs. Guardianship, 33 L.A. Bar. Bull. 5 (1957). For an explanation of the new terminology, see page 6 of that article.

the need therefor."[41] Basing the appointment on the "need" for it, rather than on a finding of "incompetency," will not only tend to limit the stigma attached to the proceeding but will also add the required flexibility to the statute. A court will be free to appoint a conservator whenever it finds that the conservatee is not able to care for his property, whether the inability results from a medical disability or from some other cause and whether he is completely incompetent, in the technical sense, or suffering from some lesser impediment.

At the same time, a requirement, such as that found under the California statute, that the court make a written finding of the need for the appointment of a conservator would force it to focus on the essential question involved, instead of merely on the nonessential question whether the alleged conservatee is a certified patient in a state mental hospital, which seems to be the sole issue under Section 1374.

Furthermore, the court should be required, as it is in California, to allot to the conservator those powers and only those powers which are appropriate to the particular condition of need found. No person would then be completely deprived of his legal capacity unless he was totally incapable. And if it would clearly benefit a patient to retain some power over his property, the court, by a judicious allocation of limited powers to a conservator, would be able to aid the patient's treatment while protecting his property to the extent necessary.

If such a system should be adopted in New York, it would also be necessary to permit the court to modify the powers of a conservator readily in order to allow for continuous adjustments designed to parallel changes in the patient's condition and needs. Any such modifications, however, should require a written finding by the court of the changes needed and of the new allocation of appropriate powers.

"Any interested person," including the conservator, should

[41] Cal. Prob. Code, § 1751.

be able to present the original petition or the petition for any necessary modification in the powers of a conservator. In order to protect the conservatee fully, "all interested persons" should receive notice of the pendency of the appointment of a conservator or of any modification in powers, and the right to a hearing on these questions should be provided.

In its discretion, and especially when the petition is not presented by an employee of the Department of Mental Hygiene, the court should be able to appoint a guardian *ad litem* or a temporary conservator to represent the patient's interests. If a guardian *ad litem* or a temporary conservator is appointed, the court should be able to provide adequate compensation from the conservatee's estate, when it is substantial enough to meet the expense, or from public funds, when it is not.

A jury trial of the issue of incompetency has often been regarded as a necessity of procedural due process in a committeeship proceeding. In order to preserve this right to a jury trial without making it mandatory in every proceeding, the right to a jury trial on a motion to discharge a conservator could be provided. If such a motion to discharge were available immediately after appointment and if provision for trial by jury were provided on such a motion, the due process requirement would be met without unduly fettering the appointment proceeding.

As a final element of this suggested statutory scheme, we would favor a provision allowing a conservatee to petition for and nominate his own conservator.[42] The actual appointment, of course, would rest with the court acting under the admonition that it be "guided by what appears to be for the best in-

[42] Cal. Prob. Code, § 1752. See also State of New York Law Revision Commission, Act, Recommendation and Study Relating to Provisions Authorizing a Person of Sound Mind to Designate Another Person to Act as His Committee in the Event of Future Incompetence, submitted in 1953 (Leg. Doc. (1953) No. 65Q). The provisions of this draft of proposed legislation require any authorization to be written and signed with all the formality required for a signature on a will.

terests of the person to be placed under conservatorship."[43] It would, of course, have to determine whether or not the person requesting a conservator fully understood whom he was nominating at the time of making the nomination, and also it would have to determine the suitability of the nominee. But the scheme would alleviate some of the stigma involved. In the same way that the voluntary admission to a mental hospital preserves to a patient his sense of dignity, so the voluntary assumption of conservatorship should preserve to a conservatee an interest in himself and an interest in his property.

Such a statutory scheme as the one we have here outlined would provide a new flexibility in the law of committeeships. It would place firmly upon the court the responsibility, not only for appointing a person to act as a conservator, but also for determining exactly what the need is which requires the appointment and how much responsibility should be shifted from the conservatee to the conservator. Although the court would not be placed under a duty of continually reviewing each case, it might at any time, either on its own motion or on the motion of some interested person, be required to reevaluate the original order and, if necessary, to make a new order in the light of changed conditions.

RECOMMENDATIONS

On the basis of its conclusion that the present laws governing the property and business interests of the mentally ill need improvement, the committee recommends:

> *Recommendation No. 19 (Protection of Property of Patients)*. The director of a state mental hospital shall have the authority, under regulations to be promulgated by the Commissioner of Mental Hygiene, to provide protection for the property of patients in his hospital up to a fixed

[43] Cal. Prob. Code, § 1752.

amount without respect to the method of admission or to the power of a court to appoint a committee or other guardian.

Recommendation No. 20 (*Appointment of Conservator for Patients in Hospitals*). Section 1374 of the Civil Practice Act, relating to committees of an incompetent, should be repealed, and a new statute should be enacted to provide an inexpensive, flexible, and nontraumatic method for the appointment of a "conservator" for any person in a state mental hospital, licensed private institution, or psychiatric receiving hospital, regardless of the method of admission of the patient, if the patient cannot properly care for his property and business interests by reason of old age, mental weakness, or mental illness.

The statute shall require a written judicial finding of the need for the appointment or discharge of a conservator or for any grant of powers to or change in powers of a conservator, but it shall not require that a finding of "incompetency" be made.

The statute shall authorize the court to grant to the conservator in each case powers appropriate to the condition and needs of the patient, whether such powers are greater or less than those now granted to a committee under Article 81 of the Civil Practice Act.

The act shall also provide for a temporary conservator pending a permanent appointment and shall allow a jury trial in a discharge proceeding only.

Recommendation No. 21 (*Possible Extension of Use of Conservator*). If experience with the conservator provisions proposed in Recommendation No. 20 suggests extension of this use, a conservator should be authorized in the case of persons who are unable to care for their property and business interests whether or not they are hospitalized.

VII

Admissions in Criminal Cases

MINOR offenses or acts in the nature of disorderly conduct are sometimes used as a pretext for effecting admissions in emergency cases. Section 81(5) of the Mental Hygiene Law, as we have seen, expressly authorizes the police to arrest and confine in a safe place, until his sanity is determined, any person who appears to be mentally ill and who is acting in a disorderly manner.[1] The arresting officer is required to notify the health officer immediately, so that admission to a mental hospital on a health officer's certificate can be effected if the person appears in need of immediate care and treatment. In cities with receiving hospitals, the arresting officer may bring such a person directly to the receiving hospital, the "safe and comfortable place" prescribed by the statute. District attorneys in many parts of the state have reported extensive use of these procedures.

District attorneys have also reported that in order to protect the authorities against suits for false imprisonment the police sometimes arraign such a person on a technical violation of law before a magistrate, who then issues a criminal order of examination under Section 870 of the Code of Criminal Procedure. Some hospital directors expressed disapproval of the practice of arresting and arraigning a person in order to effect his hospitalization by means of a criminal order of examination, because a patient forced into a hospital under threat of criminal

[1] See Chapter IV.

action is not disposed to cooperate in his therapy. In all these cases the disorderly or criminal conduct is more or less an incident—a means availed of—for sending an unwilling patient to the hospital. Under these circumstances, as one director said, the hospital is forced into the role of jailer.

If minor offenses are loosely used as a pretext for hospitalization, the remedy may lie in greater education of police officers as to methods of civil admission under the Mental Hygiene Law, including the authority which the police now have under its Section 81(5) to restrain an apparently mentally ill person who is acting in a disorderly manner, pending examination by a physician as to the need for hospitalization. A more effective remedy may lie with the local magistrate if such an apparently mentally ill person is arraigned. Instead of resorting to a formal criminal order of examination, the magistrate may set in motion a civil admission, either admission to a receiving hospital under Section 81(5) or admission by a health officer under Section 72. If the defendant is certified to a state hospital and the complaint pending before the magistrate charges an offense or misdemeanor, such commitment is deemed a final disposition of the offense charged.[2]

In this chapter we are concerned with antisocial conduct resulting in criminal proceedings and with admissions to mental hospitals which become necessary at various stages in those proceedings. The patients so admitted may, for brevity, be referred to collectively as "criminal-law patients."

Our *first* concern will be with admission for observation as to the mental ability of a defendant to stand trial for the crime or offense charged, and with his further hospitalization if found not able thus to stand trial. It may be a proceeding

(a) for an offense or minor misdemeanor;
(b) for an indictable crime (anywhere in the state) on which no indictment has yet been returned, or in New

[2] Code Cr. Proc., § 873.

York City for a misdemeanor on which no information has yet been filed; or

(c) for a crime (anywhere in the state) on which an indictment has been returned, or in New York City for a misdemeanor on which an information has been filed.

The possible termination of the further hospitalization of patients found unable to stand trial will also be considered.

Secondly, we shall consider the sending to a mental hospital of a defendant who has been acquitted of crime on the ground of insanity, and also his subsequent possible discharge.

Thirdly, we shall consider transfer and commitment to a mental hospital of a convicted prisoner who, while a prisoner, is found to be mentally ill, and also his retransfer therefrom or possible discharge. The procedures will be discussed for three classes of prisoners: (a) male prisoners in state penal or correctional institutions, (b) female prisoners in state penal or correctional institutions, and (c) prisoners of either sex in local penal or correctional institutions.

The statutes governing the admission to mental hospitals of criminal-law patients are a complex patchwork. The same thing is true of the statutes governing their possible discharge. For the kind of case mentioned in each of the last three paragraphs, we shall first summarize the relevant statutes and then describe the practice and the problems. At the end of the chapter we shall present the committee's findings and recommendations.

First: Admission for Observation as to Ability to Stand Trial and Commitment Where Such Ability Is Not Found; Possible Ending of Such Commitment.

The examination. Whenever it appears to a court or magistrate having jurisdiction of a defendant charged with a crime or offense that reasonable ground exists to believe that the defendant is in such a state of insanity that he is incapable of understanding the charge or proceeding or of making his defense, or whenever an indicted defendant pleads insanity to an indictment, then the court or magistrate may order the defendant to be examined to determine his sanity.[3] The psychiatrists who make the examination report to the court, advising it of their opinion.

Outside New York City this examination must be made by two qualified psychiatrists designated by the superintendent of any public hospital and from his own staff if possible. The hospital must be one certified by the Commissioner of Mental Hygiene as having the requisite facilities. In New York City the examination must be made by two such psychiatrists designated by the director of the Division of Psychiatry of the city's Department of Hospitals from the staff of such Division.[4]

Examinations may be made in the place where the defendant is detained or, if the superintendent or director in question so recommends, the court may send the defendant to another place or to a mental hospital designated by the superintendent or director for not more than sixty days "for observation and examination." [5] In New York City the examination is conducted at the prison wards of Bellevue, Kings County, or Elmhurst Hospitals.

In practice, many courts throughout the state first request an informal and preliminary examination of a defendant before issuing a formal order directing the examination and a report to the court.[6] Such an informal and preliminary examination

[3] Code Cr. Proc., §§ 658, 870. Practice for the commitment of defendants thus charged with crimes or offenses is set forth in Code Cr. Proc., §§ 658–662-f, 870–876.

[4] Code Cr. Proc., § 659. In either place the director who appoints the two psychiatrists may serve as one of the two. The law provides that in New York City the two psychiatrists shall be aided by an assistant corporation counsel, but this provision is a dead letter.

[5] Code Cr. Proc., § 660.

[6] See People v. Esposito, 287 N.Y. 389, 39 N.E. 2d 925 (1942); People v. Pershaec, 172 Misc. 324, 15 N.Y.S. 2d 215 (Ct. Gen. Sess. N.Y. Co., Collins, J., 1939).

of the defendant is one way of demonstrating that reasonable ground exists for the belief that the defendant is mentally ill. Sections 658 and 870, as noted, require that such a reasonable ground for belief exist before the formal examination is ordered. To explore the procedures for meeting this condition, our staff asked district attorneys about the practices followed in their counties. The replies showed that the district attorney, or defense counsel, or the court may ask for an informal opinion from a private psychiatrist, or from a psychiatrist on the staff of a state hospital, or from a mental health clinic. In one upstate city psychiatrists from a receiving hospital go to the jail on certain days each week to examine defendants whose mental ability to stand trial has been questioned; only if the psychiatrists believe further observation in a hospital necessary is the defendant sent to the hospital on a criminal-order admission for observation and examination. (In a few counties the lower court judges never take it upon themselves even to order an examination for a defendant who is charged with a felony.)

In some areas, however, the court sends defendants to the state hospital on a criminal-order admission without asking the hospital whether, in its opinion, the patient needs to be hospitalized for the examination. This practice is not in accord with the Code of Criminal Procedure, which, as we have seen, lets the court determine whether an examination is needed, but lets the hospital superintendent or director determine whether it should take place in a hospital and designate the particular hospital. One director of a state hospital told our staff that when he began to insist on the hospital's right to agree to any criminal-order admission and began to send psychiatrists to the jail to decide whether hospitalization was necessary, criminal-order admissions to his hospital dropped from about thirty a month to about three.

Directors of state hospitals are divided in opinion on the best place for such an examination. Some say that a proper examination can be made only in a hospital setting, where the defendant can be observed twenty-four hours a day by experienced personnel. Others say that examination at a jail is satisfactory and that attendants at the jail can give adequate supplementary reports on the defendant's behavior when the psychiatrist is not there.

The increasing number of mental-hospital wards which are unlocked and so afford "minimum security" is strengthening the preference of hospital directors for examination at a jail or, if at the hospital, without admitting the defendant there as an in-patient. District attorneys express concern, too, about sending certain defendants to hospitals with inadequate facilities for guarding them. In 1958, when St. Lawrence State Hospital was to become completely "open," the director wrote to the district attorneys in the area served by his hospital suggesting a procedure for criminal-order admissions in the light of the "minimum security" afforded by his hospital. He noted the serious disruptions caused by the presence in his open wards of up to fifteen criminal defendants at once, who often arrive late at night. At least 75 to 80 per cent of these, he said, would be found sane and returned to stand trial. He proposed that the district attorneys suggest to the courts that the defendant

> be brought to the hospital by appointment and a preliminary examination, or a final examination, [could] be done at that particular time, if it were possible to make a complete decision. If the man were found to be sane, he could be returned immediately with the deputies who brought him. On the other hand, if he were out and out psychotic, we would keep him here. If there was any question as to what should be done and still the man appeared sane, he could still be returned to the jail and after our social workers gathered the information, either from the probation officers or the courts or the relatives concerned, we could then see the prisoner again. This would mean that the man would be detained in jail at maximum security rather than at the hospital for 10, 15 or 20 days, a place of minimum security. I feel that if this plan were allowed

to work you would find that satisfactory examinations and opinions would be rendered to the Court and it might even work out better than the present plan.[7]

That changed conditions in mental hospitals are inducing changes in the ways of carrying out examinations on ability to stand trial is indicated by a recent revision of the *Policy Manual of the Department of Mental Hygiene*. This stresses the legal requirements: an order for the examination by the court, a request by the court to the hospital director that the examination be made, and recommendation by the hospital director to the court if the defendant should be sent for examination to the hospital or to any other place of detention.[8] The *Manual* adds:

> Note: Such a recommendation should be based upon all the facts including the welfare of the defendant and the patients in the hospital, as well as suitability for purposes of the examination. The director may require the sheriff of the county where the defendant is under indictment, to furnish sufficient officers to guard the defendant. The director or person in charge may elect to examine the defendant at the place where he is detained, eliminating the need for an order of commitment or guards for the defendant.[9]

Treatment during examination. In 1961 Section 870 of the Code of Criminal Procedure was amended so as to permit a defendant under examination or hospitalized for this purpose to receive psychiatric or medical treatment at the discretion of the superintendent or director.[10] Several district attorneys, who were asked to comment on this amendment before it passed, opposed it on the constitutional ground that a de-

[7] Letter of May 14, 1958, from Dr. Herman B. Snow to district attorneys, reprinted in Snow, The Open Door Hospital, 35 Psychiatric Quarterly 1, 11 (1961).

[8] Department of Mental Hygiene, Policy Manual, § 409(b)(3) (revised April 10, 1961).

[9] *Ibid.*

[10] N.Y. Sess. Laws 1961, ch. 96, § 1, eff. March 13, 1961.

fendant who had neither been convicted of a crime nor judicially determined to be mentally ill should not be given treatment against his will. Some opposed it on the ground that treatment might interfere with the later conduct of the trial. Others favored the amendment on condition that such treatment should not render the psychiatrists' report or testimony inadmissible; one district attorney, however, dismissed this point as highly legalistic.[11] Still other district attorneys favored the amendment without qualification, as a humane measure.

Reports to the court. Some judges and district attorneys told our staff that the psychiatric examinations are not sufficiently thorough; they pointed to the short time devoted to them. They complained that the reports by the psychiatrists to the court are too brief, although Section 662 of the Code of Criminal Procedure requires "a full and complete report." Often the report contains only a formal statement that the defendant is found to be mentally ill. A detailed report[12] would help both the district attorney and the court in handling the case. One district attorney said, "I think a full and complete report should be submitted by the examining psychiatrists. This would not be a waste of time because if the defendant is convicted, such a report could be utilized by the probation officer in his presentence report."

Hospitalization of defendants found unable to stand trial. If the psychiatric examination indicates that the defendant is

[11] See American Law Institute, Model Penal Code, Tentative Draft, No. 4, § 4.09, and Comments thereon at p. 201 (1955) to the effect that a statement made by a person subject to psychiatric examination or treatment for determination as to fitness to stand trial "shall not be admissible in evidence against him in any [criminal] proceeding on any issue other than that of his mental condition but it shall be admissible upon that issue, whether or not it would otherwise be deemed to be a privileged communication."

[12] See People v. Whitman, 149 Misc. 159, 168–69, 266 N.Y.S. 844, 854–55 (Ct. Gen. Sess. N.Y. Co., Collins, J., 1933) for a statement of the practical uses of this report.

incapable of standing trial and if the court agrees, the court's disposition of the defendant will depend on the place where the court sits, the nature of the charge, and the status of the criminal action at the time of the examination.[13] As noted above, these cases fall into three general groups.

(a) *Defendants found unable to stand trial: Cases involving a charge of an offense or a nonindictable misdemeanor.*

When the defendant is charged anywhere with an offense which is not a crime or when he is charged outside New York City with a misdemeanor over which the local courts of special sessions [14] have exclusive jurisdiction—and when he is found unable to stand trial—the superintendent or director in charge of the defendant's examination, if he thinks immediate care and treatment beneficial, must notify the court and those officials made responsible by Section 81(1) and 81(2), or, presumably, one of those officials. This official then institutes civil proceedings for the defendant's certification under Section 74 of the

[13] A jury trial has been held not to be a constitutional requirement in a determination of the issue of insanity rendering a person incapable of standing trial. People *ex rel.* Klesitz v. Mills, as Sup't of Creedmoor State Hospital, 179 Misc. 58, 61–65, 37 N.Y.S. 2d 185, 189–91 (Sup. Ct. Queens Co., Froessel, J., 1942).

[14] These are city courts, justices of the peace courts, and village police justice courts. Code Cr. Proc., §§ 56, 56-a (jurisdiction, with certain qualifications, of courts of special sessions outside New York City over many misdemeanors specified, over offenses, and over violations of ordinances and infractions); § 11 (mentioning, among others, city courts outside New York City authorized to act in criminal matters, courts of special sessions, and police courts); city court acts for the various cities other than New York City; Town Law, § 31; Village Law, § 182 (jurisdiction with certain qualifications, over any misdemeanor). A new section of the Code of Criminal Procedure, § 61, empowers the grand jury to direct a district attorney to file an information in case of a misdemeanor or offense in a court of special sessions in the town within the county, or in the village police court in the village within the county, where the act was committed. N.Y. Sess. Laws 1962, ch. 613, § 1, eff. Sept. 1, 1962.

Mental Hygiene Law, as for a person not confined on a criminal charge.[15] Thus the defendant will be sent to a civil mental hospital of the Department of Mental Hygiene, not to Matteawan State Hospital. (Matteawan is under the jurisdiction and control of the Department of Correction, although it is visited and inspected by representatives of the Department of Mental Hygiene.[16]) The certification under Section 74 is deemed a final disposition of the offense or misdemeanor charged.[17] If certification does not take place, the court in which the case is pending has discretion to dismiss the charge.[18] Our staff found that most district attorneys are satisfied with these provisions of the law.

(b) *Defendants found unable to stand trial: Cases involving a charge of an indictable crime in which no indictment has been returned or, in New York City, a charge of a misdemeanor on which no information has been filed.*

When the defendant is charged with an "indictable" crime [19] and has not yet been indicted or when he is charged with a misdemeanor in the City of New York but the district attorney has not yet filed an information against him in the Court of Special Sessions—and when he is found unable to stand trial—then civil proceedings are similarly instituted for the defendant's certification "as provided in the mental hygiene law for the commitment of a person not in confinement on a criminal charge." [20] But, unlike the situation described in (a) above, here the court handling the certification under Section 74 of the Mental Hygiene Law "may commit the defendant to any

[15] Code Cr. Proc., § 873. See People v. Hyatt, 187 Misc. 1031, 68 N.Y.S. 2d 903 (Sup. Ct. Erie Co., Ottaway, J., 1946).

[16] Correction Law, § 400.

[17] Code Cr. Proc., § 873.

[18] Code Cr. Proc., § 873.

[19] Code Cr. Proc., § 4(4) states that all crimes must be prosecuted by indictment, so far as here relevant, except those made cognizable by courts of special sessions, police courts, or city courts.

[20] Code Cr. Proc., § 872.

appropriate state *institution of the department of correction or the department of mental hygiene.*"[21] (Emphasis supplied.) Thus the court which hears this petition for civil certification has absolute discretion to commit a defendant charged with any felony (or, in New York City, with a misdemeanor still pending in City Magistrates' Courts) either to Matteawan or to a civil hospital.

In New York City the practice is that when a defendant, not yet indicted or informed against, is found incapable of understanding the charge or participating in his defense the superintendent of Bellevue or Kings County Hospital institutes a proceeding in the Supreme Court for a certification. Although the court has absolute discretion to certify either to Matteawan or to a civil hospital, it usually selects the civil hospital unless the charge is one of homicide, armed robbery, or other serious felony. (If the charge is serious, the district attorney will invariably present the case to a grand jury to obtain an indictment before a petition for certification is submitted to the Supreme Court, and the procedure set forth in point (c) below will then be followed.)

When a defendant is certified in any part of the state prior to being indicted or informed against, all proceedings in the court which had jurisdiction of the criminal charges and which ordered the examination terminate automatically.[22] The district attorney may, however, present the charge to a grand jury thereafter. If the defendant is then indicted, or if in New York City an information is then filed against him for a misdemeanor in the Court of Special Sessions at the direction of a grand jury, the warrant will be lodged, pursuant to Section 872 of the Code of Criminal Procedure, with the director of the hospital where he is confined. In 1960 this section was amended so as to provide that if the prosecutor shall not have reopened the matter or have presented his evidence to a grand jury within

[21] Code Cr. Proc., § 872.

[22] Code Cr. Proc., § 872.

six months of the date of the certification, and if he shall have stated in writing his decision not to do so, then he may not reopen the matter or present it to a grand jury thereafter.

If the defendant has been indicted anywhere, or if in New York City an information for a misdemeanor has been filed against him before the certification proceedings have been instituted, then the psychiatrists' report on the defendant's condition must be presented, not to the court which ordered the examination, but to the court in which the indictment or information is to be tried. (The procedure there and then will be that for a person under indictment; it is discussed in point (c) below.[23])

Outside New York City the practice appears to be that district attorneys almost invariably present a charge of any indictable crime to a grand jury before a certification proceeding has been instituted. This is done regardless of the seriousness of the offense charged. One prosecutor commented that since justices of the peace are not well schooled in the law a defendant is assured of all his legal rights by a transfer "to a court of competent jurisdiction."[24] A few prosecutors, however, depart from the practice just mentioned when the charge is a minor one. Their practice, instead, is to present a case of this kind to a grand jury after the defendant has been certified, and then to lodge a warrant at the state hospital after an indictment has been returned.

Another factor in the decision on the kind of hospital to which such a defendant may be sent is the matter of payment for care in the hospital. When a defendant is certified to a civil hospital, his maintenance, care, and treatment while confined in the hospital must be paid for by the county from which

[23] Code Cr. Proc., § 871.

[24] See, for an example of bungling by a justice of the peace, Mierop v. State of New York, 22 Misc. 2d 216, 201 N.Y.S. 2d 2 (Ct. of Claims, Del Giorno, J., 1960).

he was committed.[25] The county incurs no such expense when a defendant is committed to Matteawan.[26] Several district attorneys told our staff that they make very sure, in all cases involving an indictable crime, that the defendant will be committed to Matteawan in order to avoid this expense to their county. One prosecutor remarked that the requirement of payment for care of a defendant in a civil hospital puts an unfair burden on a county.

(c) *Defendants found unable to stand trial: Cases involving a crime for which an indictment has been returned or, in New York City, a misdemeanor for which an information has been filed.*

If the defendant has been indicted anywhere, or if in New York City the district attorney has filed an information against him for a misdemeanor in the Court of Special Sessions—and if such defendant has been found unable to stand trial—proceedings will be instituted for the defendant's commitment in "the court having jurisdiction of the person" of the defendant, i.e., the court in which the indictment or information is pending.[27] This means that no separate proceeding for certification under Section 74 of the Mental Hygiene Law will be instituted in the Supreme Court or a county court. If the criminal court confirms the report of the examining psychiatrists, either after a hearing or on motion without opposition, then the defendant "shall" be committed

> to an appropriate *institution of the department of correction.*[28] A defendant so committed may at any time during the period of his

[25] Mental Hygiene Law, § 79; Application of Eaton, 196 Misc. 648, 92 N.Y.S. 2d 461 (Sup. Ct. Onondaga Co., Searl, J., 1949).

[26] Correction Law, § 412 (last sentence).

[27] Code Cr. Proc., §§ 658, 662-b, and 875. Effective Sept. 1, 1962, the Magistrates' Courts of the City of New York and the Court of Special Sessions of the City of New York are abolished, and a new Criminal Court is established (N.Y. Sess. Laws 1962, ch. 697).

[28] This mandatory provision was enacted by N.Y. Sess. Laws 1953, ch. 785, § 3, eff. July 1, 1953. Before its enactment the criminal court

commitment be transferred to any appropriate state institution of the department of mental hygiene or of the department of correction, as may be approved by the heads of such departments.[29] [Emphasis supplied.]

Thus, to repeat, where a defendant has been indicted anywhere, or has been informed against for a misdemeanor in New York City, and has been found incapable of understanding the charge or making a defense, it is *mandatory* that he be committed to Matteawan. Despite any possible extenuating circumstances, the court in which the indictment or information is pending has no discretion whatsoever to order his certification to a civil hospital[30] (or, since the 1961 amendment, to the jurisdiction of the Department of Mental Hygiene[31]).

This inflexible rule has led to a practice in New York City which mitigates its harshness for misdemeanors, though not for felonies. Our staff found that when a defendant is informed against in the Court of Special Sessions for a misdemeanor and he is found too ill to stand trial, the district attorney will invariably discharge the defendant on his own recognizance so that the Supreme Court may acquire jurisdiction to certify him to a civil hospital. In such a case the defendant, who is already in the prison ward at Bellevue or Kings County, will stay there for the necessary three or four days until the Supreme Court certifies him, instead of being transferred to a ward for civil patients. This practice is justified because the phenomenon of a discharge on a defendant's own recognizance—unknown outside New York City—does not terminate the pendency of the criminal charge. The charge remains quiescent and is usually revived if the defendant is not certified by the Supreme Court judge.

---

had discretion to commit either to a civil state hospital or to an institution of the Department of Correction.

[29] Code Cr. Proc., § 662-b. [30] Code Cr. Proc., § 662-b.

[31] N.Y. Sess. Laws 1961, ch. 504, § 6, eff. April 11, 1961.

Let us compare cases under point (b), a felony anywhere in New York State before indictment or a misdemeanor in New York City before information, with others under point (c), a felony anywhere after indictment or a misdemeanor in New York City after information. If a defendant is informed against in a Court of Special Sessions in New York City for any misdemeanor,[32] such as petit larceny,[33] the court *must* commit him to Matteawan. If he is charged with the same criminal act in a court of special sessions outside New York City, a court *must* certify him to a civil hospital. If he is charged with the same criminal act in the Magistrates' Court in New York City (before being held by the City Magistrate to answer in the Court of Special Sessions), the Supreme Court *may choose to* certify him either to Matteawan or to a civil hospital. If he is charged with any felony anywhere in the state but has not been indicted, the court which handles the certification *may choose to* certify him either to Matteawan or to a civil hospital, regardless of the gravity of the crime. Once he has been indicted, however, the court which handles the indictment *must,* regardless of the circumstances, commit to Matteawan.

The statutory provisions have thus created a situation in which some defendants charged, for example, with petit larceny must be confined at Matteawan, whereas others charged with rape or homicide may occasionally be confined in civil hospitals. The accidents of geography and of the stage in the proceeding at which a psychiatric examination is sought are likely to determine where the defendant will be hospitalized, regardless of the nature of the charge or the violence of the patient.

[32] Other than libel. For a criminal libel, indictment is required by N.Y. Const. art. 1, § 8. Doyle v. Police Court of The City of Niagara Falls, 177 Misc. 359, 3 N.Y.S. 2d 324 (Sup. Ct. Erie Co., Swift, J., 1941); Trombetta v. Van Amringe, 156 Misc. 307, 280 N.Y. Supp. 480 (Sup. Ct. N.Y. Co., Cohn, J., 1935).

[33] Penal Law, §§ 1298–99.

Such differing results are hard to justify, in the absence of any showing that they are based on the medical needs of the patient or the needs of society. Statutory provisions which allow accidental circumstances to determine such results might well be subject to attack on constitutional grounds as denying equal protection of the laws.[34]

Our staff inquired of judges and prosecutors, therefore, whether all courts having jurisdiction of returned indictments, and also the Court of Special Sessions of New York City after an information is filed, should be given the same discretionary power now enjoyed by a court operating under Mental Hygiene Law Section 74 to send a defendant either to Matteawan or to a civil hospital.

A questionnaire asked New York State judges whether the Code of Criminal Procedure should be amended to eliminate this disparity. Of the 50 judges replying, 25 said they would "strongly favor" such an amendment, 12 said they would "mildly favor" it, 7 said they would "mildly oppose" it, and 6 said they would "strongly oppose" it. Thus 37 judges favored such an amendment and 13 opposed it.

The judges' comments explain their views. One wrote that judges can be trusted to be discreet in their exercise of the discretionary power suggested; another said that no logical reason occurred to him for the distinction, since indictment raises no presumption of guilt; another agreed that indictment makes little difference, because it merely expresses the opinion of the district attorney (and, presumably, the opinions of the grand jurors led by his views); another judge said that a court should have power to deal with such a situation summarily in order to reach a just and humane result. Only one judge who was strongly opposed to the amendment commented; he said

[34] See U.S. *ex rel.* Carroll v. McNeill, 294 F. 2d 117 (2d Cir. 1961), discussed *infra* note 69.

that until the matter has been presented to a grand jury no one has examined the facts, and that existing law gives the public a necessary protection.

Although three-fourths of the judges answering the questionnaire favored some amendment of the present law to ensure equal treatment for persons accused of similar crimes, no agreement appeared on what this equal treatment should be. Some thought that all such defendants should be sent to Matteawan the better to protect themselves and others. Others thought that all should go to a civil hospital because they are not criminals.

The opinions of prosecutors about such an amendment were sharply divided. Those favoring the present mandatory provision for commitment to Matteawan gave one or another of the following reasons: that security arrangements are not satisfactory in the civil hospitals; that mandatory commitment to Matteawan creates no problem; that the present law promotes uniformity throughout the state, with all defendants going to the same "staging area," while interhospital transfers remain available to remedy any resulting hardship; and that the place of confinement should be determined by doctors, not by judges.

Those prosecutors favoring some such amendment commented variously: that more flexibility should be written into the law to permit commitment to civil hospitals both before and after indictment; that the judges can be trusted to exercise a sound discretion; that if a defendant becomes unmanageable in a civil hospital he can be transferred to Matteawan by an administrative decision without a court order; and that only those defendants who are charged with serious crimes should be committed to Matteawan. One prosecutor qualified his support of such an amendment by saying that the judge's discretion to send to a civil hospital should be exercised only when the hospital director tells the court that the defendant would be suitable for his hospital.[35]

[35] Before the amendment of 1953, *supra* note 28, Section 662 of the

In 1958 Section 662-b of the Code of Criminal Procedure was amended to provide that an indictment or proceeding might be dismissed by the court having jurisdiction of a defendant's case after he had been confined continuously for two years, on the consent of the district attorney. The amendment provided further that if the indictment or proceeding were so dismissed and if the defendant were then in a state hospital and required continued treatment and confinement, the director of that hospital should notify a public officer of the locality from which the defendant had been received.[36] This officer, or a person mentioned in Section 74 of the Mental Hygiene Law (as a possible petitioner, no doubt) must then apply under Section 74 for a certification of the defendant as "for the certification of a person not in confinement on a criminal charge." The Department of Mental Hygiene, however, reported its "experience . . . that there has been much difficulty in having the local authorities . . . petition for the certification of a defendant."[37] In 1959, accordingly, Section 662-b of the Code of Criminal Procedure was amended again.[38] The present law is that if the defendant has been confined to a civil hospital, and if the indictment or proceeding has been dismissed under the two-year rule, and if the defendant needs continued treatment and confinement, he shall be certified under Section 74 of the Mental Hygiene Law.[39]

If, however, a defendant has been confined to Matteawan

Code of Criminal Procedure provided that the psychiatric report should include a recommendation as to the appropriate institution to which the defendant should be sent if committed.

[36] N.Y. Sess. Laws 1958, ch. 705, § 1, eff. April 14, 1958; see N.Y. State Legislative Annual 468 (1958).

[37] N.Y. State Legislative Annual 6 (1959).

[38] N.Y. Sess. Laws 1959, ch. 337, § 1, eff. April 13, 1959.

[39] See N.Y. Ops. Atty. Gen. 320 (1943) for an opinion given to the Department of Mental Hygiene that a defendant committed to a civil hospital who needs hospitalization after the dismissal of the indictment against him should be treated as a civil patient.

State Hospital, and if the indictment or proceeding has been dismissed under the two-year rule, and if the defendant needs continued treatment and confinement, Section 662-b provides that he "shall be retained therein as provided in section four hundred and nine of the correction law." That section of the Correction Law, however, by its express terms is applicable only to convicted prisoners who continue to be mentally ill at the expiration of their sentence. Thus no clear statutory authority exists for the retention at Matteawan of a defendant against whom an indictment has been dismissed and who needs continued treatment and confinement.

Examination of these complex provisions on commitment of defendants found unable to stand trial because of their mental condition and the views of judges and prosecutors on the problem led our committee to conclude that the Code of Criminal Procedure should be so amended as to eliminate the present unequal treatment in commitment of defendants accused of similar crimes and to clarify the procedures for the possible termination of such a commitment.

Second: Commitment of Defendants Acquitted of Crime on Ground of Insanity and Subsequent Possible Discharge.[40]

Excluded from the scope of this study is the broad question of insanity as a defense in criminal actions.[41] The more limited

[40] The material in the *Second* and *Third* parts of this chapter represent phases of our study which are somewhat peripheral to its main purpose. In those phases little or no investigation of actual practices has been made; the analysis and recommendations are based chiefly upon the statutes themselves.

[41] A distinguished committee under the chairmanship of Dr. Richard V. Foster undertook a three-year study of the M'Naghten rule and a new definition of insanity in relation to responsibility for criminal conduct. As a result of its work, bills to amend the test for insanity as a defense in criminal actions, now provided by Section 1120 of the Penal Law, were introduced in the New York State legislature in 1961 and 1962, but failed to pass. See also Subcommittee on Constitutional Rights,

question of the procedures for commitment to a mental hospital of criminal defendants acquitted by reason of insanity was included, however, as being one method of admission.[42]

Before 1960 the Code of Criminal Procedure directed any court which should acquit a defendant on the ground of insanity to commit him to a state hospital if the court deemed "his discharge dangerous to the public peace or safety." [43] A defendant thus committed might be discharged later, upon a certificate of recovery made by the director of the hospital and approved by the court.[44]

In 1960 New York State adopted a new procedure for the commitment and the subsequent discharge of defendants acquitted of crime on the ground of insanity.[45] Under it the court must commit such a defendant to the custody of the Commissioner of Mental Hygiene in all cases. The defendant must then be confined, either at Matteawan State Hospital or at a civil state hospital. If the Commissioner of Mental Hygiene is of the opinion, later, that the defendant "may be discharged or released on condition without danger to himself or to others," a report to that effect will be submitted to the court which originally ordered the commitment.[46] Or the defendant himself may apply to the court for his discharge or release.[47]

The court may then order that the defendant be examined by

Committee on the Judiciary, U.S. Senate, 87th Cong., 1st Sess., Hearings, Part 2 (1961).

42 For an excellent analysis of this problem, see Weihofen, Institutional Treatment of Persons Acquitted by Reason of Insanity, 38 Texas L. Rev. 849 (1960).

43 Code Cr. Proc., § 454 (prior to amendment by N.Y. Sess. Laws 1960, ch. 550, § 1, eff. Sept. 1, 1960).

44 Mental Hygiene Law, § 87(3) (last sentence thereof repealed by N.Y. Sess. Laws 1960, ch. 550, § 2, eff. Sept. 1, 1960).

45 N.Y. Sess. Laws 1960, ch. 550, eff. Sept. 1, 1960, amending Code Cr. Proc., § 454 and Mental Hygiene L., § 87(3).

46 Code Cr. Proc., § 454(2).

47 Code Cr. Proc., § 454(5).

two qualified psychiatrists.[48] If the court is satisfied that the defendant may be discharged or released on condition without danger to himself or others, the court may order his discharge or his release on such conditions as the court determines to be necessary.[49] If the court is not thus satisfied, a hearing must be held. This is deemed a civil proceeding. After the hearing, the court may discharge the committed person, may release him on condition, or may recommit him to the Commissioner of Mental Hygiene.[50]

If the defendant is released conditionally, the defendant may, under this new procedure, receive care and supervision to be provided by the Department of Mental Hygiene.[51] If within five years after such a conditional release the court decides, after a hearing, that the release must be revoked for the safety of the defendant or for that of others, the court must revoke it and order the defendant recommitted.[52] Such a defendant has available to him the writ of habeas corpus.

It may be objected to these new provisions that an acquittal on the ground of insanity involves a determination of the defendant's mental condition only at the time of the commission of the crime. The effect of Section 454—even before its 1960 amendment and more likely after it—might be, accordingly, to compel detention of some persons not mentally ill at the time of their commitment.

A leading New York case (a sequel to the acquittal of Harry K. Thaw for murder on the ground of his insanity) considered a similar problem and held that it was not fatal to the constitutionality of a law requiring commitment of persons acquitted but dangerous that it contained no provision for a determination of the defendant's mental condition at the exact moment of commitment—and required no notice to the defendant and

[48] Code Cr. Proc., § 454(2).
[49] Code Cr. Proc., § 454(3).
[50] Code Cr. Proc., § 454(3).
[51] Code Cr. Proc., § 454(3).
[52] Code Cr. Proc., § 454(4).

gave him no opportunity for a hearing to determine his condition.[53] The court said that the defendant had had notice and a hearing in a proceeding which involved the possibility of commitment from the time when he pleaded the defense of insanity against the charge, and that the provisions for discharge on his recovery also furnished him a safeguard.[54] The court also said, as an additional ground for its decision, that inasmuch as Section 454 (in its form at that time) provided for no more than the commitment of a defendant found dangerous to the public peace or safety, constitutionality flowed from the police power of the state to protect society:

> In fine, I think that the Legislature contemplated that upon the trial for a crime the investigation into the insanity of the defendant at the time of the commission of a crime, pleaded by the defendant, might satisfy the court that if the defendant were entitled to be freed absolutely upon an acquittal based upon such insanity, the verdict would not only exonerate the defendant, but in effect might let loose one then so insane as to be a menace to public peace and safety, and that, therefore, the Legislature expressly limited the effect of such an acquittal in the exercise of the police power, so that it might not be an absolute discharge in course, but that the court might order the detention of the defendant as a dangerous insane person until his reason was restored.[55]

Under the new procedure of Section 454, however, commitment is not confined to cases in which a defendant is dangerous. Every defendant acquitted on the ground of insanity must be committed to the custody of the Commissioner of Mental Hygiene, whether he is dangerous or not.

The 1960 change in the New York statutes would thus cast some doubt on the constitutionality of the scheme for automatic

[53] People *ex rel.* Peabody v. Chanler, Sheriff of Dutchess County, 133 App. Div. 159, 117 N.Y. Supp. 322 (2d Dept. 1909), aff'd on opinion below, 196 N.Y. 525, 89 N.E. 1109 (1909).

[54] *Id.* at 164–65, 117 N.Y. Supp. at 326.

[55] *Id.* at 164, 117 N.Y. Supp. at 326.

commitment of persons acquitted if such constitutionality had to depend entirely upon Harry K. Thaw's case. But it does not. The *Coates* case,[56] decided recently by the New York Court of Appeals, held that a compulsory detention without notice or hearing was constitutional because relief had at all times been available from a judge and jury under Section 76 of the Mental Hygiene Law. (This was the only method of discharge, as Judge Froessel's opinion remarked, with which the court was there concerned.) It is now clear, therefore, that in the opinion of the New York Court of Appeals an involuntary admission without notice or opportunity for a hearing is not *ipso facto* unconstitutional. The inquiry shifts, therefore, to the reasonableness of the opportunities for review and release and to the reasonableness of the original admission. Review and release are discussed elsewhere in this report (Chapter V). The involuntary admission of Thaw was based on a jury's verdict that he had not been proved sane, beyond a reasonable doubt, at the time of the alleged crime. Although this verdict fell far short of an affirmative finding that he was clearly insane at the time of his admission, it did raise a doubt sufficient, perhaps, to prevent the admission from being arbitrary or unreasonable.

The constitutionality of a federal statute for automatic commitment of a person acquitted of crime because of insanity has recently been upheld, in affirming the denial of a writ of habeas corpus, in *Ragsdale* v. *Overholser* in the District of Columbia.[57] The court's opinion, by Judge Burger, said that

> the public interests sought to be protected outweigh appellant's claimed right to be set free the instant a verdict is returned. It is hardly asking too much to require that a defendant who is absolved from punishment by society because of his mental condition at the

[56] 9 N.Y. 2d 242, 173 N.E. 2d 797 (1961), *supra* note 18 to Chapter V.

[57] 108 U.S. App. D.C. 308, 281 F. 2d 943 (Burger, J., 1960) rehearing en banc den. (Bazelon, J., diss.). But cf. Lynch v. Overholser, —— U.S. —— (May 21, 1962).

time of the criminal act should accept some restraint on his liberty by confinement in a hospital for such period as is required to determine whether he has recovered and whether he will be dangerous if released.[58]

The court noted that in a majority of the cases which had considered statutes similar to that under consideration the statutes had been held constitutional. He referred to those collected in 145 American Law Reports at page 892 (1943).

In the opinion of our committee, the statutory provisions on commitment of a defendant acquitted for insanity are sound and flexible. Moreover, such a defendant's constitutional rights are adequately protected, giving due consideration to the reason for his original detention, by his right to a hearing on his request for discharge and by his right to seek a writ of habeas corpus. If there is any constitutional vice in such a statutory scheme, it probably lies less in the automatic commitment as such than in a possibly insufficient guaranty that the patient will receive good medical treatment, will be followed up with continuing solicitude for his freedom, and will be released as soon as his welfare and that of the community allow.[59]

To this end, consideration might be given to the advisability of providing periodic court review of the retention in mental hospitals of defendants in criminal cases—not only those acquitted by reason of insanity but also any other person held by a hospital under an order of a criminal court.

In view of the establishment of the Temporary State Commission on Revision of the Penal Law and Criminal Code, our committee recommends to that Commission that it consider the wisdom of applying to these defendant-patients the recommendations of our committee concerning authorization by the

[58] *Id.* at 314, 281 F. 2d at 949.

[59] Krash, The Durham Rule and Judicial Administration of the Insanity Defense in the District of Columbia, 70 Yale L. J. 905, 938–48 (1961).

courts for the retention of civil patients by hospitals for limited periods of time and concerning periodic court review of such authority. The extension of this principle to defendants hospitalized for mental illness, if deemed appropriate by the Temporary State Commission, would supplement and greatly strengthen the present safeguards consisting of the right to a hearing on request for discharge and the right to seek a writ of habeas corpus.

Third: Transfers to Mental Hospitals of Convicted Prisoners Certified to Be Insane and Retransfer or Discharge Therefrom.

Male prisoners in state penal or correctional institutions. Whenever the physician or psychiatrist of any state penal or correctional institution certifies to the warden that a male prisoner confined because of conviction for a felony is insane, the warden must transfer such prisoner to the Dannemora State Hospital.[60] This hospital admits convicted male prisoners only. It is under the jurisdiction and control of the Department of Correction, but is visited and inspected by representatives of the Department of Mental Hygiene.[61]

Prior to 1962, a transfer to Dannemora State Hospital was designed to be an administrative transfer without notice to the prisoner or any opportunity to contest the certification of the physician or the decision of the administrative officer. The decision was not to be subject to the examination, approval, or disapproval of any court before the transfer. And until recently confinement at Dannemora State Hospital was not even reviewable, until after the expiration of the maximum term of im-

[60] Correction Law, § 383. After the committee concluded its study, this section was repealed and a new Section 383 was enacted, which is in accord with the committee's Recommendation No. 33, set forth in Chapter VII, *infra* (N.Y. Sess. Laws 1962, ch. 393, § 1, eff. April 9, 1962).

[61] Correction Law, § 375.

prisonment, by a writ of habeas corpus grounded upon a claim that the prisoner's mental condition did not justify his detention there.[62]

On April 27, 1961, the New York Court of Appeals unanimously decided that a court may not refuse, on a Dannemora prisoner's application for habeas corpus, to inquire into the legality of his transfer there from a state prison even though his maximum term of imprisonment had not yet expired.[63] The court said:

> Although under ordinary circumstances a mere transfer (as distinguished from a commitment for insanity) is purely an administrative matter, and a prisoner has no standing to choose the place in which he is to be confined, we do not feel that the courts should sanction, without question, removals, in cases of alleged insane prisoners, which can conceivably be uncontrolled and arbitrary.
>
> . . . . .
>
> Since the writ of habeas corpus has traditionally been relied upon to alleviate the oppression of unlawful imprisonment and abuses of similar character, it can be invoked to obtain a hearing to test the validity of a commitment in an institution for the criminally insane [9 N.Y. 2d at 484–485, 174 N.E. 2d at 726].

If the male prisoner recovers before his sentence expires, he must be transferred back to the penal or correctional institution from which he came or to some other one.[64] If he does not recover by that time, there are three possible dispositions.

First disposition: Thirty days or less before the term's expiration, the director of Dannemora may apply to a judge of a court of record for an order directing that the prisoner be com-

[62] People *ex rel.* Washington v. Johnston, as Director of Dannemora State Hospital, 12 App. Div. 2d 673, 207 N.Y.S. 2d 698 (3rd Dept. 1960); People *ex rel.* Sacconanno v. Shaw, as Director of Dannemora State Hospital, 4 App. Div. 2d 817, 164 N.Y.S. 2d 750 (3rd Dept. 1957).

[63] People *ex rel.* Brown v. Johnston, as Director of Dannemora State Hospital, 9 N.Y. 2d 482, 174 N.E. 2d 725 (1961).

[64] Correction Law, § 386.

mitted to the custody of the Commissioner of Mental Hygiene, who may then place him either in a civil hospital or in a hospital under the jurisdiction of the Department of Correction.[65] Before such an order may issue, the same procedures must be followed as for the certification of a person not in confinement on a criminal charge, i.e., those of Section 74 of the Mental Hygiene Law.[66]

SECOND DISPOSITION: If the prisoner is not recovered by the expiration of his maximum term but if in the opinion of the director of Dannemora he is "reasonably safe to be at large," he may be released.[67]

THIRD DISPOSITION: If he is not recovered by that time and if,

[65] Correction Law, § 384, as amended by N.Y. Sess. Laws 1961, ch. 429, § 1, eff. Sept. 1, 1961.

[66] Before the 1961 amendment to Section 384 of the Correction Law, the director of Dannemora State Hospital was required by it to apply for an order authorizing him to retain the prisoner at Dannemora in accordance with the procedure prescribed in Section 408 of the Correction Law. Notice and an opportunity to be heard had in 1943 been held to be a constitutional prerequisite to such an order, and so to be required by implication (though not expressly) by Section 384. People *ex rel.* Morriale v. Branham, 291 N.Y. 312, 52 N.E. 2d 881 (1943), adhered to on reargument, 292 N.Y. 127, 54 N.E. 2d 331 (1944). In 1948 Section 384 had been amended to conform its requirements expressly to these constitutional requirements. N.Y. Sess. Laws 1948, ch. 377, § 1, eff. July 1, 1948. In 1960 an unreported decision by Mr. Justice Main, Supreme Court, Fourth Judicial District, brought to light a case in which a prisoner had been kept at Dannemora for twenty years after the expiration of his maximum term on an order of detention secured prior to the 1943 *Morriale* case and just before the end of his maximum term, without notice to him or to any relative or friend. After this decision Attorney General Lefkowitz reported (New York Post, Jan. 5, 1961) that the records at Dannemora showed that 215 of the 1,935 inmates had been committed before 1943 without proper legal notice. The Attorney General announced that the procedure for examination, notice, and hearing now prescribed expressly by Section 384 would be applied to these 215 cases.

[67] Correction Law, § 385, as amended N.Y. Sess. Laws 1961, ch. 429, § 2, eff. Sept. 1, 1961.

in the opinion of the Commissioner of Mental Hygiene, his discharge would be detrimental to the public safety or welfare or injurious to the patient, and the Commissioner so certifies in writing, then the patient may apply for discharge to a court of record in the area where the hospital is located. The court may appoint two qualified and disinterested psychiatrists to examine the patient and may call for other evidence. If the court is satisfied that the discharge or conditional release of the patient will not be detrimental to the public safety or welfare or injurious to the patient, then the court may order his discharge or his release on such conditions as the court determines to be necessary.[68] Within five years after such a conditional release, the court has power to order the patient recommitted to the custody of the Commissioner of Mental Hygiene. All patients not retained, whether discharged absolutely or released conditionally, may be granted convalescent status in accordance with the rules prescribed by the Commissioner.

Female prisoners in state penal or correctional institutions and all prisoners in local penal or correctional institutions. Female prisoners who become mentally ill while serving a sentence in state penal or correctional institutions and prisoners of either sex who become mentally ill while serving a sentence in local penal or correctional institutions are transferred to Matteawan State Hospital for treatment.[69] But no transfers of

[68] Mental Hygiene Law, § 87(3), as amended N.Y. Sess. Laws 1961, ch. 429, § 3, eff. Sept. 1, 1961.

[69] Also transferred to Matteawan State Hospital are certain civil patients under Section 85 of the Mental Hygiene Law and Section 412 of the Correction Law.

Section 85 of the Mental Hygiene Law provides that where the director of any state hospital ascertains that a patient has committed or is liable to commit an act which if committed by a sane person would constitute homicide or felonious assault, or is so dangerously mentally ill that his presence in the hospital is dangerous to the safety of other patients or the staff or the community, then he must forthwith apply to a court within the county where his hospital is located for the ap-

convicted prisoners to Matteawan can be made administratively without court order, as could transfers of male convicted prisoners to Dannemora until the Court of Appeals spoke in 1961.[70]

---

pointment of a commission to determine the dangerous mental illness of such patient. The court then appoints a commission of not more than three disinterested persons to examine the patient and report to the court. The patient may be represented by counsel in the proceedings. If the commission finds that the patient is dangerously mentally ill and if the court is in substantial agreement with this report, then the patient must be admitted to Matteawan State Hospital.

Section 412 of the Correction Law provides, however, that the Commissioner of Mental Hygiene may, without a court order, transfer to Matteawan any patient in a state mental hospital (1) who is held at the civil hospital by other than civil process; (2) who has been previously sentenced to prison "and who still manifests criminal tendencies," or (3) who has previously been an inmate of Matteawan.

On July 26, 1961, the United States Court of Appeals for the Second Circuit unanimously decided that Section 412 is unconstitutional as applied to patients who have fully served prior sentences for crimes and have subsequently been admitted by civil process to a state civil hospital (within group (2) above). United States *ex rel.* Carroll v. McNeill, 294 F. 2d 117 (1961), vacated and appeal dismissed as moot, 369 U.S. 149 (1962). The court noted that except for patients initially committed upon civil process to the care of the Department of Mental Hygiene and transferred to Matteawan under Section 412, every patient legally at Matteawan is there pursuant to a court order specifically directing that he be there. The court held "that the denial of a judicial transfer procedure arbitrarily discriminates against those patients who have fully served prior sentences for crimes and have subsequently been admitted by civil process to a state institution of the type of Pilgrim [a civil state mental hospital], and denies to this class of patients the equal protection of the laws guaranteed to them by the Fourteenth Amendment." 294 F. 2d at 120.

The constitutionality of Section 412 as applied to a civil patient who was previously an inmate of Matteawan (of group (3) above) is under attack in a case now pending in the Supreme Court, Albany County, *In re* Gomillion. In that case a notice of appeal has been filed from an order of Justice Bruhn directing the transfer of the patient back to Hudson River State Hospital from Matteawan. Although the unconstitutionality of Section 412 was urged by counsel, the court's order was based on a statutory construction of the Correction Law.

[70] This disparity in treatment was referred to by the Court of Appeals

Whenever the physician of any of these penal or correctional institutions reports to the warden or officer in charge that any of the prisoners is "insane," that official must apply to a court of record under a section of the Correction Law entitled "Commitment of insane prisoners to the Matteawan state hospital"[71] for an order committing the prisoner there. This section specifies the procedure for obtaining the court order, including designation of two examining physicians, neither of whom may be connected with such penal or correctional institution, and service of notice of the application, with a copy of the warden's petition, on the prisoner and on his nearest relative or friend.[72]

---

in a footnote in People *ex rel.* Brown v. Johnston, as Director of Dannemora State Hospital, *supra* note 63, 9 N.Y. 2d at 486, 174 N.E. 2d at 726.

[71] Sec. 408.

[72] Under Section 408 (2) of the Correction Law, three days' written notice of the application, with copy of the director's petition, must be served personally on the prisoner. In addition, notice and a copy of the petition must be served on the nearest relative or friend of the prisoner, if any.

Prior to 1960 Section 408 required only one day's notice to be given to the nearest relative known to be within the county where the prisoner is confined. In 1960 this section was amended so as to provide for three days' notice (N.Y. Sess. Laws 1960, ch. 528, eff. April 14, 1960). The title of this Chapter 528 reads: "An act to amend the correction law in relation to requiring the appointment of a special guardian of a person to be committed to Matteawan State Hospital, and providing for the payment of expenses and allowances therefor." In approving this bill the Governor wrote:

"The law now requires that one day's notice must be given to the nearest relative known to be within the county where the prisoner is confined. Not only is one day insufficient to insure time for such a relative to retain a lawyer and arrange to appear in the proceedings, but the limitation that only a relative within the county need be notified is unfair, particularly in the case of prisoners confined involuntarily in institutions outside the county of their residence.

"This bill will properly extend the notice requirements to provide for three days' notice to the appropriate relative anywhere in the State.

"It will be noted that the title to the bill refers to the appointment

The prisoner or his nearest relative or friend may demand a hearing before the court issues its order.

One judge in New York City told our staff that he never orders a mentally ill prisoner in a local penal institution committed to Matteawan when the conviction is for an offense or a misdemeanor and when the sentence is about to expire. In order to avoid mandatory commitment to Matteawan (Correction Law, § 408) in such a situation, this judge generally suggests that the prisoner be held in the prison ward of Bellevue Hospital until the expiration of his sentence. Then at the expiration of his sentence such a person is certified to a civil hospital under Section 74 of the Mental Hygiene Law.[73]

If a convicted prisoner at Matteawan State Hospital recovers before the expiration of his sentence, he may be transferred by the Commissioner of Correction to the penal or correctional institution from which he came or some other one.[74] If he con-

---

of a special guardian. Such appointment was provided for in an earlier print of the bill, but it is not in the amended form. In each of the last two years, bills containing provision for special guardians were disapproved. This bill, in its amended form, no longer contains such a provision. The failure to amend the title would not seem to be a fatal defect. . . .

"Reservations have been expressed regarding the requirement that notice be served by the sheriff, rather than by registered mail, upon the relatives of the prisoner. If in practice this procedure proves unduly burdensome the statute may be appropriately amended at a later time." (New York State Legislative Annual 512 (1960).)

See also amendment of Section 408 by N.Y. Sess. Laws 1962, ch. 799, § 1, eff. April 30, 1962.

[73] For optional transfer of such prisoners in New York City for observation at Bellevue or Kings County Hospital, see the 1957 amendment which is Correction Law, § 408(1-a). (For New York City it omits the requirement that the court designate the two examining physicians.) If such a prisoner were committed to Matteawan State Hospital, he could, at the expiration of his term, be transferred to a civil hospital at the discretion of the Commissioner of Mental Hygiene. Correction Law, § 409.

[74] Correction Law, § 410.

tinues to be mentally ill at the expiration of his sentence, there are three possible dispositions. *First Disposition:* He may be retained at Matteawan without an additional court order. *Second Disposition:* He may be transferred to a civil hospital at the discretion of the Commissioner of Mental Hygiene.[75] *Third Disposition:* He may be discharged if, in the opinion of the superintendent of Matteawan State Hospital, he is "reasonably safe to be at large" and his relatives or friends are able and willing to maintain him comfortably without further public charge.[76]

The statute governing the disposition of unrecovered convicted prisoners at Matteawan at the expiration of their sentence thus differs from the statute governing the disposition of such male prisoners at Dannemora in three respects: (1) No court order is necessary for such unrecovered prisoners at Matteawan, presumably because their initial admission to Matteawan was on court order. (2) Such unrecovered prisoners at Matteawan who, in the opinion of the superintendent, are reasonably safe to be at large may be discharged only if relatives or friends are able and willing to maintain them comfortably without further public charge, whereas such unrecovered prisoners at Dannemora who, in the opinion of the director, are reasonably safe to be at large may be discharged without any such requirement of care by relatives. (3) There is no such provision for conditional release or discharge by court order of unrecovered prisoners at Matteawan as there is for unrecovered prisoners at Dannemora (Section 87(3), Mental Hygiene Law, as amended in 1961). Of course, such unrecovered prisoners at Matteawan may resort to the remedy of habeas corpus to seek discharge.

The variations and inequities in the procedures relating to the admission to mental hospitals of convicted prisoners certified to be insane, the retention and release of such prisoners, and

[75] Correction Law, § 409.

[76] Correction Law, § 409.

their transfer to a civil hospital after the expiration of the prisoner's sentence should be eliminated. Admission to both Dannemora and Matteawan State Hospitals from penal institutions should be on a court order after notice to the prisoner and his nearest relative or friend and an opportunity for a hearing. The former disparity in admission procedures to both hospitals was eliminated in 1962 (N.Y. Sess. Laws 1962, ch. 393, eff. April 9, 1962). This legislation is in accord with the committee's recommendation. Similarly, the provisions of Section 87(3) of the Mental Hygiene Law for discharge and conditional release of unrecovered male prisoners at Dannemora should apply also to all unrecovered convicted prisoners in Matteawan (Correction Law, §§ 384 and 409). Finally, the provisions of Section 409 of the Correction Law concerning retention of prisoners, release to relatives, and transfer to a civil hospital after expiration of the prisoner's sentence should apply explicitly, not only to prisoners whose sentences have expired, but also to defendants unable to stand trial with respect to whom indictments or proceedings have been dismissed. Elimination of these irrational variations would assure all criminal-law patients similar treatment and similar procedural safeguards.

RECOMMENDATIONS

On the basis of its investigation of present law and practice in admissions in criminal cases, the committee makes the following findings and recommendations:

Admission for Observation Concerning Ability to Stand Trial, and Commitment When Such Ability Is Not Found

The committee finds that the law conferring authority on hospital directors to recommend the place for holding a mental examination on ability to stand trial (Code Cr. Proc., § 660) is sound. Examination in such criminal-order cases does not present a problem in New York City, where defendants are examined at the prison wards of Bellevue, Kings County, and Elmhurst Hospitals. Elsewhere, however, hospital directors are not always consulted on the place for examination, and a number of difficulties may be created thereby, notably when defendants are sent for examination to hospitals which afford only "minimum security." The committee therefore recommends:

> *Recommendation No. 28 (Place of Examination)*. The practice concerning examination of defendants on ability to stand trial should be brought into line with the provisions of the law (Code Cr. Proc., § 660) so that the place of examination in criminal-order cases will not unnecessarily retard the trend toward open hospitals.

> *Recommendation No. 29 (Full and Complete Report of Examination)*. The law requiring "a full and complete report" after psychiatric examination on ability to stand trial (Code Cr. Proc., § 662) should be strictly enforced so that a comprehensive report based on a thorough examination is always provided to the court.

> *Recommendation No. 30 (Elimination of Unequal Treatment of Similar Defendants)*. The provisions of the Code of Criminal Procedure (§§ 658–662-f; 870–876) relating to commitment to mental hospitals of defendants found incompetent to stand trial should be simplified and clarified so that the unequal treatment now present in commitment of defendants accused of similar crimes will be eliminated (and thus make unnecessary the procedural measures often adopted to mitigate the harshness of this unequal treatment), and so that the kind of hospital to which the defendant is committed will depend on the needs of the

patient and his suitability for a particular hospital, and not upon accidents of geography or the stage of the proceeding at which the psychiatric examination is sought, as it often does today.

Specifically, the committee recommends:

(a) That Section 873 of the Code of Criminal Procedure continue to provide that a defendant who is charged with an offense which is not a crime and who is found unable to stand trial should be certified in a civil proceeding to a civil hospital, and the charge against him thus disposed of.

(b) That a defendant who is charged with a crime or indicted or informed against for a crime and who is unable to stand trial should be committed to a civil hospital or to Matteawan, and that the decision on the kind of hospital should be made by the court, taking into consideration the recommendations of the examining civil hospital. In the case of a crime which is not serious (not involving violence against a person or other crimes equally dangerous), the statute should state a policy in favor of commitment to a civil hospital.

Recommendation No. 31 (Payment for Care). Section 79 of the Mental Hygiene Law (which now provides that payment for care of a defendant found unable to stand trial and committed to a civil hospital be made by the county from which the patient is admitted) should be amended so that payment for care of such a defendant shall be made by the state, as it is now made under Section 412 of the Correction Law when such a defendant is committed to Matteawan State Hospital. Such an amendment would obviate the practice, obviously unfair to the patient, of arranging his commitment to Matteawan primarily for the purpose of saving expense for the county.

Commitment of Defendants Acquitted of Crime on Ground of Insanity

The committee finds that the law (Code Cr. Proc., § 454) on commitment of defendants acquitted for insanity is sound from the point of view of the defendant-patient and of society, and that the defendant-patient's right to a hearing on his request for discharge and his right to seek a writ of habeas corpus adequately protect his constitutional rights, giving consideration to the reason for his original detention. The committee therefore makes no recommendation for change in this provision of the law except to the extent that Recommendation No. 34 would affect defendants acquitted of crime on the ground of insanity.

Admission to Matteawan State Hospital and Release of Convicted Prisoners and Defendants Unable to Stand Trial

> *Recommendation No. 32 (Admission and Release Procedures for Matteawan).* Section 409 of the Correction Law (relating to retention of convicted prisoners at Matteawan State Hospital) should be amended to apply not only to prisoners whose sentences have expired but also to defendants unable to stand trial with respect to whom indictments or proceedings have been dismissed (Code Cr. Proc., § 662-b) and the discharge and conditional release procedures prescribed in Section 87(3) of the Mental Hygiene Law for unrecovered male prisoners in Dannemora State Hospital should be made applicable to all such prisoners and such defendants in Matteawan State Hospital.

Transfer of Prisoners to Dannemora State Hospital

Recommendation No. 33 (*Transfer to Dannemora on Court Order*). The transfer to Dannemora State Hospital from state penal or correctional institutions of male prisoners who are certified to be insane should be on a court order after notice to the prisoner and his nearest relative or friend and an opportunity for a hearing (Correction Law, § 383), as is now provided in admissions to Matteawan State Hospital of female prisoners from state penal or correctional institutions or of prisoners of either sex from local penal or correctional institutions (Correction Law, § 408).[77]

Possible Added Safeguard of the Right of Defendant-Patients to Release

The committee considered the advisability of providing periodic court review of the retention in mental hospitals of convicted prisoners and defendants held by a hospital upon an order of a court but took no position on this proposal in view of the establishment of the Temporary State Commission on Revision of the Penal Law and Criminal Code. Any such proposal to supplement present safeguards of the right to release of defendant-patients is properly within the purview of that Commission. This committee therefore recommends:

Recommendation No. 34 (*Retention of Persons Admitted in Criminal Cases*). The Temporary State Commission on Revision of the Penal Law and Criminal Code should be requested to take under consideration the recommendations of this committee concerning authorization by the courts for retention of civil patients by hospitals for limited

[77] This recommendation was enacted into law by N.Y. Sess. Laws 1962, ch. 393, eff. April 9, 1962.

periods of time and concerning periodic court review of such authority, with a view to determining whether these recommendations should apply likewise to convicted prisoners and defendants held by a hospital upon an order of a court, either at all times, after expiration of the convicted prisoner's term of imprisonment, or after dismissal of an indictment or proceeding pending against a defendant unable to stand trial. The details of the operation of any such procedure for patients in criminal cases should be determined by that Commission.

Appendixes and Index

Appendix I. Statistical Tables

TABLE 1. VOLUNTARY ADMISSIONS TO STATE MENTAL HOSPITALS, 1949–1960

This table gives numbers and percentages of the total admissions that were voluntary at selected New York State mental hospitals for the years specified and provides data for Chart 1.

Year	St. Lawrence State Hospital		Harlem Valley State Hospital		Hospitals serving upstate area		Hospitals serving New York City area		All hospitals (excluding Psychiatric Institute)	
	Number	Per cent	Number	Per cent	Number	Per cent	Number	Per cent	Number	Per cent
1949	159	35.6	25	3.9	742	11.2	381	2.9	1,123	5.7
1955	159	28.8	15	1.7	933	11.7	425	3.2	1,358	6.4
1956	202	34.6	13	1.6	1,405	16.8	670	5.2	2,075	9.8
1957	245	43.2	31	3.6	1,644	19.6	956	7.2	2,600	12.0
1958	328	46.6	45	4.4	2,048	23.1	1,324	9.3	3,372	14.6
1959	372	54.5	70	7.0	2,850	30.1	2,282	14.7	5,132	20.5
1960	413	56.3	67	6.7	3,164	31.1	2,489	15.2	5,653	21.3

Source: New York State Department of Mental Hygiene, Division of Statistical Services.

TABLE 2. Voluntary Admissions and Patients on Open Wards for the Year Ending March 31, 1960

This table gives numbers and percentages of voluntary admissions and percentages of patients on open wards in New York State mental hospitals at the time specified.

State hospital	Total number of admissions	Number of voluntary admissions	Per cent of voluntary admissions	Per cent of patients on open wards
All hospitals (excluding Psychiatric Institute)	26,512	5,653	21.3	63.4
Hospitals serving upstate area	10,188	3,164	31.1	62.2
Hospitals serving New York City area	16,324	2,489	15.2	64.2
St. Lawrence	733	413	56.3	100.0
Marcy	1,002	372	37.1	26.0
Middletown	900	332	36.9	91.0
Binghamton	1,051	373	35.5	72.5
Hudson River	1,514	510	33.7	93.5
Manhattan	1,320	403	30.5	54.8
Rochester	1,121	318	28.4	46.9
Willard	720	195	27.1	57.1
Gowanda	821	189	23.0	64.1
Buffalo	1,426	298	20.9	48.0
Central Islip	2,620	530	20.2	71.5
Utica	900	164	18.2	22.7
Brooklyn	1,652	281	17.0	80.2
Creedmoor	2,970	485	16.3	77.8
Rockland	2,058	285	13.8	46.4
Pilgrim	3,097	327	10.6	55.0
Kings Park	1,602	111	6.9	68.6
Harlem Valley	1,005	67	6.7	48.9

Source: New York State Department of Mental Hygiene, Division of Statistical Services. Percentages of patients on open wards were from New York State Department of Mental Hygiene, *Monthly Statistical Report* 5 (Dec. 1959).

TABLE 3. TOTAL ADMISSIONS TO NEW YORK STATE MENTAL HOSPITALS FROM EACH COUNTY, BY METHOD OF ADMISSION, FOR THE FISCAL YEAR ENDING MARCH 31, 1960

County	Legal status of admission							
	Total	Certified	One physician's certificate	Health officer's certificate	Voluntary certificate	Emergency certificate	Examination under Code of Crim. Proc.	Commitment under Code of Crim. Proc.
Total	26,783	14,485	2,110	1,960	5,912	1,429	518	369
New York State	26,417	14,267	2,103	1,924	5,856	1,420	505	342
New York City	13,685	9,513	1,711	45	2,034	46	18	318
Bronx	1,866	1,160	312	7	319	12	0	56
Kings	4,951	3,583	777	9	475	10	4	93
New York	4,476	3,307	189	23	808	13	7	129
Queens	2,217	1,341	420	5	397	8	7	39
Richmond	175	122	13	1	35	3	0	1
Rest of state	12,732	4,754	392	1,879	3,822	1,374	487	24
Albany	258	199	2	8	45	3	1	0
Allegany	65	17	0	7	27	4	8	2
Broome	543	59	47	145	196	87	9	0
Cattaraugus	149	56	2	4	46	16	20	5
Cayuga	128	48	0	30	30	15	5	0
Chautauqua	255	92	7	15	85	31	22	3
Chemung	224	82	2	27	86	22	5	0
Chenango	75	23	2	17	26	4	3	0
Clinton	85	34	0	11	35	1	4	0
Columbia	62	27	0	17	15	3	0	0
Cortland	53	14	0	25	13	1	0	0
Delaware	56	7	1	19	20	5	4	0
Dutchess	515	29	19	253	201	12	0	1
Erie	1,416	982	18	6	275	130	5	0
Essex	47	13	0	6	26	1	1	0
Franklin	103	43	1	7	47	4	1	0
Fulton	66	34	0	12	17	1	2	0

TABLE 3 (*Continued*)

County	Legal status of admission							
	Total	Certified	One physician's certificate	Health officer's certificate	Voluntary certificate	Emergency certificate	Examination under Code of Crim. Proc.	Commitment under Code of Crim. Proc.
Genesee	52	18	0	9	18	4	3	0
Greene	44	25	0	11	7	0	0	1
Hamilton	3	0	0	3	0	0	0	0
Herkimer	119	29	2	46	35	2	5	0
Jefferson	173	35	1	23	105	7	2	0
Lewis	42	5	0	7	25	1	4	0
Livingston	47	9	1	0	14	11	12	0
Madison	92	11	0	42	29	2	8	0
Monroe	820	428	67	7	220	66	31	1
Montgomery	86	25	1	17	21	14	7	1
Nassau	1,072	588	62	4	266	87	62	3
Niagara	349	74	2	61	56	144	12	0
Oneida	609	59	7	245	205	71	22	0
Onondaga	476	237	5	35	135	59	5	0
Ontario	98	25	1	22	26	11	13	0
Orange	532	66	9	217	200	30	9	1
Orleans	40	22	0	1	13	3	1	0
Oswego	107	29	6	27	41	1	3	0
Otsego	93	24	1	10	37	15	6	0
Putnam	47	3	2	17	20	4	1	0
Rensselaer	89	70	0	3	16	0	0	0
Rockland	224	4	5	155	57	2	1	0
St. Lawrence	276	38	5	10	169	31	23	0
Saratoga	84	43	1	14	21	1	3	1
Schenectady	219	105	0	56	23	22	13	0
Schoharie	49	24	1	5	14	0	5	0
Schuyler	38	13	0	5	16	0	4	0
Seneca	53	8	0	18	10	11	6	0

TABLE 3 (*Concluded*)

County	Legal status of admission							
	Total	Certified	One physician's certificate	Health officer's certificate	Voluntary certificate	Emergency certificate	Examination under Code of Crim. Proc.	Commitment under Code of Crim. Proc.
Steuben	159	52	2	48	46	6	5	0
Suffolk	926	58	77	2	330	382	77	0
Sullivan	137	47	1	44	42	3	0	0
Tioga	29	3	1	4	13	7	1	0
Tompkins . . .	102	29	2	30	32	4	5	0
Ulster	234	69	1	28	126	10	0	0
Warren	76	32	3	2	23	1	14	1
Washington . .	52	27	0	7	16	0	2	0
Wayne	87	21	3	19	20	6	18	0
Westchester . .	834	628	21	14	164	3	1	3
Wyoming . . .	39	7	1	0	12	11	7	1
Yates	24	5	0	2	9	2	6	0
N.Y.S., county unknown	1	0	0	1	0	0	0	0
Other states in U.S.	333	205	7	31	45	8	12	25
Other countries .	9	6	0	2	0	0	0	1
Unascertained . .	23	7	0	2	11	1	1	1

Source: New York State Department of Mental Hygiene, Division of Statistical Services.

Note: The subtotal figures in this table do not correspond exactly with those in Tables 2 and 6, because of minor differences in computation methods.

TABLE 4. Disposition of Patients Released from Psychiatric Receiving Hospitals outside New York City, 1960

Hospital	Released to home or community		Transferred to state hospitals		Transferred to other mental institutions		Other disposition		Total
	Number	Per cent	Number	Per cent	Number	Per cent	Number	Per cent	Number
Grasslands	720	48.0	737	49.1	33	2.2	11	.7	1,501
Meadowbrook	727	55.7	478	36.6	77	5.9	23	1.8	1,305
Meyer Memorial	847	33.1	954	37.3	170	6.7	586	22.9	2,557
Monroe County Infirmary	436	32.0	458	33.6	62	4.6	406	29.8	1,362
Mosher Memorial	1,449	83.3	279	16.0	1	.1	10	.6	1,739

Source: Information furnished to the committee by these receiving hospitals.

TABLE 5. Importance of Notice to Patient of Application for Court-ordered Admission

This table gives percentages of New York State judges and physicians considering such notice (when not detrimental to the patient) important or unimportant.

Location of judge	Percentage of judges considering notice to patient:	
	Important	Unimportant
New York City (N = 17)	100	0
Upstate (N = 18)	72	28
All judges (N = 35)	86	14

Location or kind of physician	Percentage of physicians considering notice to patient:	
	Important	Unimportant
New York City (N = 30)	57	43
Upstate		
Practitioners (N = 97)	34	66
Community mental health directors * (N = 19)	37	63
All physicians (N = 146)	39	61

Source: Replies to questionnaires addressed by the committee to judges and physicians in New York State (1960).

* All the directors of community mental health services were outside New York City; their opinions are entitled to separate consideration as coming from specialists in this field.

TABLE 6. Emergency Admissions to New York State Mental Hospitals for the Year Ending March 31, 1960

This table gives numbers and percentages of such admissions to each hospital, by kind of emergency admission, for the time specified.

Hospital	Total admissions	Nonemergency admissions		Emergency admissions			
				Health officer		Incomplete court-order	
	Number	Number	Per cent	Number	Per cent	Number	Per cent
All state hospitals	26,512	23,125	87.2	1,960	7.4	1,427	5.4
Hospitals serving N.Y.C. area	16,324	15,610	95.6	197	1.2	517	3.2
Hospitals serving upstate area	10,188	7,515	73.8	1,763	17.3	910	8.9
Binghamton	1,051	656	62.4	263	25.0	132	12.6
Brooklyn	1,652	1,652	100.	0	0	0	0
Buffalo	1,426	1,088	76.3	67	4.7	271	19.0
Central Islip	2,620	2,208	84.3	2	.1	410	15.6
Creedmoor	2,970	2,970	100.	0	0	0	0
Gowanda	821	741	90.3	24	2.9	56	6.8
Harlem Valley	1,005	975	97.1	23	2.3	7	.7
Hudson River	1,514	1,176	77.6	319	21.1	19	1.3
Kings Park	1,602	1,562	97.5	0	0	40	2.5
Manhattan	1,320	1,320	100.	0	0	0	0
Marcy	1,002	751	74.9	190	19.0	61	6.1
Middletown	900	548	60.9	309	34.3	43	4.8
Pilgrim	3,097	3,042	98.2	0	0	55	1.8
Rochester	1,121	974	86.9	37	3.3	110	9.8
Rockland	2,058	1,881	91.4	172	8.4	5	.2
St. Lawrence	733	618	84.3	65	8.9	50	6.8
Utica	900	473	52.5	322	35.8	105	11.7
Willard	720	490	68.	167	23.2	63	8.8

Source: New York State Department of Mental Hygiene, Division of Statistical Services.

TABLE 7. Admissions of Nonobjecting Patients on a Single Physician's Certificate, 1949–1960

This table gives numbers and percentages of such admissions at selected state mental hospitals under Section 73 of the New York Mental Hygiene Law for the period specified; it provides data for Chart 2.

Year	Hospitals serving upstate area		Hospitals serving New York City area		All hospitals (excluding Psychiatric Institute)	
	Number	Per cent	Number	Per cent	Number	Per cent
1949	124	1.9	153	1.2	277	1.4
1955	86	1.1	150	1.1	236	1.1
1956	71	.8	152	1.9	223	1.1
1957	81	1.0	635	4.8	716	3.3
1958	79	.9	2,459	17.3	2,538	11.0
1959	161	1.7	2,267	14.6	2,428	9.7
1960	235	2.3	1,865	11.4	2,100	7.9

Source: New York State Department of Mental Hygiene, Division of Statistical Services.

TABLE 8. Physicians' Opinions about Admission of Nonobjecting and Senile Patients on a Single Physician's Certificate

This table gives percentages of New York State physicians holding various opinions about such admissions.

Location or kind of physician	Percentage considering such admissions:		
	Satisfactory	Unsatisfactory	No opinion
New York City (N = 28)	89	7	4
Upstate			
Practitioners (N = 93)	61	39	0
Community mental health directors * (N = 17)	76	18	6
All physicians (N = 138)	69	30	1

Source: Replies to questionnaires addressed by the committee to physicians in New York State (1960).

* All the directors of community mental health services were outside New York City; their opinions are entitled to separate consideration as coming from specialists in this field.

TABLE 9. Importance of Hearings with and without Patients Present

Location of judge	Percentage of judges considering hearing with Patient:		Relative:	
	Important	Unimportant	Important	Unimportant
New York City (N = 34)	94	6	79	21
Upstate (N = 57)	35	65	60	40
All judges (N = 91)	57	43	67	33

Location or kind of physician	Percentage of physicians considering hearing with Patient:		Relative:	
	Important	Unimportant	Important	Unimportant
New York City (N = 28)	36	64	61	39
Upstate				
Practitioners (N = 96)	24	76	44	56
Community mental health directors * (N = 18)	33	67	48	52
All physicians (N = 142)	27	73	48	52

Source: Replies to questionnaires addressed by the committee to judges and physicians in New York State (1960).

* All the directors of community mental health services were outside New York City; their opinions are entitled to separate consideration as coming from specialists in this field.

TABLE 10. IMPORTANCE OF REPRESENTATION BY ATTORNEY IN CASES OF CERTIFICATION

Location of judge	Percentage of judges considering representation by attorney: Important	Unimportant
New York City (N = 17)	82	18
Upstate (N = 38)	40	60
All judges (N = 55)	53	47

Location or kind of physician	Percentage of physicians considering representation by attorney: Important	Unimportant
New York City (N = 27)	56	44
Upstate		
Practitioners (N = 94)	23	77
Community mental health directors * (N = 19)	21	79
All physicians (N = 140)	29	71

Source: Replies to questionnaires addressed by the committee to judges and physicians in New York State (1960).

* All the directors of community mental health services were outside New York City; their opinions are entitled to separate consideration as coming from specialists in this field.

TABLE 11. Use of Special Procedures by Judges to Decide Doubtful Cases of Certification

Procedure	Percentage of judges					
	Upstate (N = 35) *		New York City (N = 11 †)		All places (N = 46)	
	Often or sometimes	Rarely or never	Often or sometimes	Rarely or never	Often or sometimes	Rarely or never
Re-examination and reconsideration of the need for hospitalization by examining physicians	15	85	92	8	36	64
Extending period of observation and treatment in hospital	14	86	100	0	35	65
Examination by independent psychiatrist	19	81	55	45	29	71
Paroling patient to custody of relatives provided patient takes psychiatric treatment on out-patient basis	17	83	73	27	31	69

Source: Questionnaire addressed by the committee to New York State judges (1960).

* Not all the 35 upstate judges commented on each procedure: 33 upstate judges commented on the first procedure; 31 on the third; and 34 on the fourth.

† Twelve New York City judges commented on the first procedure.

TABLE 12. Proper Medical and Legal Roles in Admission according to Judges and Physicians

Roles of judges and doctors	Judges * (percentage)			Physicians * (percentage)				
	Upstate (N = 61)	New York City (N = 35)	All judges (N = 96)	Upstate (N = 98)	New York City (N = 30)	Community m.h. directors (N = 21)	Health officers and designees (N = 98)	All physicians (N = 247)
a) Admission by doctors' certificate only, with right to court hearing after admission	25	23	24	56	47	67	49	53
b) Admission by court-appointed commission of doctors or doctors and lawyers	27 †	28 †	27 †	5	20	5	11	9
c) Admission by court order given routinely if judge determines that requisite procedures have been followed and that there is evidence to support doctors' findings	39	14	30	15	33	19	26	22
d) Admission by court order with doctors giving their diagnosis and recommendations and judge deciding whether facts warrant admission	64	57	62	28	3	14	17	19
e) Admission by court order with judge having full authority to decide question of admission regardless of medical recommendations	30	46	35	0	0	0	4	2

Source: Questionnaires addressed by the committee to New York State judges and physicians (1960).

* The judges and doctors were asked to express their opinions on each of the five formulations of the roles of judges and doctors in compulsory admission. The figures given represent the percentage of the total respondents in each category who "strongly agreed" or "agreed" with the formulation. The columns add up to more than 100 per cent because most of the respondents agreed with more than one formulation.

† This formulation was not included in the second questionnaire addressed to judges. The percentages for this formulation are based solely on the replies to the first questionnaire addressed to judges. In that mailing, 41 replies were from upstate judges, and

Appendix II. Some Observations on the Hospitalization of the Mentally Ill under European Laws

by Ruth Roemer

INFORMATION on the operation of the laws governing hospitalization of the mentally ill was gathered in England, France, Switzerland, Yugoslavia, and Norway during the summer of 1960. Everywhere the medical and legal problems in admissions to mental hospitals were similar to those faced in the United States. A review of the foreign problems may, therefore, provide perspective on some of those in New York State. Here are summarized, by method of admission, the high lights of the operation of the laws in these five countries.

Voluntary Admissions

All the countries visited, except England, have a system of voluntary admission similar to that in the United States, although some still retain formalities beyond the written application of the patient. *Norway* and *Yugoslavia* both require the signature of two witnesses, although this requirement is eliminated in Norway's proposed bill covering hospitalization of the mentally ill. In *Yugoslavia* (that is, in *Slovenia*, the only part of Yugoslavia visited) the medical director of the hospital customarily signs. *Norway* and certain cantons of *Switzerland* also require a medical certificate to accompany an application for a voluntary admission. The Swiss, however, do not insist on a medical certificate for simple cases, and as a matter of practice in most cases a doctor recommends the admission of voluntary patients.

In *France* and *Switzerland* a voluntary patient is free to leave at any time, but many statutes in other European countries, like that in New York, require written notice of intention to leave. In *Norway* a voluntary patient may be detained for fourteen days under present law, but the proposed bill extends this period for twenty-one days. Norway has had an explicit provision that the legal status of a voluntary patient may not be changed because of a deterioration in his condition; consequently, when a voluntary patient who needs further care refuses to remain, he must be discharged and put outside the hospital gate before he can be readmitted as a compulsory patient. The new bill will do away with this subterfuge and permit change of status of a hospitalized patient when it is necessary.

Informal Admissions

By way of contrast to the approach of most countries, *England* has abolished the voluntary admission as we know it and has substituted the nonstatutory or informal admission. (*France* also uses this method, called the *service libre*, and one-third of all admissions are by this method.) Section 5 of the British Mental Health Act of 1959 provides that nothing in the act shall prevent the admission of a patient without any application or order or direction rendering him liable to be detained. This is an admission without any formalities, like an admission to a general hospital. The patient admitted informally is free to leave at any time, but the act authorizes compulsory admission of hospitalized patients, thus permitting informal patients to be changed to the status of detained patients quickly, if that should be necessary.

Informal admissions in England started long before the passage of the new act on July 29, 1959. In 1952 Dr. R. C. Freudenberg, Consulting Psychiatrist, Netherne Hospital, Coulsdon, Surrey, asked to be permitted to admit patients without any formality. The Ministry of Health de-certified part of his hospital and renamed it Fairdene; patients were then admitted informally to that part of the hospital. Today in England 80 per cent of all admissions are informal. In many hospitals only 2 to 3 per cent of patients are certified, and Mapperly Hospital at Nottingham has had no certified patients since 1935. The director of Mapperly believes that even one certified patient prejudices the therapeutic milieu of the hospital. Many patients who are first admitted by compulsion agree to stay as informal patients once their treatment is under way, and then their status is changed. From 1959 to 1960 the number of compulsorily detained patients declined by more than five thousand.

Voluntary admissions have risen everywhere in the world when mental hospitals have been made open, but the increase in informal admissions in England has been of a totally different order of magnitude. This has been accomplished through the creation of a new public attitude toward hospitalization for mental illness—through case-by-case education of patients and their families by general practitioners, through visits to the homes of patients by mental welfare officers and hospital psychiatrists, and through out-patient care of the mentally ill in clinics attached to general hospitals and in day hospitals. For instance, when the day hospital called "The Acre" was established at Worthing to serve part of the catchment area of

Graylingwell Hospital at Chichester, a general practitioner would call The Acre and say that he had a patient who should receive care. Then a psychiatrist from The Acre, who was also on the staff of Graylingwell, would visit the patient with the general practitioner and convince him to come to the day hospital or to enter Graylingwell informally. (Admissions to Graylingwell from the area of Worthing were halved by the full range of therapeutic services offered to day patients at The Acre.)

The new public attitude is, of course, fostered by the open hospitals, which are becoming more and more a part of the community,[1] and by the short stays of many new patients. The medical director of one hospital summarized the attitude toward informal admissions by pointing out that in the past the greatest enemy was the law that said you could not have treatment until you were so sick that you had to be certified.

Compulsory Admissions for an Indefinite Period

In all five countries visited, compulsory admission is a medical matter, with varying provisions for legal safeguards after admission. None of the countries visited required an order of a court *before* admission.

England had become disenchanted with routine orders for admission by magistrates who uniformly endorsed the doctors' decisions. Under the new act the order of a justice of the peace before admission is eliminated, and an application by a relative

[1] An unusual effort to integrate the mental hospital into the community occurred at Colchester, where the director of Severalls Hospital invited the general hospital to locate its maternity ward temporarily in a wing of the mental hospital when a stubborn infection spread among the newborn. The director of Severalls seized the opportunity to give this dramatic demonstration to the community that mothers and babies could be kept happily and safely in a mental hospital.

and the certificates of two physicians are sufficient to give the hospital authority to admit the patient. One of the physicians, if possible, shall have known the patient previously, and the other must be approved by the local health authority as having special experience in the diagnosis and treatment of mental disorder. Additional safeguards are: (1) examination and admission by the hospital; (2) the requirement for periodic renewal of authority for detention; (3) medical discharge; (4) the patient's right to appeal to the lay management committee of the hospital for discharge; (5) the power of the nearest relative to order discharge, which becomes effective unless the hospital blocks it; and (6) the patient's right of recourse to the Mental Health Review Tribunal, a new body established in each of the fifteen hospital regions.

The Mental Health Review Tribunals are tripartite bodies, with legal members, medical members, and others with relevant experience, which began to function on November 1, 1960. The patient or his nearest relative may appeal to the Tribunal for discharge at any time within the first six months of his hospitalization, thereafter once each year for the next two years, and thereafter once in each two-year period. It is anticipated that very few appeals will be made to the Tribunals, first, because of the small number of compulsorily detained patients (only detained patients need use the Tribunals; others may leave the hospital at will) and, secondly, because of the effective system of discharge described in (3), (4), and (5) above.

The judicial system of admission was not abandoned lightly. The National Council for Civil Liberties strongly urged its retention. A number of psychiatrists and others were concerned about the lack of a legal proceeding before admission and so testified at the hearings before the Royal Commission on the Law Relating to Mental Illness and Mental Deficiency. It should also be noted that Scotland's new act retains approval of an application by a sheriff, who is a barrister and like the county court judge in England (Mental Health Act of Scotland, § 28).

But the Royal Commission and Parliament unanimously supported the medical admission. In explanation of the approval of this change by psychiatrists, a representative of the Ministry of Health said that it is much more honest if the psychiatrist says to the patient, "I as your doctor think you should be hospitalized," than if he blames it on the magistrate. A psychiatrist at one hospital which is rapidly being transformed from a custodial to a therapeutic institution said, "The patient may apply to the Tribunal the day he enters the hospital. What adds to a patient's illness is not a wrongful admission, though it may cause distress, but remaining in the hospital for a long time." Another psychiatrist stated that a medical admission is sufficient for the vast majority of patients; he questioned the advisability of making the majority suffer for the few whose admission needs special attention. Opinion is best summarized by a statement of Dr. W. S. Maclay, Medical Senior Commissioner, Board of Control, Ministry of Health:

> There has been some criticism of the abolition of the judicial order particularly by those doctors who feel that it may damage the relationship between them and their patients if the main responsibility for recommending compulsory detention in hospital is clearly seen to fall on them. The great majority of the profession, however, welcome the change. They feel that the assessment of the patient's mental condition and of his need for treatment, which is the essential basis for action, is a matter of medical judgment and that it is no advantage to the patient and little to the doctor if the doctor shelters behind a magistrate. A far better safeguard is the requirement for two medical opinions, one of which is by an expert.[2]

England's new act must be viewed against the dynamic changes that have occurred in mental hospitals—what Dr. T. P.

[2] Maclay, The New Mental Health Act in England and Wales, 116 Amer. J. of Psychiatry 777, 780 (1960).

Reese has epitomized as the "humanisation" of mental hospitals.[3] Further changes are envisaged. Patients today may be divided into three groups—short-stay patients for whom the average stay is six weeks; medium-stay patients for whom the stay is three months to two years; and long-stay patients who remain for more than two years. At present, 80 per cent of all patients are short-stay patients, and it is anticipated that in the future these patients will be treated mainly in general hospitals. For patients who are medium-stay cases, rehabilitation units will be established. It is thought that only 5 to 6 per cent of cases should be long-stay cases, although at present in England 9 per cent are long-stay cases. Of this 9 per cent, 38 per cent are over the age of sixty-five.

England is looking forward to more and more treatment of the mentally ill in the community—in general hospitals, outpatient clinics, and day hospitals. The real concern, as a prominent medical officer of health said, is whether the country will be able to develop quickly enough the resources needed in the community for caring for the patients who can be treated there instead of in hospitals and for patients who will be released from the hospital. Planning has probably averted any crisis that might have been caused by dumping patients on the community prematurely, but nevertheless there is a serious shortage of psychiatric social workers and other personnel. Some psychiatrists, while recognizing that facilities for the care of chronic patients will always be necessary, predict the end of the huge mental hospital within the next twenty years. The present temper of England is reflected in the statement of Dr. Joshua Carse:

> Now that we are no longer obsessed with the idea that psychiatric treatment automatically means in-patient treatment in a mental hospital, we can place the hospital in its right perspective in re-

[3] Reese, The Changing Pattern of the Mental Health Services, 79 Royal Soc. of Health J. 354–56 (1959).

lation to other treatment services available. What we are trying to provide is a comprehensive scheme which will best meet the needs of all kinds of patients. From experience we have found that 4 out of 5 of the patients referred to us can be successfully treated while still remaining in the community. For the remaining 20%, however, in-patient treatment was essential and there will always be a number of patients in this category. Having an out-patient service, however, does make it easier for patients to be discharged from hospital and continue their follow-up treatment while at home. . . . It is felt, therefore, that a psychiatric service is better assessed on how well it meets the needs of the patients and the community rather than place all the emphasis on a massive reduction of the admission rate.[4]

The compulsory medical admission in *France* is based on the application of a relative and a single medical certificate, the safeguards being the need for renewed medical certificates, medical discharge, power of family to order release, and right of application to a court for discharge. The additional medical certificates required after admission constitute a review of the case. The problems in France concern not improper admissions but inadequate facilities, limited financial resources, and the need for new kinds of services, such as day hospitals. Nevertheless, the French system has been criticized because the only precaution before hospitalization is the single medical certificate, which need not be given by a psychiatrist and can be obtained easily in the large cities. Proposals that have been put forth to reform the French law to afford greater protection for individual liberty include requiring a certificate signed by two physicians, assigning a provisional character to admissions to institutions, and organizing better supervision of patient care.[5]

In *Switzerland* compulsory admission is also medical, based on the application of a relative and on a single medical certif-

[4] Carse, The Community Services of Graylingwell Hospital 9–10 (1959).

[5] Colin and Capitant, Traité de Droit Civil, vol. I, 1005 (1957).

icate. In Geneva, in addition, the Department of Health issues a certificate of admission based on the medical certificate. Discharge is medical, with provision for appeal to the Conseil d'État. In Geneva, a patient may also apply to the Board of Psychiatric Supervisors (Conseil de Surveillance), made up of doctors and judges. The psychiatrists interviewed all favored the lack of formality in compulsory admissions in Switzerland; one commented that arbitrary internment in mental hospitals occurred only in detective stories. It should be noted that this attitude was associated with dynamic therapeutic policies in the hospitals visited. For instance, the director of the Clinique Universitaire de Bel-Air had refused money for more beds on the ground that additional funds should provide support for community facilities for psychiatric care; for if more beds are provided, the tendency is to fill them.

In *Yugoslavia*, compulsory admission is medical (a petition from a relative and one detailed medical certificate), but detention is a legal matter. The same day that the patient enters the hospital the hospital writes to the court informing it that the patient has arrived. A commission, made up of a judge and a psychiatrist not attached to the part of the hospital where the patient is located, is required to come to visit the patient at the hospital within three days. In practice, the commission comes every two weeks. Before its visit the judge writes to the relatives of the patient and obtains information on the case. When the commission arrives at the hospital, the patient is examined, and the psychiatrist proposes to the judge the maximum amount of time that the patient should be detained—from one month to one year. If at the end of that time the patient is not well, then his detention can be renewed. Patients have a right of appeal from the decision of the commission to a court.

The psychiatrists at the Llubljana Mental Hospital felt that the procedure for detention was essential because mental hospitals are still completely closed in Yugoslavia, although all the new methods of therapy are being used. Yugoslavia suffers from a serious shortage of beds for mental patients—1.5 per thousand population compared with about 4 beds per thousand in the United States. The establishment of aftercare clinics is a top priority in the mental health field, but the shortage of psychiatrists (only three towns in Slovenia have resident psychiatrists) stands in the way.

Norway has operated with a medical admission since 1848. Under this law patients are admitted compulsorily on the application of a relative and on a medical certificate of a single physician. The certificate is sufficiently detailed to enable the hospital to judge the need for hospitalization from its face. After the patient's admission, a Control Commission, set up for each hospital, consisting of a doctor, a lawyer (usually the county judge), and a woman visits the hospital, reviews each new admission, and asks the patients whether they have any complaints. A patient may apply to the Control Commission for discharge on any of its visits to the hospital. At Dikemark Hospital, the Municipal Mental Hospital of Oslo, the Control Commission sees about fifteen new patients each time it comes. At Lier Hospital, a hospital for chronic mental patients, the Commission sees about twenty-five to thirty patients in one day.

Norway's proposed mental health bill, in addition to providing for grants to mental hospitals and making certain changes in the financing of care, amends the provisions governing admissions. These amendments were provoked by Norway's having signed the European Convention for the Protection of Human Rights and Fundamental Freedoms, which provides in Article 5:

(1) Everyone has the right to liberty and security of person. No one shall be deprived of his liberty save in the following cases and in accordance with a procedure described by law:

. . . . .

(e) the lawful detention of persons for the prevention of the spreading of infectious diseases, of persons of unsound mind, alcoholics or drug addicts or vagrants.

. . . . .

(4) Everyone who is deprived of his liberty by arrest or detention shall be entitled to take proceedings by which the lawfulness of his detention shall be decided speedily by a court and his release ordered if the detention is not lawful.

Norwegian lawyers feel that the 1848 law does not comply with this convention. Moreover, the Norwegians are still bridling at the memory of the Nazi occupation of Norway and as a matter of principle want to be sure that their own law affords every safeguard. The new bill proposes the following changes:

(1) To increase to four the number of members of the Control Commission in order to permit the inclusion of a representative of business and to require that the lawyer-member be the county judge;

(2) To permit the Control Commission to sit as a court with all the powers of a court, if so requested;

(3) To establish a new appellate court in Oslo for the entire country, this court to be made up of a judge of the highest court of Norway, two persons with the qualifications of such a judge, and two psychiatrists. Patients would have the right to apply to this court for discharge once every six months, but the matter of detention would be decided on papers and argument, without the patient's appearance before the court. The Norwegians have rejected as medically undesirable the Danish system, which they examined, whereby patients appear in person for hearings before regular courts of law.

There is some feeling that Norway, having long operated successfully with a medical form of compulsory admission, may be taking a step backward with this new bill, especially in view of Norway's open hospitals and other advances in care of the mentally ill. But the hope is that the legal procedures will not hinder patient care and that there will be few applications to the appellate court. One psychiatrist commented that legal safeguards are advisable because psychiatrists are prone to take the family's rather than the patient's point of view. The director-general of the Health Services of Norway, Dr. Karl Evang, stressed that even though there had been no abridgment of civil liberties or improper hospitalizations, the mere existence of court procedures constitutes a preventive measure. The fact that there have been no abridgments is no guarantee that there will be none.

Emergency Admissions

Emergency admissions in the countries visited generally involve an admission similar to an involuntary admission for an indefinite period, but compliance with some formalities is deferred. Thus *England* provides for the admission of a patient in an emergency on the certificate of a single physician, but the patient may be detained only seventy-two hours unless an additional medical certificate is supplied within that time. One of the significant changes of the new act is that the mental welfare officer can no longer take a patient to the hospital without a medical certificate. In *Switzerland* (Geneva) a patient is admitted in an emergency on a medical certificate, and then the authority of the Department of Health is secured within twenty-four hours after admission. *Norway* uses the regular medical admission, except that the supplying of all the papers is delayed. Thus a patient may be accepted in an emergency by a hospital provided a statement from his nearest relative accompanies him, and the next day the medical certificate is supplied.

France is unusual in permitting an emergency admission initiated by a public official, the prefect, without any medical certificate. The *placement d'office* is an emergency order for hospitalization and is supposed to be used only for dangerous patients, but it is not always limited to such cases. Although no medical certificate is required, often one is secured because of the fear of a charge of *sequestration arbitraire*. It has been recommended that this method be avoided because it is a police measure, lacks flexibility, and needs the confirmation of the prefect for discharge.[6]

Admissions for Observation

England provides a special method of compulsory admission for observation for twenty-eight days on the certificates of two physicians. The practice in London is similar to that in New York City: patients are admitted to observation wards and kept for seventeen days before transfer to a mental hospital. Outside London, patients are admitted directly to a mental hospital. Representatives of the Ministry of Health commented that it is more satisfactory if a patient can be admitted directly to a mental hospital than if he is admitted to a receiving hospital first. It has been found that when the patient goes directly to the mental hospital he is more likely to agree to stay.

France has no compulsory admission for observation. It handles observation in its out-patient clinics, where patients are persuaded to enter mental hospitals if necessary. *Yugoslavia* has an admission for observation for three months to determine the need for a declaration of incompetency. *Norway* has a judicial admission for observation in criminal cases; the police may initiate what is called an administrative observation in psychiatric clinics, but not in mental hospitals.

[6] Henne, L'Entrée en placement d'office des malades mentaux dans les établissements psychiatriques, L'Information Psychiatrique, no. 6, 691–714 (1960).

Special Problems

Criteria for compulsory admission. England's criterion for compulsory admission (mental illness and need of care and treatment) is based on the therapeutic orientation of its hospitals. The standard for admission is need for treatment, not protection of the community. The British say that if hospitals are not custodial the standard for admission should not be custodial. In the present climate of opinion in which large numbers of mental patients are treated in the community, there is no concern about unjust hospitalizations based on this standard. Some psychiatrists conceded that if public opinion should change an overzealous doctor could be influenced by the need for treatment and thus certify patients who perhaps should not be certified. In that event, of course, the patient would have recourse to the Mental Health Review Tribunal.

The new bill in Norway specifies "grave mental illness" as a requirement, and its drafters are seeking language to permit compulsory hospitalization of persons who are dangerous to themselves or others or who may be a risk to the health or life of the family. The aim is to find language, which is not too broad, authorizing compulsory hospitalization when the patient is sick, needs treatment, cannot get it in the community, and is an intolerable and destructive force in his family.

Senile patients. In every country senile patients represent an increasing proportion of the mental hospital population. Depending on their resources, the countries visited are striving to establish special geriatric centers, some connected with mental hospitals and some not. *England* frowns on a compulsory admission of older patients. The practice there is to admit these patients for observation, and then they generally stay voluntarily.

Alcoholics. Alcoholism is not a large problem in *England* or *Norway*. Both countries admit alcoholics with psychosis, and in

Norway nonpsychotic alcoholics may be forced to take treatment in special institutions (there are 800 beds in the country for this purpose). Alcoholism is, of course, a serious problem in *France* and also in *Yugoslavia.* France has a new law, enacted in 1954, which makes the procedure for compulsory hospitalization of alcoholics more strict than the procedure for compulsory hospitalization of the mentally ill. As a French mental health official said of this procedure, "One has the right to get drunk in France. It has to be the extreme case, where the person is dangerous, before admission can be compelled." Yugoslavia is considering a similar law (40 per cent of the male patients at the Llubljana Mental Hospital are alcoholics) and is experimenting with out-patient treatment of alcoholics.[7]

Psychopaths. Lively discussion has centered around *England's* new provision authorizing compulsory admission for observation of persons with psychopathic personality at any age and compulsory admission for treatment of such persons under the age of twenty-one. This provision stems from the general feeling that if there is any hope of helping these patients it must be done while they are young. There is great concern, however, lest these provisions establish a new criminal code for psychopaths before they have been convicted of any crime. In view of these concerns and the differences of opinion among psychiatrists as to whether these patients should and can be treated in hospitals, it is interesting to know that the admission of psychopaths to mental hospitals will start slowly, in research centers, where the results can be evaluated.

Conclusion

Methods of admission and detention of mental patients in the various countries seem closely related to the resources for

[7] Petrovic, Recent Progress in Yugoslavia in the Prevention and Treatment of Alcoholism, Mental Health, vol. XIX, no. 2, 51–57 (1960).

care and the practices that exist in the hospitals and the communities. England illustrates this most vividly, since the new British Mental Health Act did not precede but followed practices that had already been tried and established in care of the mentally ill. Norway's legislative developments will be interesting to watch because there the effort is being made to retain the benefits of a medical admission but to surround detention with effective legal safeguards.

Index